THE IDENTITY-CONSCIOUS EDUCATOR

Building Habits & Skills *for a* More Inclusive School

Liza A.
TALUSAN

Solution Tree | Press

a division of
Solution Tree

555 North Morton Street
Bloomington, IN 47404
800.733.6786 (toll free) / 812.336.7700
FAX: 812.336.7790

email: info@SolutionTree.com
SolutionTree.com

Visit **go.SolutionTree.com/diversityandequity** to download the free reproducibles in this book.

Printed in the United States of America

Library of Congress Cataloging-in-Publication Data

Names: Talusan, Liza, author.
Title: The identity-conscious educator : building habits and skills for a
   more inclusive school / Liza A. Talusan.
Description: Bloomington, IN : Solution Tree Press, [2022] | Includes
   bibliographical references and index.
Identifiers: LCCN 2021058193 (print) | LCCN 2021058194 (ebook) | ISBN
   9781952812712 (paperback) | ISBN 9781952812729 (ebook)
Subjects: LCSH: Multicultural education--United States. | Inclusive
   education--United States. | Reflective teaching--United States.
Classification: LCC LC1099.3 .T358 2022 (print) | LCC LC1099.3 (ebook) |
   DDC 370.117--dc23/eng/20220125
LC record available at https://lccn.loc.gov/2021058193
LC ebook record available at https://lccn.loc.gov/2021058194

Solution Tree
Jeffrey C. Jones, CEO
Edmund M. Ackerman, President

Solution Tree Press
President and Publisher: Douglas M. Rife
Associate Publisher: Sarah Payne-Mills
Managing Production Editor: Kendra Slayton
Editorial Director: Todd Brakke
Art Director: Rian Anderson
Copy Chief: Jessi Finn
Production Editor: Paige Duke
Content Development Specialist: Amy Rubenstein
Acquisitions Editor: Sarah Jubar
Copy Editor: Jessi Finn
Proofreader: Elisabeth Abrams
Text and Cover Designer: Abigail Bowen
Editorial Assistants: Charlotte Jones, Sarah Ludwig, and Elijah Oates

To Jorge, who continues to be one of my favorite teachers.
To Joli, Jay, and Evan, who often advocate for their identities to be
made visible in the classroom. Thank you for inspiring this work.

ACKNOWLEDGMENTS

Thank you to the many teachers who have leaned into building an identity-conscious practice throughout the years. I have had the great fortune to work with thousands of educators across the United States and around the world who have committed to having difficult and courageous conversations about identity in the classroom. Thank you for creating spaces for people to talk about and explore issues of identity in your classrooms.

I have had the privilege of partnering with principals, heads of school, diversity directors, and administrative teams who have known the importance of this work of identity consciousness. You continue to lean into the research and practice that support building skills for a more inclusive community. I know that this pressure, especially during our divided times, is a risk you have to navigate carefully and strategically. Thank you for preparing our teachers and students for an increasingly diverse community today and a more inclusive one tomorrow.

I am grateful for the educators of color I have met through the People of Color Conference—my chosen family. Hearing your stories is a key reason why I wrote this book. I hope this book can serve as a springboard for your colleagues and your school communities to build a strong foundation for this work so that you, as teachers and leaders of color, can thrive.

Thank you to the students who continue to encourage teachers, school leaders, and parents and caregivers to do this work. You are often ahead of us, the adults. You have grown up in a world that is more connected, more open to difference, and more ready to talk about identity. Thank you for your patience and also your urgency as we support you, respond to you, and take responsibility for our own learning.

My scholarship related to race, ethnicity, and education is rooted in my educational journey. I am grateful for the University of Massachusetts Boston's Department of Leadership in Education, in which I earned my doctorate and currently serve as an instructor. I continue to be inspired by the students in the program— all teachers, school leaders, and practitioners—who are confronted each day with the desire to be more inclusive educators. I hope this book serves as an affirmation for the work you are doing.

Thank you to my acquisitions editor, Sarah Jubar, who never gave up on this book. Our very first conversation was just days before the winter holiday break in 2019, and from that day on, you have been consistently encouraging, patient, and thoughtful throughout the whole process. Your feedback throughout the writing process pushed my thinking, developed my style as a more organized writer, and posed helpful, probing, and clarifying questions. I am forever grateful for your mentorship and skill. I certainly could not have done this without you.

Thank you to my brilliant production editor, Paige Duke. During the long weeks I spent revising the manuscript, I sat in awe of your contributions to both the content and flow of this book. Your tireless encouragement was so important, and I appreciate the kindness and care with which you treated this work.

In March 2020, just as the global pandemic of COVID-19 hit the United States, my writing partners—Jorge Vega, Amy Collinsworth, and Leslie Gonzales—formed what became known as the Saturday Writing Team. This group encouraged and uplifted me and other writers to disrupt academic norms of competition and to develop the steady practice of writing, revising, rinsing, and repeating.

Thank you to my parents, Eduardo and Araceli Talusan; my siblings and their partners, Mary and JP, Grace and Alonso, Paul and Kirsten, and Jonathan and Jenny; my children, Joli, Jay, and Evan; and my husband, Jorge. Thank you to Eva, Andy, Marie, and Pedro. And thank you to my incredible nieces, nephews, and niblings—I wrote this book inspired by your stories about school experiences and your desire to be seen and heard in your classrooms.

Thank you to the K–12 student version of me who never had the opportunity to learn about myself, my people, and my history. In many ways, I wrote this book in honor of my childhood experiences when I longed for a teacher who taught from an identity-conscious lens.

Finally, I'd like to thank my readers. I am grateful for your choice to pick up this book, to work through these activities, and to take action toward a more inclusive community.

Solution Tree Press would like to thank the following reviewers:

Jennifer Abrams
Communications Consultant
Jennifer Abrams Consulting
Palo Alto, California

Laura Hesson
Washington County School District
Board Member
Washington County School District
St. George, Utah

Thomas Krawczewicz
Director of Educational Resources
DeMatha Catholic High School
Hyattsville, Maryland

Jenny McMaster
Special Education Resource Teacher
Sacred Heart School
Sioux Lookout, Ontario

Brett J. Novick
School Counselor, Marriage
and Family Therapist, Adjunct
Instructor
Rutgers University
New Brunswick, New Jersey

Darian Thrailkill
Teaching Assistant Professor,
College of Education
East Carolina University
Greenville, North Carolina

Ringnolda Jofee' Tremain
PK3–8 Principal
Trinity Basin Preparatory
Fort Worth, Texas

Visit **go.SolutionTree.com/diversityandequity**
to download the free reproducibles in this book.

TABLE OF CONTENTS

Reproducible pages are in italics.

ABOUT THE AUTHOR

 **Liza A. Talusan, PhD,** is a strategic partner in areas of diversity, equity, inclusion, and justice to schools and organizations both domestically and internationally. She is a faculty member at the University of Massachusetts Boston in the Department of Leadership in Education, where she teaches courses on anti-racist leadership and identity-conscious leadership skills.

Liza has held a number of leadership positions in educational organizations, including the American Educational Research Association, the National Association of Student Personnel Administrators, and the Association for the Study of Higher Education. Liza's scholarship has been published in the *Journal of Critical Scholarship on Higher Education and Student Affairs* as well as in book collections (such as *Privilege Through the Looking-Glass* and *UnCommon Bonds*). She was a featured facilitator in the documentary *I'm Not Racist . . . Am I?* (with Point Made Productions) and has appeared on a number of education-related podcasts, including *Third Space With Jen Cort*, *Leading Equity* with Sheldon Eakins, and *Organizing for Change* with Amanda Decker.

Liza earned a bachelor's degree from Connecticut College, a master's degree from New York University, a human resources certificate from Stonehill College in Easton, Massachusetts, a doctorate in higher education from the University of Massachusetts Boston, and her certified coaching credentials from the Institute for Professional Excellence in Coaching. She is also a qualified administrator of the Intercultural Development Inventory (IDI). To view Liza's list of courses and resources, visit www.lizatalusan.com.

To book Liza A. Talusan for professional development, contact pd@SolutionTree.com.

PREFACE

In March 2020, the COVID-19 global health pandemic changed how we experience the world around us. Essential employees—first responders, health care workers, food service and grocery employees, and government and city workers, among others—were on the front lines of the pandemic. Teachers and students were thrust into online platforms and away from their classroom desks, learning new tools and implementing them in real time.

While people worldwide engaged with this crisis, certain populations had significant differences in how they experienced the pandemic. Data from the U.S. Centers for Disease Control and Prevention (CDC, 2021) revealed populations that were considered at higher risk for COVID-related illness and death: those who had significant pre-existing health conditions and those who experienced inequities in social determinants of health. The CDC (2021) issued guidelines such as hand washing, social distancing, and mask wearing that helped decrease the risk.

Structural inequities also contributed to level of risk. In particular, identity informed and impacted how people experienced the global pandemic in terms of care, follow-up, and even health advice. The Office of Disease Prevention and Health Promotion (2021) states:

> Race or ethnicity, sex, sexual identity, age, disability, socioeconomic status, and geographic location all contribute to an individual's ability to achieve good health. It is important to recognize the impact that social determinants have on health outcomes of specific populations.

The disparities exposed by COVID-19 require us, as educators, to become conscious of identity and the role it plays in our lives, our schools, and our communities.

Since 2008, I have traveled around the United States and worked with over 275 schools, organizations, corporations, associations, and leadership teams as they engage in difficult conversations about teaching and learning. While I focus on creating actionable teaching plans, lesson plans, leadership plans, and strategic plans with them, I spend a significant amount of time asking participants, "Who are you?" I encourage them to reflect on how their identities inform and impact what they do, how they act, and how they interact with the world around them.

Attentional bias, the tendency to focus on certain elements while ignoring others, accounts for the way people create preferences for what they pay attention to (Cherry, 2020). For example, as an Asian American woman, I am often thinking about how decisions at school impact Asian American students. As a child of immigrants, I am often thinking about how students and families from immigrant backgrounds experience school, curricula, and teaching practices rooted in Eurocentric ways of teaching and learning. In order to move closer to a more identity-conscious, culturally relevant, and reflective classroom or work environment, we educators must explore how our identities impact our work, what and whom we advocate for, and what we pay attention to in our decision making.

I'll illustrate this point by sharing my identities. I am an educator, a mother, an Asian American woman, a child of immigrants, and a parent to a child with a disability. My partner and I have a middle-class lifestyle. We have three children. I am a member of a racially diverse family and community. I am Catholic. I am English speaking. I earned a terminal degree (a PhD) through formal education structures. I am heterosexual. I am able bodied. I have lived with depression.

I have spent my entire career working with and within schools. I have taught in middle and upper school classrooms, and I have served as a school administrator at both a preK–8 school and a preK–12 school. I have worked with large school systems and districts and spent much of my time navigating a large, urban research university as both a student and a faculty member. I have mentored students who identify as Black, Latinx, Indigenous, Asian, multiracial, and White. My students come from extreme privilege and from extreme challenges and trauma. Some are living with chronic illness while continuing their education. My students identify as transgender, gender nonconforming, nonbinary, and gender fluid. I have worked with first-year teachers who want to quit and master teachers who thrive on the everyday challenges of the profession.

While my identities make up the core of who I am, what I experience, and what I have achieved, I live, learn, and teach in a world where my identities interact with the identities of my students. There are identities that I feel closer to—that connect me to my students in a deep and profound way. For example, with my students of color, I share an understanding of racism from personal experience and an understanding of how the social consequences of race have impacted us. My students also hold identities that I have no experience with and that create distance in our relationships. For example, as a heterosexual and cisgender woman, I do not know what my LGBTQ and transgender students experience. I do not know their highs and their lows. I do not know how they experience the classroom or how they see me and my identities. However, through identity-conscious practice, I become aware of those identities that bring me closer and those that serve as barriers; that awareness helps me be a better teacher, advisor, mentor, and leader to and for my students.

Through building the habits and skills of an identity-conscious practice, I understand where I need to grow and learn. I know where I might make missteps or mistakes. I am aware of my language and the impact of my words. I am aware of my identity and conscious of how it shows up in the decisions I make and what I pay attention to each day. Throughout my lifetime, I've been on a journey of engaging, sustaining, and deepening my understanding of how identity shows up in my teaching and learning.

I intend for this book to support you in practicing identity awareness. Wherever you are on that path, I am grateful for your journey to become a more identity-conscious educator. The events of 2020, particularly connected to racial injustice and COVID-19, deepened our collective awareness that identity matters. For teachers and school leaders, identity matters in the school community. We must build the skills for talking about identity and for recognizing how to shape a more inclusive school environment for our students, colleagues, and families to thrive.

INTRODUCTION

Identity matters; it has always mattered. But the global pandemic brought that truth into the spotlight in a multitude of ways. Class differences (as evidenced by access to technology, internet, and food security) affected how quickly and successfully students transitioned to online learning environments. Americans witnessed the rise of racial injustice and the resulting public outcry in communities, towns, and schools across their nation. Many teachers were unsure how to talk to their students about inequity, race, racism, injustice, protest, and identity. Some teachers chose to lean into dialogues about these topics, while others chose to leave these issues out of the classroom.

CNN reports that, in response to the focus on systemic and institutionalized racism, Black students and alumni began sharing "Black at" Instagram posts highlighting micro- and macroaggressions they had experienced in majority-White schools, at times naming teachers and administrators who had negatively impacted them (Holcombe, 2020). From both an accountability lens and a communications lens, school leaders were forced to respond. In return, stakeholders (students, families, boards, alumni, faculty, and staff) demanded that schools address a culture and a climate that weren't acknowledging race, racism, and identity. Teachers and school leaders began to confront how school curricula, policies, practices, programs, and procedures contributed to a school culture that failed to be diverse or inclusive of identity.

Within a few months, school communities made some progress by hosting book clubs, professional development, and online workshops to raise awareness of identity in schools. Scholars, such as Kimberlé Crenshaw, hosted webinars to address policies impacting Black communities (www.aapf.org/media-gallery). Learning for Justice (formerly Teaching Tolerance) also posted content to address issues of race in K–12 schools (www.learningforjustice.org/professional-development/webinars) to support teachers and school leaders in this work. White teachers, parents, and school leaders engaged in the dialogue, such as in the *New York Times* podcast *Nice White Parents* (Joffe-Walt, 2020). Even *Sesame Street* and CNN hosted a town hall to talk about race and racism with a young audience (Chaet, 2020).

In this introduction, I'll make the case for why teachers should be talking about identity in school and I'll discuss how they can get started exploring identity. For educators who are just beginning that journey, the first step is understanding how their identities shape their lives. By developing their identity-conscious practice, they open the door for their students, their peers, and their schools to talk about identity and work toward more inclusive environments. Educators can build this connection to their peers and communities by bringing people together to discuss issues of identity and inclusion. Finally, I'll discuss setting shared intentions and guidelines to create positive group environments.

Talking About Identity in School

While there was a social push to talk about race, racism, and identity in schools, many educators, White educators in particular, found themselves unprepared to do so. Research indicates that White educators and school leaders tend to avoid discussing race and racism in the classroom (Gere, Buehler, Dallavis, & Haviland, 2009; Haviland, 2008). Some teachers avoid such conversations for fear of saying the wrong thing (Keengwe, 2010). They might lack the skills to engage in challenging conversations or perhaps learned to avoid conflict. However, others take the view that racial distinctions don't matter, an ideology called *color blindness*. Researchers Terri Peters, Marcia Margolin, Kristi Fragnoli, and Diane Bloom (2016) find that "color-blind racial attitudes have negative effects on teaching and learning, negating the history of racism and discrimination in the United States and its continued influence on people of color" (p. 13). While 2020's racial climate pushed teachers to engage in identity-conscious practices, many were underprepared and too overwhelmed to talk about what they were experiencing.

In addition to hosting conversations about identity, schools have begun adjusting their curriculum to better reflect an inclusive history, providing counternarratives to largely Eurocentric, male-dominated perspectives of history. Through my work, I've seen teachers providing more diverse mathematics, science, technology, and engineering examples for students to create more inclusive structures and approaches. Students are hearing more voices and stories of people of color, of LGBTQ families, and of people with disabilities. In some cases, these efforts have been met with resistance—mostly in response to a changing demographic, a changing society, and a changing community (Zwicky & Walls, 2020).

The events of 2020 set education on a path toward increased identity consciousness and greater inclusion. However, as students return to in-person learning and schools try to resume business as usual, educators must guard against reverting to practices where identity-conscious learning is an afterthought. The COVID-19 global pandemic and ongoing racial injustice gave us a collective awareness that identity matters. If we as educators are to continue the important work of building skills for identity-conscious practice, we need to create meaningful pathways for learning and growing. I wrote this book to help teachers and school leaders commit to greater inclusion in their schools and communities, develop an identity-conscious practice, and cultivate skills for engaging in difficult conversations. When we understand ourselves and the impact of belonging, we can provide more responsive classroom experiences that benefit not only our students but also our schools and communities.

In 2019, Sesame Workshop and NORC at the University of Chicago conducted a study examining how parents and educators in the United States view the importance of social identity in children's future success. Researchers Jennifer Kotler, Tanya Haider, and Michael H. Levine (2019) note that "children fare better when they feel valued and respected by the people who surround them and by the institutions that serve them" (p. 6). Their research also indicates that "healthy social development—including a strong appreciation of individual and group identity factors—can be influenced (both positively and negatively) by home and peer interactions, as well as in community and school experiences" (Kotler et al., 2019, p. 9). By extension, having a positive identity is crucial to children's development, and classrooms and school communities play a major part in this development.

The research team also found that 60 percent of teachers discuss race and ethnicity in their classroom at least sometimes, while 37 percent of parents do so at home (Kotler et al., 2019). And "at least half of teachers discuss their students' family make-ups, genders, and countries of origin in their classroom" (Kotler et al., 2019, p. 23). The topic of social class appears to be largely off-limits; just one in five teachers says they regularly discuss this in their classroom, "despite teachers' belief that social class is the most impactful identity on later success in life" (Kotler et al., 2019, p. 23).

When the research team asked teachers whether a student, a student's family, or a teacher had complained of differential treatment due to race or ethnicity, gender, social class, family makeup, country of origin, religion, or immigration or documentation status during the 2018–2019 school year, about 25 percent of teachers reported having experienced an incident of differential treatment. This percentage suggests that tens of thousands of differential treatment incidents occurred in schools and early learning settings across the United States in that school year (Kotler et al., 2019). A study drawing data from the Toronto District School Board (TDSB), the nation's largest public board of education, suggests teachers and students in Canada share similar experiences (Parekh, Brown, & Zheng, 2021).

Getting Started Exploring Identity

Schools are spaces of learning, critical thinking, and discourse where people wrestle with new ideas, concepts, and experiences. All of this happens through the lens of identity. Who people are informs what they do, how they act and interact with others, and how they see the world around them. So, how can teachers talk with their peers and school leaders about working toward greater equity and inclusion? How can they have more conversations about identity with their students? What do educators need to know, learn, and experience to do this work with students?

While some professional development focuses on how to expand content and curricula related to issues of identity, a key missing component toward building identity-conscious educators is a focus on the educators themselves. Educators' lives are not identity neutral. Supporting teachers to make content and curriculum changes is important, but it doesn't go far enough. Educators also need tools to explore how their identities inform their work—how they interact with students, what they pay attention to, and how proximate they are to particular identities.

The activities, reflection questions, vignettes, and discussion guides throughout this book will support you, the reader, along your identity-conscious journey. By deepening your understanding of identity and the role it plays in your classroom and in your school, you will strengthen your engagement with your students, your curriculum, your peers, and your community. By building your capacity for difficult conversations about identity, you will begin to seek more opportunities to engage in those conversations. You will become more curious. You will become more aware of who you are and how you see the world around you. By being more conscious of identity, you can begin to shape more inclusive classrooms, schools, and communities through more meaningful connections, conversations, and collaborations.

I encourage you to complete each chapter on your own, diving deep into your reflections and thoughts about how your identity informs and impacts your personal life and professional life. While space is provided in the book for you to complete the activities, extend your practice by using a journal or digital notepad if you need extra space to write. Then, find a community in which you can talk about what you're learning. Your community can be a group of peers, your class, family, friends, a book club, an affinity group, or an online meetup of folks who are committed to this work. Share your thoughts and experiences as you go through this work together.

Bringing People Together

If you are interested in extending your learning to a discussion group, I recommend that you co-create intentions, discussion guidelines, or conversation protocols so that members can contribute to a positive discussion environment. The following are some helpful intentions to draw from as you move forward with your group. I encourage you to read through these with your group, adjusting the language to suit your group and adding or removing items as needed.

- **Approach these group sessions as a learning time:** "We must come to our sessions with a commitment to learn and to support others in their learning."

- **Believe in the first draft:** "Knowing that we are coming together in community to try on new ideas, to practice speaking up, and to better understand different experiences, we should understand that our ideas may be in first-draft form and not quite perfect."

- **Resist perfection:** "There is no single perfect way to engage in these dialogues. And there is not one linear path toward understanding identity. We must acknowledge that this work can sometimes be messy and that messiness is part of the experience."

- **Assert that allowing messiness does not give participants permission to be oppressive:** "We need to acknowledge when oppressive behavior and experiences have entered the space. We must name and interrupt the behavior and then identify a pathway to recover from and dismantle that oppressive behavior. While we may not intend to be hurtful or harmful, our actions and words might have caused harm. We should take ownership when those moments result from our actions or words."

- **Discuss the difference between *unsafe* and *uncomfortable*:** "We say, 'We want safe spaces for dialogues,' but too often, that really means, 'We don't want to feel uncomfortable.' Discomfort is part of the growth process in this work. Let's discuss what this looks like in our group."

- **Commit to a time limit:** "This work is ongoing. We might be tempted to go beyond our allotted session time because we feel the need to come to some sort of resolution. But resolution isn't always possible in identity work, so we'll prioritize respecting our time commitment. Let's create a time limit for the conversation. Knowing that we could spend forever on each chapter topic, we should limit group discussion on a chapter to sixty to seventy-five minutes, after we've done the individual work within the chapter."

- **Create social opportunities:** "This work is serious and heavy, and we can make it more sustainable if we also experience connection, community, and joy. Let's brainstorm ways to make this work social: Perhaps we can host discussions in different locations. A different person could serve as the facilitator for each meeting. We could have food and drink themes for each event. Let's make it a priority to bring joy into the space in order to connect our conversations to positive feelings and associations."

Reading This Book

The Identity-Conscious Educator: Building Habits and Skills for a More Inclusive School gives you the tools to start an identity-conscious practice in your personal life and professional life so that you may, in turn, support your students, your coworkers, and your school community in doing the same. The book uses a three-part structure, which mirrors the model I introduce for developing the identity-conscious practice: (1) build knowledge, (2) engage in reflection, and (3) move to action. Please note that I use many examples of real-life people to illustrate ideas throughout the book. People's names and the details of real-life events have been changed to protect their privacy.

In part I, chapters 1 and 2 focus on getting ready for identity work by building knowledge about the identity-conscious approach. Consider it a warm-up section where you'll reflect on your experiences with having tough conversations in general. Because people commonly feel nervous or hesitant to talk about identity, the goal of part I is to reframe your relationship with conflict as an invitation, rather than a barrier, to doing this work.

Chapter 1 discusses what it means to become identity conscious and how you can open yourself up to the difficult conversations you'll encounter along the way. You'll explore essential questions about the impact that identity has on teaching and learning, and you'll imagine how you might open the door to difficult conversations.

In chapter 2, I point to a helpful shift in perspective from avoiding conflict to inviting challenge. You'll consider why it's hard to talk about identity, how avoidance patterns keep you stuck in silence, and how inviting challenge allows you to join the conversation.

In part II, chapters 3 through 7 ask you to reflect on five core identities: (1) race, (2) class, (3) sexual orientation, (4) gender, and (5) disability. Any one person can claim many identities, and each identity is an essential part that helps make up the whole person. However, the scope of this book focuses on these five core identities to give you a starting point for cultivating an identity-conscious practice as an educator. Leaning on the three-part model, you'll build knowledge about each identity, reflect on early messages you received and how they influenced your relationship to each identity, and build action plans by engaging with the activities at the end of each chapter.

In chapter 3, you'll examine your relationship to race. You'll explore what it means to shift from color-blind attitudes to color-conscious ones and see how race shows up in the classroom. And you'll examine the impact that identity consciousness has on how you create curricula and how you talk to students about race.

Chapter 4 addresses class, socioeconomic status, and money. While talking about these matters can be uncomfortable, your relationship to class is not neutral; it impacts your life and your work. You'll explore how class differences show up in school, inform how you interact with students, and influence your ability to create greater equity.

Chapter 5 talks about sexual orientation. Because educators have a responsibility to ensure a safe environment for all students, you'll identify how sexual orientation shows up in the classroom, what it looks like to create more inclusive curricula, and how you can talk about the LGBTQ community with students.

Chapter 6 discusses gender identity, especially in relation to the gender norms students encounter in the classroom and school community. Gender has traditionally been framed as a binary, so a critical facet of the work of identity-conscious practice is building knowledge about gender diversity. You'll also have the opportunity to reflect on early messages you received about gender in order to create plans for meeting gender-diverse needs in the classroom and talk with students about gender diversity.

Chapter 7 asks you to explore your relationship with disability. You'll ask the question, "How does disability show up in school?" You'll also examine what changes are needed to create curricula that accommodate students of all abilities and to talk about disability with students.

Now that you know what the identity-conscious practice is and you have a working model for employing it in your life and work, you'll turn your focus to what to do next. In part III, chapters 8 through 12 examine how your behaviors, attitudes, and beliefs move you to action and how you should respond to success and failure along the way.

In chapter 8, you'll explore the terms *ally*, *accomplice*, *co-conspirator*, and *abolitionist* as they relate to identity-conscious teaching and learning. Becoming an ally is not the end goal; it's a first step. So, you'll examine the limits of the ally role and imagine how you might move beyond it to answer the call to become an accomplice, co-conspirator, and abolitionist.

Chapter 9 allows you to reflect on the role of failure in the identity-conscious practice. Despite their commitment to just action, educators will make mistakes and recognize harm in the course of their work with students and peers. The guidance in this chapter calls you to embrace failure as a path to growth and deeper connection with others on the journey.

The focus of chapter 10 is gaining tools to extend your learning beyond the scope of this book. How do you keep learning about identity-conscious practice when you have so many competing priorities? How do you create structures of accountability in your work? Together, we'll identify tools to help you answer these questions.

My hope for you in this identity-conscious journey is that you build your practice to the point that you're able to share it with others. To that end, chapter 11 prepares you to facilitate conversations about identity. You'll learn a framework for noticing participants' cues, and you'll encounter six strategies for responding to challenges that arise in conversation so that you can keep the discussion moving forward.

In chapter 12, you'll review the model we've built for the identity-conscious practice so that you can incorporate other identities as you move beyond this book. My intention is to provide you with the habits and skills you need to become comfortable with the model's framework and adapt it for your unique practice as you move beyond *The Identity-Conscious Educator*.

This work of identity-conscious practice starts with us educators. And it starts here.

Part I
GETTING READY FOR IDENTITY WORK

The work of an educator—teaching, leading, advising, coaching, and collaborating—is not identity neutral. In fact, identity informs and impacts how you act, how you interact with others, and how you see the world around you. In the following chapters, you will build knowledge, engage in reflection, and create action toward an identity-conscious practice. Throughout this book, you will have opportunities to dive deeper into issues of identity. But first, you have to lay the groundwork to understand why identity consciousness is important and what makes it difficult.

CHAPTER 1

The Journey to Identity Awareness

Growing up, I did not have the opportunity to engage in many difficult conversations. The relationships my siblings and I had with our parents were ones of obedience—we did as they told us, we did not argue with our elders, and they encouraged us to "stay out of trouble." For my parents, this approach was culturally rooted in our identities as Asians and Asian Americans. Probably more influential than our ethnic identity, though, was that my parents had fled their home country of the Philippines in the mid-1970s during martial law, when the government took control in response to civil unrest. They had seen what happened to people who spoke out against the government or who challenged authority and the status quo. Soon after martial law began, they left the Philippines for the United States and a promise of freedom.

In the United States, my parents did their best to have our little Filipino family fit in with their new American life. After a few years, they moved us from the crowded city of Boston to the sprawling suburbs. We moved from an apartment to a five-bedroom home. We moved from the city streets with cars to almost an acre of land with cows and sheep grazing behind our back fence. We moved from a city full of immigrants and Black and Brown people to a small town of mostly White Irish and Italian people.

As I tried to fit into this new environment, I learned that being Filipino, being different, would not be easy. My brown-skinned family stood out among a sea of White peers, classmates, teachers, and families. I lived among people who had never heard of the Philippines. At school, I was called a *chink*. In church on Sundays, young children stared at my family and pulled the corner of their eyes, whispering "*Chinese eyes*," while the congregation recited the Our Father. I was asked if I spoke *ching chong* and if I even knew how to speak English.

When I was growing up, I just assumed this was the cost I paid for being different. Later in life, I learned the name for these daily acts: microaggressions (Sue, 2010; Sue et al., 2019). In their initial work about this topic, Columbia University professor of counseling psychology Derald Wing Sue and colleagues (2007) define *microaggressions* as "brief and commonplace daily verbal, behavioral, and environmental indignities, whether intentional or unintentional, that communicate hostile, derogatory, or negative racial slights and insults to the target person or group" (p. 273). The work on microaggressions has evolved over time to address the meaning of "micro" in the term. Namely, "micro" does not refer to how small an act is, but rather it symbolizes the covert and individual manner in which this type of discrimination occurs. Microaggression theory (Torino, Rivera, Capodilupo, Nadal, & Sue, 2019) expanded this definition to recognize the impact of microaggressions on other historically marginalized identities (for example, gender, sexual orientation, ability, religion, size, age, social class, and others). Nadal, Erazo, and King (2019) note that a greater frequency of racial microaggressions was significantly associated with greater traumatic stress symptoms, and that incidents experienced in a school or workplace were the type of microaggressions most associated with traumatic symptoms.

Even though many microaggressions I experienced happened at school or where adults were present, no teacher, school leader, bus driver, playground monitor, or parent or guardian ever intervened. Decades later, my most salient memories of school are not what I learned or what I achieved; instead, I most remember when teachers and other adults failed to see me. I remember when they failed to support me. I remember most when they failed to include me in their teaching, in the curriculum, and in our class conversations.

> Decades later, my most salient memories of school are not what I learned or what I achieved; instead, I most remember when teachers and other adults failed to see me. I remember when they failed to support me. I remember most when they failed to include me in their teaching, in the curriculum, and in our class conversations.

I do not have a single memory of adults speaking up on my behalf. I remember their silence.

In hindsight, I wonder if the adults overheard any of these moments that impacted me so much. I wonder if my teachers ever thought about me or what it must have felt like to be the only Asian American student in their class. I wonder if they thought about how I felt, never seeing myself reflected in their teaching. I wonder if they tried to change their curriculum but feared they might not do it right.

And so, this is where we begin our journey.

In this chapter, you'll learn what it means to become aware of identity and to embrace an identity-conscious practice. I'll highlight the differences in identity-blind and identity-conscious approaches, specifically in regard to cultivating inclusive environments for students. Then I'll talk about how to open the door to tough conversations about identity. I acknowledge that each person has a unique relationship to difficult conversations. The activities at the end of the chapter will allow you to reflect on the early messages you received about identity, conflict, and difficult conversations. Finally, I'll show you how to engage in discussion with your community as one way of moving into action.

ESSENTIAL QUESTIONS

- How does identity impact my teaching and learning?

- How do I build identity consciousness?

- What impact do I have on my students when I do not notice identity?

Reflecting on Your Identity

There exist two broad approaches to diversity: (1) an identity-blind approach (O'Brien & Gilbert, 2013) and (2) an identity-conscious approach (Plaut, Thomas, Hurd, & Romano, 2018). An *identity-blind* approach emphasizes that differences do not impact who people are or how they interact. It might sound like this: "My students are just my students—I don't see their race." This approach minimizes differences, focusing instead on similarities between groups (Leslie, Bono, Kim, & Beaver, 2020). On the surface, this approach may feel unifying because we prioritize what makes us the same. However, an identity-blind approach means that people fail to see that differences matter and that these differences may impact how others experience the world. When we, as teachers and leaders, fail to see differences, we fail to respond to the diverse needs of our community. O'Brien and Gilbert (2013) note three approaches to identity-blind practice: (1) ignoring differences, (2) treating everyone the same, and (3) requiring non-dominant groups to assimilate to dominant identities and practices.

In contrast, an *identity-conscious* approach emphasizes that differences matter. In the classroom, it sounds more like this: "I meet my students where they are at and pay attention to what they need." Leslie et al. (2020) describe this approach as (1) acknowledging differences, (2) supporting groups to maintain their cultures and cultural practices, and (3) valuing differences. This approach is most commonly understood as multiculturalism, the practice of valuing differences in classes and communities, and it results in improved intergroup relationships.

Whether people adopt an identity-blind approach or an identity-conscious approach is itself influenced by their personal identities. To begin building your awareness of identity, take time to reflect on your thoughts, attitudes, behaviors, and beliefs. A range of experiences can shape your perception about identities (such as the five core identities you'll explore in part II [page 37]: (1) race, (2) class, (3) sexual orientation, (4) gender, and (5) disability, including what you have been taught, how you have been treated, who you know, what your family values are, what your culture has told you, and more. Identity consciousness raises your awareness of what is present and what is missing. As you build an identity-conscious practice, the activities in this book can help you explore and understand your approach, identify areas that may be challenging for you, and support you as you build an action plan for your teaching and leading.

Identity-conscious practice is a process of realizing that who you are informs and impacts how you act, how you interact with others, and how you see the world around you. For you, as an educator, this awareness of identity shows up in how you interact with students, what kinds of literature you select, the perspective through which you teach history and social studies, or what language you use in mathematics sets. Consider the following examples.

- In a worksheet created for students, a teacher uses examples referring to "mom and dad." The language fails to be inclusive of a student who has two moms, a student who has two dads, or a student who lives with guardians.

- A teacher privileges social studies texts told from the viewpoints of White explorers. This approach misses an opportunity to provide critical information about the negative impacts of colonization or the contributions of Black, Indigenous, Asian, Latinx, or multiracial people.

- A teacher dialogues with the class about students of color who are labeled "at risk." The discussion neglects to question whether systems are at risk of failing students; instead, it relies on suggesting students have to "build grit" or "work hard."

In each of these scenarios, slight changes in language and perspective create a more inclusive approach. For example, when teachers broaden their understanding of family structure, they include students who are raised with grandparents, have a single-parent home, or live with a caregiver. When teachers honor diverse family structures, they give students space to share about their families, relationships, and connections, which opens the door to knowing them better. Working from an identity-conscious practice means that teachers move away from the limited viewpoint of a deficit model and broaden their understanding of structural and organizational impact. As educators, we must be mindful of the identities we privilege and those that we erase or make invisible. That invisibility can impact a student's sense of belonging in their classroom and their school.

> Identity-conscious practice is a process of realizing that who you are informs and impacts how you act, how you interact with others, and how you see the world around you.

Opening the Door to Difficult Conversations

As you continue on the journey of your identity-conscious practice, you'll inevitably be drawn into conversations about identity with others. Sometimes, these conversations will be comfortable; oftentimes, they will not. To engage in identity-conscious work requires us to have difficult conversations about how we act, interact with others, and see the world (or the classroom) around us. But not everyone has had positive messages about difficult conversations. Some people really like engaging in difficult conversations while others prefer to avoid them. Here again, your identities have likely informed your relationship with difficult conversations.

A characteristic of difficult conversations that we can examine through the lens of identity is *conflict*. Think about some of the earliest messages you received about conflict. Did you learn that engaging in conflict is good, healthy, and productive? Or did you learn that engaging in conflict is hurtful and negative and only leads to bad outcomes? How have those messages about conflict informed and impacted who you are or what you think? If you grew up with messages that conflict is good, healthy, and productive, then you likely feel comfortable in difficult conversations. You might even look forward to difficult conversations because you have experienced that conflict can lead to growth and change. If you learned that conflict is hurtful and negative and only leads to bad outcomes, then you likely avoid or disarm difficult conversations. You might use humor to decrease the anxiety you feel in difficult conversations, or you might agree to disagree to find a quick ending.

Consider the following example of two very different experiences of the same event. During a workshop I facilitated for teachers at a K–12 school, participants discussed how they felt about difficult conversations. Paul, a science teacher who taught across multiple grade levels, shared that he loved getting into difficult conversations with his colleagues. He enjoyed the back-and-forth dialogue, particularly about controversial topics. Paul was often in the faculty room with a newspaper in one hand and his coffee in the other, always ready to have a good conversation with anyone who walked into the room. Paul especially loved discussing topics about identity; these discussions sometimes became heated. Paul described those moments as "passionate and exciting," saying they made him feel energized.

Mia, a fifth-grade teacher, spoke up and said she typically felt intimidated when conversations took on this tone. She recalled a conversation with Paul that turned out this way. Mia said during that conversation, Paul began to argue with her, which made her uncomfortable because she felt the conversation had become a disagreement. She recalled saying to Paul, "I guess we have to just agree to disagree," and "We all have our own opinions," and then walking away. Mia had very negative connections to disagreement. She would rather conversations stopped before they became too much for her to handle. What Paul saw as energizing, passionate, and exciting, Mia saw as difficult, argumentative, and disagreeable.

Conversations about identity often open the door to conflict because people are sharing personal experiences informed by who they are, what they have experienced, and how they see the world around them. If you learned that talking about identities (such as race, class, sexual orientation, gender, and disability) is impolite, improper, or unsafe, then that door is open only a tiny bit, if at all. If you learned that talking about identities is important, healthy, and necessary, then you might be more open and willing to have difficult conversations, knowing that they are an essential part of the identity-conscious practice.

As educators, we create conditions in our classrooms and in our schools that leave the door to difficult conversations either wide open or barely ajar. The opportunities you create for students to have conversations about identity in the classroom are informed by *your* ability to engage in conversations about identity and *your* willingness to have difficult conversations. Do you want to be remembered as an educator who created space for students to talk about issues of identity? Or do you want to be remembered for your silence?

Activities for Developing Identity Awareness

What do K–12 educators need to know, do, and demonstrate in order to begin the journey toward identity awareness? The two activities for this chapter guide you to reflect on your relationship with difficult conversations and raise awareness of various identities.

Activity 1: Engaging in Reflection

In this work of building identity consciousness and opening the door to difficult conversations, it is important to think about the first and early messages you received that inform and impact who you are today. Read the following reflection questions, and record your thoughts and experiences in the space provided.

1. Building identity consciousness requires engaging in difficult conversations. What do you notice about yourself in difficult conversations? What do you notice about others?

   _____

   _____

   _____

2. Conflict is a characteristic of difficult conversations. What do you notice about yourself during conflict? Did you have positive messages about engaging in conflict? Negative messages? How do you think those early messages about conflict inform and impact how you approach difficult conversations today?

   _____

   _____

   _____

3. The Opening the Door to Difficult Conversations section ends with these two questions: (1) Do you want to be remembered as an educator who created space for students to talk about issues of identity? and (2) Do you want to be remembered for your silence? (page 20). How would your current students describe you? How would they respond to your efforts to talk about identity? What is your next step?

   _____

   _____

   _____

Activity 2: Raising Identity Consciousness

Building identity consciousness means you are actively reflecting on issues of identity and the impact of identities on your life. Use the chart for this activity to list identity categories. Take the following three steps to fill out the chart. There are also a few blank spaces at the end of the figure's first column so you have the option to add more identity categories.

1. Go through the list, and in the Familiarity column, make note of the categories you are *familiar* with and the ones you are *less familiar* or *unfamiliar* with.

2. In the space provided in the Identity column, make note of how categories can be further broken down. For example, the category of race consists of identities such as Black, Asian, Latinx, Native American, and White, and the category of disability consists of experiences that may involve emotional disabilities, visible disabilities, invisible disabilities, physical disabilities, and learning disabilities.

3. On a scale of 1 (not very) to 10 (very), how comfortable are you talking about each of these identities? How comfortable are you talking about these identities with (a) friends, (b) family, (c) coworkers, and (d) students? Why, if at all, does your level of comfort change when you talk to these different people? Note your level of comfort in the Friends, Family, Coworkers, and Students columns.

Identity	Familiarity	Friends	Family	Coworkers	Students
Race (for example, Black, Asian, Latinx, Native American, and White)					
Socioeconomic status (for example, working class, middle class, and upper class)					
Gender _____ _____ _____					
Sexual orientation _____ _____ _____					

Identity	Familiarity	Friends	Family	Coworkers	Students
Political beliefs _____ _____ _____					
Mental health _____ _____ _____					
Religion _____ _____ _____					
Disability _____ _____ _____					
Gender identity _____ _____ _____					
Immigration status _____ _____ _____					
Family structure _____ _____ _____					
Health experiences _____ _____ _____					

The Identity-Conscious Educator © 2022 Solution Tree Press • SolutionTree.com
Visit **go.SolutionTree.com/diversityandequity** to download this free reproducible.

Identity	Familiarity	Friends	Family	Coworkers	Students
Body size and shape _____ _____ _____					
Language _____ _____ _____					
Employment experiences _____ _____ _____					
Education _____ _____ _____					
Age _____ _____ _____					
Relationship status _____ _____ _____					
Sex _____ _____ _____					

Discussion

This guide provides structures for you to think deeply about identity and difficult conversations. To advance this beneficial work, engage in conversations with others using the following discussion prompts.

1. Have a conversation with a partner or a small group of three to four people. Go through each activity in this chapter together. Leave enough time to engage in conversation that does not rush learning. Be sure to create intentions for the conversation and expectations for participation. See Bringing People Together on page 8 to help set expectations.

2. In a larger group, engage with the following questions.

    ○ What did you experience as you did the activities in this chapter?

    ○ What did you notice about yourself as you completed these activities?

    ○ What do you believe is your next step as you continue this learning process?

The Identity-Conscious Educator © 2022 Solution Tree Press • SolutionTree.com
Visit **go.SolutionTree.com/diversityandequity** to download this free reproducible.

CHAPTER 2

The Shift From Avoiding Conflict to Inviting Challenge

As the middle child in a large family, I grew up navigating different social relationships. At times, I was too young or too little to hang out with the older siblings and too old or too big to be with my younger siblings. I spent most of my life navigating these relationships where I didn't always fit in. Even as an adult, I still find myself in these types of relationships. Because I often served as the bridge between the older siblings and the younger siblings, I had to pay attention to relationships. Oftentimes, being that bridge builder was rewarding, fun, and made me feel connected to different types of people. But it also made me feel anxious when there was conflict; after all, conflict created tension, and I desired to keep peace in the family. As an adult, I easily recognized this tension in my workplace, on teaching teams, and on school leadership teams. I shied away from this tension and, as a result, gave up a lot in my relationships. Most notably, I gave in to the needs of others instead of sticking up for my own needs. I sacrificed some of my emotional needs to keep conflict from escalating. In order to protect myself, I developed patterns of avoidance.

As my career evolved, I had to confront my avoidance tactics. When I started teaching graduate students in an education and leadership program, the department chair told me that she wanted to more explicitly address the role of teachers and school leaders in confronting race and racism in education. I was nervous about developing a curriculum and syllabus that were designed around confrontation, discomfort, and tension. I worried that these difficult topics would alienate my students, and they wouldn't like me. I feared the conflict that would occur in class and the honesty that would be required of my students. I voiced my fears to my department chair: "What if I make students uncomfortable?" She replied, "That's exactly what needs to happen."

Though I had this permission and directive, I was still tempted to avoid the conflict I knew would come. My remedy: Dive in headfirst. My action items: Create an entire syllabus filled with authors of color, with topics that centered on issues of race, and with activities that explicitly called out racism in education. On the first day of class, I said, "Our educational systems are built on and upheld by racism. Are you ready to tackle this?" The students shifted in their seats, and then they smiled. "We are nervous, but we are ready," they replied. We made it through the semester—with some difficult discussions, big emotions, and even bouts of frustration. But courageously diving into this conflict was a necessary and powerful learning experience. Instead of fearing conflict, I learned to see it as an invitation to grow my capacity and connect with others. The following year, those same students asked for another class in which they could strengthen their educational leadership skills. In response, I developed a course called Anti-Racist Leadership Skills. Together we dove even deeper into conflict, and these emerging school leaders prepared to tackle some of the most pervasive issues of systemic racism. If I hadn't been able to face my fear, I wouldn't have been open to these opportunities.

Addressing your relationship to conflict is an important step in building an identity-conscious practice. In this chapter, I'll talk about why interrupting your avoidance patterns is critical to this process. Many educators avoid having difficult conversations because they're uncomfortable. But what if, instead of seeing difficult conversations as barriers to comfort, you saw the discomfort they cause as an invitation to learn, explore, and examine different ways of knowing or being? These opportunities for growth can lead educators to new conversations, readings, and interactions in the classroom. From there, you'll discover how to build the skills you'll need for engaging in those difficult conversations. Being able to move through discomfort is key to talking about challenging issues. As you work through the three activities at the end of the chapter, you will create action plans for moving through discomfort in productive ways.

ESSENTIAL QUESTIONS

- How does avoidance show up in my personal life and professional life?

- What do I risk by not talking about identity?

- What steps can I take to be more identity conscious?

Interrupting Your Avoidance Patterns

While leaning on avoidance as a coping mechanism is natural, it severely limits a person's capacity for engaging in important issues. And when it comes to creating more inclusive environments in classrooms and schools, avoidance makes progress difficult.

Research demonstrates that when teachers, trainers, and parents are unable to facilitate a successful dialogue on race, they fail to engage in empathy, dim awareness and accuracy of differences, and invalidate experiences associated with race and racism (Sue, 2015). For example, Porosoff and Weinstein (2021) note that social-emotional learning (SEL) practices are a powerful driver in shaping educational experiences and current classroom approaches to learning, management, and behavior. And yet, many of us as teachers and school leaders have failed to state how outcomes of SEL are racially biased. Dena Simmons (2021), a leading researcher in SEL, states that, when not situated in a racialized context, SEL can simply be "White supremacy with a hug." Therefore, we should "honor the full range of emotions as expressions of our common humanity, and use emotional experiences as opportunities to discover the values underneath" (Porosoff & Weinstein, 2021). That range of emotions includes the discomfort we might feel when addressing issues of race and racism.

When I began a dialogue on race in the graduate-level course I taught, my students noted patterns of avoidance in the education they had previously received and the education they themselves provided. These were public and private school teachers, school administrators, university leaders, and nonprofit directors; each one had significant experience as a student and as an educational professional. They told me, "Dr. Talusan, this is the first time I have ever heard about racism in education in this way." They couldn't believe that this information had not been required in their undergraduate curriculum, that it hadn't been discussed in their high school classes. Their comments confirmed what Derald Wing Sue (2015) reports in *Race Talk and the Conspiracy of Silence: Understanding and Facilitating Difficult Dialogues on Race*: "Race talk is often silenced, ignored, diluted, and/or discussed in very superficial ways for fear of offending others or creating potentially explosive situations" (p. 17).

So, it was no surprise when my students were initially uncomfortable with the content of my class. They worried about their words, their statements, and their perspectives. But the deeper we went into the literature, the more they understood that part of the discomfort was that the content was new, different, and unfamiliar. As the year went on, they expanded their vocabulary for an identity-conscious practice, and they normalized discomfort as part of the learning process. They saw how their daily lives in the classroom and in schools are informed by identity. Through these new concepts, we engaged in conversations that challenged their ideas about teaching, leading, and education. And, these conversations helped them develop the skills they needed to engage in difficult conversations. By the time they finished the course, my students had grown more confident and courageous. As a result, most had begun to talk more explicitly about identity in their classrooms and teaching teams; and all of them had created action plans for how to bring this work into their teaching. With practice, my students shifted from their learned avoidance to courageous connection.

With better tools, deeper understanding, and practice, teachers and leaders can see discomfort as an invitation to learn, do, and engage more.

That shift wasn't unique to my first group of graduate students; it's a pattern I've witnessed year after year with diverse student groups. With better tools, deeper understanding, and practice, teachers and leaders can see discomfort as an invitation to learn, do, and engage more. Next, let's look at how you can take your first steps toward inviting difficult conversations.

Inviting Difficult Conversations

You've seen how avoiding conflict limits opportunities to build an identity-conscious practice. But interrupting avoidance patterns doesn't instantly empower teachers to have difficult conversations. We educators sometimes avoid topics because we do not have enough information about or experience with the content. We tend to avoid challenging experiences because we have not developed the skills to engage in productive conflict (Patton, 2017; Singleton, 2014). To get to the point of inviting difficult conversations, we need to learn how to have effective disagreements and productive discourse; we have to acquire tools for engaging in a critical way. Rather than avoid difficult conversations, we should ask ourselves, "What skills do I need in order to guide students to have difficult conversations?"

A great way to start building those skills is by expanding your capacity to engage with discomfort as conversations naturally arise in the classroom. When I ask students if their teachers provide opportunities for difficult conversations in their classes, students overwhelmingly respond, "No. When a difficult conversation is about to happen, a teacher says, 'We aren't talking about this right now,' or shuts it down with, 'OK, moving on . . .' without allowing for opportunities for discussion." When I relay this to teachers, they tell me that they worry about the direction those conversations will take or that they're afraid they won't have the right tools to facilitate the discussion or they won't have the right answers to students' questions. The most comfortable approach, therefore, is to avoid the difficulty. What might happen if, instead of avoiding the discomfort, the teachers moved through it and allowed the conversation to play out?

Imagine this scenario in class: You are covering a lesson about voting. As an in-class activity, you ask your students to create something to vote on: "favorite candy" or "best school lunch option" or "favorite sports team." This leads you to talking about the role of voting in a democracy. The students begin sharing conversations they have heard from adults about certain political candidates and their platforms. You hear them use some of the name-calling tactics that are common in political commercials. You are nervous about where this conversation is going and say, "OK, students. That's enough. Let's go back to voting on your favorites."

What happened here?

Out of worry and fear, you shut down the conversation and returned to safer subject matter. What would this look like if, instead of returning back to the starting line, you guided the students to think critically, to engage in reflection, and to move to action?

Let's try this again: You hear them use some of the name-calling tactics that are common in the kinds of attack ads in political commercials. You are nervous about where this conversation is going, so you say, "Before we go much further, let's talk about what's happening right now in our class process. I'm noticing you are all excited about this topic—I am, too. It's great to see you so invested in this conversation. Let's check in with everyone's comfort level. On a scale of 1 (not very comfortable) to 10 (very comfortable), how comfortable do you feel talking about this topic? Write that number on a piece of paper and hold it up so I can see it. Great, thanks. So I'm seeing a range of comfort around this topic. As we move forward, let's find ways as a class community to make sure we can have conversations that keep everyone engaged. We've been talking about who gets a voice in democracy. What are you noticing about voice and participation even in this conversation right now?"

By leaning into this conversation, revealing that discomfort is present, and checking in about the processes of conflict, you engage students in the difficult conversation instead of avoiding it. This is how teachers and students build skills for moving through challenging topics and taking responsibility for the classroom community.

While these opportunities for conflict happen more often in later grades than earlier, research suggests being open to conflict in the early years is beneficial. In their book *Courageous Leadership in Early Childhood Education: Taking a Stand for Social Justice*, editors Susi Long, Mariana Souto-Manning, and Vivian Maria Vasquez (2016) report, "Messages received in early childhood . . . impact how children see one another. From their earliest days, children can learn to value people from backgrounds different from their own or they can learn to enact negative biases" (p. 17). Early childhood educators also need to know how to engage in this discomfort as they set the foundation for the type of learning that students will seek out, expect, and experience in education.

Researchers Mary E. Dankoski, Janet Bickel, and Maryellen E. Gusic (2014) note that:

Training in communication skills is imperative to counteract the costs of organizational silence. Indeed, effective communication and the ability to manage difficult conversations are core competencies for all faculty members, and relational communication skills development is essential for all leaders, faculty, and staff. (p. 1613)

One way teachers can build skills for inviting challenge instead of avoiding conflict is by imagining how they could have responded differently during a past conversation. This exercise allows them to practice in a low-stakes environment and enables them to build confidence. Figure 2.1 provides a series of five steps for reflecting on an experience and identifying different possible outcomes; then the figure shares an example of how a teacher reflected on a conversation with a colleague and wrote an alternate ending in which they invited the challenge.

Step 1: Describe in detail an interaction, comment, or experience related to identity.

Step 2: Underline words or phrases that highlight the discomfort or the conflict you experienced.

Step 3: Circle opportunities where something could have happened in a more positive way.

Step 4: Add to or change the story to reflect how you would shift to a different response.

Step 5: Revisit the new conversation and reflect on how you were engaged rather than avoidant.

I was sitting at the lunch table with a colleague. She identifies as Jewish, and she was talking about a situation that her family was in. She began to describe that she felt it was a good idea to buy a new bedroom set, but her husband didn't want to spend the money. She used the phrase, "He was being so Jewish about it." As I sat and listened to her, I knew that the comment was not appropriate and it leaned into existing stereotypes that people have and make about people who are Jewish. Yet, I knew my friend and her family identify as Jewish. I was immediately uncomfortable about her comment, but I was more uncomfortable about the decision I had to make to say something or not say something. I am not Jewish, and I began to wonder, Is it my place to say something to someone who is commenting about their own identity, an identity I do not share?

In hindsight, I would have responded by saying, "Maya, so that sounds like a difficult decision you have about the bedroom set. I hope you and your husband can work out that difference. I just wanted to share a reaction I had when I heard you use the phrase, 'He was being so Jewish about it.' I'm not Jewish, so I don't have closeness to that comment, but it just felt like it was leaning into some negative stereotypes that I've heard about people who are Jewish. How did it make you feel to use that phrase?"

Working through this framework makes it so easy to see where I could have addressed this discomfort. Maya is a friend of mine, and I didn't want to offend her by bringing up the comment she made. I also worried because I don't know if it's appropriate to give that kind of feedback to people who hold an identity they make a comment about. But writing it down makes it seem doable without coming off as being offensive myself. I was really uncomfortable not saying anything, so speaking up next time I hear something like this comment is a good way for me to take action.

FIGURE 2.1: Steps and example of writing a new narrative.

Activities for Shifting From Avoiding Conflict to Inviting Challenge

What do K–12 educators need to know, do, and demonstrate in order to shift from avoiding conflict to inviting challenge? The three activities for this chapter guide you to reflect on your avoidance tactics, examine your relationship with discomfort, and build skills for inviting challenging conversations.

Activity 1: Engaging in Reflection

In this work of building identity consciousness and opening the door to difficult conversations, it is important to think about the first and early messages you received that inform and impact the way you relate to conflict or avoid discomfort. Read the following reflection questions, and record your thoughts and experiences in the space provided.

1. Think back to a time when you avoided a conversation about identity. What were the benefits of avoiding the conversation? How might you have benefited from engaging in the conversation?

   _____

   _____

   _____

   _____

2. What topics were emphasized in your teacher preparation program? What topics did you not learn about or not learn enough about in your training or educational program?

   _____

   _____

   _____

   _____

3. What do you notice about your behavior as a teacher or leader when difficult or controversial topics come up in your class? How would your students describe your approach to these moments?

   _____

   _____

   _____

   _____

Activity 2: Seeing Discomfort as an Invitation

Experiencing discomfort is a key component of engaging in conversations about identity. Yet, discomfort is also a common reason that people avoid tough conversations. The chart for this activity provides space for you to reflect and write about how you experience discomfort in the classroom. You can add other identities in the blank space provided in the chart's first column.

For each identity category, record your thoughts about the following.

- **Comfort level:** On a scale of 1 (not very) to 10 (very), how comfortable are you talking about each of these identities? Note your level of comfort in the Comfort Level column.

- **Causes of comfort or discomfort:** Note causes that contribute to your comfort or discomfort around the identity.

- **Action plan:** Note one action you can take to become more comfortable with the identity.

- **Next step:** Note one step you can take to have more conversations about the identity in your classroom.

Identity Category	Comfort Level	Causes of Comfort or Discomfort	Action Plan	Next Step
Race				
Social class				
Sexual orientation				
Gender				
Disability				

Activity 3: Writing a New Narrative

As you build the habits and skills of an identity-conscious practice, you'll find it easier to address the discomfort that comes with difficult conversations. Writing about a time when you experienced discomfort related to a conversation about identity and imagining a different response are a great way to practice these skills. The box provided for this activity lists a series of five steps for reflecting on an experience and identifying different possible outcomes. Refer to figure 2.1 (page 32) for an example version of this tool.

Step 1: Describe in detail an interaction, comment, or experience related to identity.

Step 2: Underline words or phrases that highlight the discomfort or the conflict you experienced.

Step 3: Circle opportunities where something could have happened in a more positive way.

Step 4: Add to or change the story to reflect how you would shift to a different response.

Step 5: Revisit the new conversation and reflect on how you were engaged rather than avoidant.

Discussion

This guide provides structures for you to think deeply about identity and difficult conversations. To advance this beneficial work, engage in conversations with others using the following discussion prompts.

1. Have a conversation with a partner or a small group of three to four people. Go through each activity in this chapter together. Leave enough time to engage in conversation that does not rush learning. Be sure to create intentions for the conversation and expectations for participation. See Bringing People Together on page 8 to help set expectations.

2. In a larger group, engage with the following questions.

    ○ What did you experience as you did the activities in this chapter?

    ○ What did you notice about yourself as you completed these activities?

    ○ What do you believe is your next step as you continue this learning process?

Part II

BUILDING YOUR IDENTITY-CONSCIOUS PRACTICE

Part I of this book (page 13) was about building the knowledge you need to be ready to undertake an identity-conscious practice. In part II, you will reflect on five core identities: race (chapter 3, page 39), class (chapter 4, page 51), sexual orientation (chapter 5, page 67), gender (chapter 6, page 83), and disability (chapter 7, page 99). In each chapter, you'll explore how that identity shows up in the classroom, how educators might work toward greater inclusion, how teachers can open the door to difficult conversations with their students, and how that identity intersects with other identities. Each chapter models a helpful three-part framework for thinking about identity and experience: (1) build knowledge, (2) engage in reflection, and (3) move to action. Each chapter ends with a series of activities intended to help you build awareness and create action plans for engaging in difficult conversations.

It's important to note that these chapters and this book cannot cover all the possibilities and nuances of identity. Your students, peers, and community members who hold these identities each have unique experiences and perspectives. A single story cannot represent an entire experience. While individuals might share similarities within their identity groups, it is not accurate to believe that all Asian people or all LGBTQ people or all working-class people have the same experiences. Along those lines, remember to honor the language and terms people use to refer to themselves.

CHAPTER 3

Race

I identify racially as Asian American and ethnically as second-generation Filipina. I grew up in a middle-class town outside of Boston in a suburb that was over 90 percent White. Only a handful of students in my high school identified as Asian or Asian American, Black or African American, Latina or Latino.

I did not have any classroom teachers who identified as people of color. All my school leaders were White, and every sports coach I had was White. I knew about Martin Luther King Jr., but we only discussed him in the context of a school holiday. I heard about Rosa Parks as an example of a courageous person, with no mention of the context of community organizing, the fight for civil rights, and the movement for equality (Theoharis, 2015). Names like Dolores Huerta, Larry Itliong, Cesar Chavez, Frida Kahlo, Angela Davis, and Georgia O'Keeffe would not appear in my education until college and beyond.

In high school, I learned quick facts like, "The Chinese helped build the railroads," but I would not learn about the racism, brutality, and death suffered by Chinese workers until I was an adult (Chang, 2019). I learned about Pearl Harbor Day and when the Japanese attacked the United States, but I did not learn about Japanese internment, systemic disenfranchisement, and the incarceration of innocent Americans of Japanese heritage (Nagata, Kim, & Wu, 2019; Trickey, 2017). My teachers, who were all White, taught history, English, social studies, science, mathematics, and writing from a Eurocentric perspective. I grew up twenty miles from Plimoth Plantation, the site where—teachers told me—Pilgrims came to these shores, befriended Native Americans, and gave us our national tradition of Thanksgiving. I would later learn—on my own and from the labor of Native and Indigenous people—that there was a very different narrative, one that centered the voices of Native and Indigenous people and included stories of destruction, war, and illness (Silverman, 2019).

My life at a school of Eurocentric stories, viewpoints, and perspectives was different from my life at home with my family. While the world outside our doors was White, my parents kept a very Filipino household. We ate Filipino foods, like adobo rice, sinigang, nilaga, and longanisa. Our home was decorated with the traditional wooden spoon and fork in the dining room, and I swept the kitchen floor each night with a *walis tambo*, a feather-like fan for smooth indoor floors. Though my parents kept many traditions from their home country, they chose not to teach my siblings and me Tagalog, the melodic language they spoke, because they worried that we would develop accents or get it confused with English. We were Filipino inside our home; we tried our best to fit into White America when we stepped outside.

This is a behavior called *code-switching*: "when the person 'temporarily' enacts behavioral codes of the mainstream group with the hope [of] demonstrating one's capacity and motivation to 'fit-in'" (Cross et al., 2017, p. 5). The challenge with always code-switching is that it feels impossible to fit in all the time.

> The challenge with always code-switching is that it feels impossible to fit in all the time.

I was constantly navigating and negotiating my identity. And yet, it didn't put an end to the microaggressions I experienced. It didn't remove the personal burden I carried of being and feeling so different from those around me. When children on the playground called me racial slurs, I often wondered, "Who taught them to call me those words?" At church, at restaurants—wherever I ventured in my predominantly White environment—people looked at me and pulled at the corners of their eyes. Sometimes, they stayed silent. Other times, they affected an Asian-sounding language, certainly one I did not speak. All the way through college, I was told that I "spoke English so well." These aggressions happened so frequently that I did not even realize they were wrong. I internalized the events, feeling it was somehow my responsibility—if only I were White, I could erase the problem. Those daily assaults, combined with a lack of affirmation of my identity in my school, curriculum, and classes, contributed to these feelings of alienation. I can't change my childhood; in many ways, the experiences I had during that time shaped my commitment to building skills for more inclusive schools. Because these experiences shaped me, they are a part of my identity-conscious practice. I reflect on those experiences and allow them to inform the way I collaborate with communities to create more inclusive environments. Through the activities in this book, you can build the habits and skills of working from an identity-conscious framework to shape confident, capable, and identity-conscious communities.

In this chapter, I'll talk about why it's important for teachers to shift from color-blind to color-conscious attitudes. Students are not identity neutral; acting as though they are, even when that behavior is rooted in good intentions, does not create healthy learning environments. Teachers must acknowledge that race shows up in their interactions with students and in their choices about the curriculum. I'll also assure readers that it's OK for students to talk about race, sharing research about what kinds of topics are age appropriate. Finally, you'll have a chance to explore how race intersects with other identities. In the activities at the end of the chapter, you'll reflect on early messages you received about race and form action plans for engaging in difficult conversations.

- What were some of the earliest messages I received about race?
- How does my racial identity inform and impact my actions and interactions in my personal life and professional life?
- What steps can I take to be more aware of race?

Shifting From Color Blind to Color Conscious

Teachers need to build the habits and skills of including students' identities in their teaching, leading, and learning. This can be especially challenging for teachers who learned conflicting early messages, such as to not see race but to only see people or kindness or some other common human characteristic.

This attitude may stem from a positive desire to humanize relationships, but sociologists caution that a color-blind ideology rarely produces that outcome. Political sociologist Eduardo Bonilla-Silva "has written extensively about the idea of color blindness, charting the ways that it functions as an ideology that legitimizes specific practices that maintain racial inequalities—police brutality, housing discrimination, voter disenfranchisement, and others" (Wingfield, 2015). When teachers erase the identities of students, they limit opportunities to expand their own knowledge and experiences with differences. The color-blind approach fails to address the complexities that make up each unique person. By treating everyone the same, teachers fail to provide the representation students need to feel validated, affirmed, seen, heard, and appreciated in the classroom. Saying "I don't see your race" means not honoring how a student's racialized experiences have informed and impacted their education. Castro-Atwater (2016) noted that this color blind racial ideology (CBRI) can lead to problematic outcomes in the classroom.

> Teachers who adopt CBRI are likely to avoid racial questions or comments from students because they are "uncomfortable" or "sensitive" and because they believe in emphasizing "sameness" over difference. However, teachers who dismiss students' questions or comments about race, fearing that they will introduce prejudice into the child's life or assuming that differences do not matter, thwart the child's ability to engage in constructive discourse and to develop critical thinking on the subject. (p. 212)

A couple of practical realities can help people understand why engaging in dialogues about race matters. First, it's not accurate for people to say they don't see race. I'll use myself as an example: When you look at me, it's obvious that I am Asian. You see that

I have black hair and brown skin, and I have what people describe as almond-shaped eyes. If you are privileged to have eyesight, you literally see these attributes. Second, from people's earliest experiences, their racial identity informs and impacts who they are and how they interact with the world—in both positive and negative ways. Not seeing people's race is dismissive of the prejudice and discrimination they may have experienced, and the privileges they may have access to, as a result of their racial identity. Not acknowledging their race means failing to see them as whole people and honor the full range of their experience.

Shifting from color-blind attitudes to color-conscious ones is truly a practice; it takes time, self-compassion, and creativity. If this feels new and unfamiliar to you, you might start with a simple reframe: instead of saying that you don't see race, state that you don't rely on stereotypes of racial groups. Another helpful option would be to acknowledge that you do, in fact, understand the real impact of race, and therefore, you do see race. As you reflect on race, the first of the core identities you'll examine in part II of this book, an important step is raising awareness of racial identities and learning how they inform and impact your experiences with others.

> Shifting from color-blind attitudes to color-conscious ones is truly a practice; it takes time, self-compassion, and creativity.

How might you be employing a color-blind approach? What can you do to shift toward becoming color conscious? First, identify ways you might have benefited from color blind racial ideology (CBRI). For example, CBRI may have made teaching easier for you by allowing you to focus on issues of character: kindness, respect, collaboration. By focusing on common outcomes, you were able to have broad conversations on shared community goals. Another benefit may be that you typically teach material you learned in your own schooling or teacher preparation programs, which likely was not inclusive of culturally diverse approaches.

As you become aware of race and how it impacts your relationship to others, you extend your color-conscious approach by being truthful in your teaching. Prepare your students to engage in critical thinking, to identify systems of inequity, and to be problem solvers and change leaders of the future. Students cannot change a system they don't know is broken. If we as teachers are perpetuating the idea that racism is a thing of the past then we invalidate any current experiences students have with racism, and we convince them that there is nothing to work toward. The truth is that racism continues to exist today. It's not a problem that a few brave activists solved in years past; it's a challenge that each of us must work together to resolve.

Creating a More Inclusive Curriculum

In 2020 and into 2021, lawmakers in sixteen states introduced or passed legislation seeking to limit how teachers talk about racism with students (Flaherty, 2021). These bills were echoes of a defunct executive order that banned the teaching of "divisive" topics—including those related to race and gender—in schools. For a while, the order had a chilling effect. Teachers and leaders wondered if the media or parents and caregivers would target them for teaching students about race. However, many failed to understand that our current school curriculum is already shaped by race: it centers White people, White achievements, and White advancement.

Some educators retreated under the pressure; others leaned into the conversation, knowing that building habits and skills for talking about race would prepare them and their students to address some of society's toughest challenges. According to early childhood education teacher Marianne Modica (2015),

> Silence about race denies students the skills they need to talk about race openly and honestly and the opportunity to think about how racism affects them and their relationships with others. Teachers who believe it is best to be colorblind lose the opportunity to address racial inequity in their classrooms and in their overall school programs. (p. 397)

Further, Modica (2015) found that teachers who engage in self-reflection with their students "model a process of growth that blends cognitive understandings and affective dispositions in the construction of racial identity" (p. 414). Modica encourages teachers to grow alongside their students, rather than believe themselves to be steps ahead of students in their learning about race. Students benefit from seeing their teachers working through tough challenges and understanding that we are all learning about identity together.

Teachers can implement their learning about race into the classroom by practicing what Zaretta Hammond (2015), teacher educator and author of *Culturally Responsive Teaching and the Brain*, calls culturally responsive teaching. *Culturally responsive teaching* is less about motivating students with racial pride and more about "mimicking students' cultural learning styles and tools. These are the strategies their moms, dads, grandmas, and other community folks use to teach them life skills and basic concepts long before they come to school and during out-of-school time." Hammond (2015) uses the example of a teacher struggling to get students to master science vocabulary using a typical approach: listing words on the board, instructing students to copy and define the words on paper, and assessing students on a vocabulary test. While this approach may be appropriate for some students, it's not ideal for diverse students who come from oral cultural traditions—which are common across African American, Latino, Southeast Asian, and

Pacific Islander communities. Hammond (2015) offers the following three suggestions for transforming any lesson to be more culturally responsive for diverse students:

1. **Make it a game:** In oral cultural traditions, the primary means of transferring knowledge and making meaning are oral and active. When teachers use a game as a means of instruction, they're tapping into that learning style: getting the brain's attention and requiring active processing. "Most games employ a lot of the cultural tools you'd find in oral traditions—repetition, solving a puzzle, making connections between things that don't seem to be related" (Hammond, 2015).

2. **Make it communal:** Organize the learning experience to align with diverse students' communal orientation. Allowing students to collaborate or compete (in a good-natured way) increases student engagement.

3. **Make it a story:** All students learn through stories; our brains use story structure to understand our environment. But this is especially true for oral traditions, where stories play a central role in passing on cultural values and moral lessons. Diverse students "learn content more effectively if they can create a coherent narrative about the topic or process presented" (Hammond, 2015).

Once teachers begin to see race and recognize the diverse identities of their students, the work extends to reshaping curricula so that instructional strategies represent and celebrate students' identities. As you build your identity-conscious practice, take a critical look at your curriculum, ask whether it recognizes and celebrates the diverse identities of all students, and make changes accordingly.

Talking to Students About Race

"At what age should I start talking with students about race?" Teachers are curious about this question; some have a set belief that there is a right stage or age to have conversations about race. Research suggests that more than designating a right age, the important factor is integrating conversations about race and identity into everyday conversations (Lingras, 2021). Researchers Sullivan, Wilton, and Apfelbaum (2020) reported an interesting causal relationship between adult perceptions of race readiness and the preference to delay conversations about race: "Our data suggest that fundamental misunderstandings about children's capacities to process race are pervasive in the United States population and may delay when adults engage children in important conversations about race" (p. 1). Professor Kang Lee found that babies as young as six to nine months notice racial difference and form race-based bias long before they enter school (Craig, 2017). Teachers have an opportunity to provide foundational knowledge to young students about skin color, the concept of race, and similarities and differences in a way that promotes respect, care, and unity. Students can build on this early learning as they progress through their education, prepared to handle increasingly more complex ideas about race and racism.

Although teachers can provide this instruction through lessons and activities, it's also helpful to bring the topic into conversations whenever the opportunity arises. This practice of talking about race and ethnicity in everyday conversations is helpful for the following reasons.

- **It normalizes the experience of talking about race:** If we wait to talk about race until a tragic experience occurs, students learn that race is connected to something negative. Instead, when students build the habits and skills for talking about race in everyday experiences, they're able to normalize these conversations, build trusting relationships with adults, and process racialized information in many different contexts.

- **It helps students know where to go for answers instead of relying on unreliable sources:** If students are curious, they often look for answers online, where misinformation abounds. Alternatively, they may turn to peers or social media for answers. While these pathways can be helpful, they should not be the only sources students go to. When teachers talk regularly about race, they create a trusting bond with young students. They learn to go to the teacher as a trusted source of information, as someone they can go to with questions.

- **It challenges single-story narratives by providing a more complex, contextual, and accurate portrait of race:** In the absence of accurate information from a trusted adult, young people draw their own conclusions about the world around them. It's all too easy for students to form false impressions about race. For example, a student might make the assumption that all poor people are people of color, or that all people of color are poor. But if this student began having regular conversations about race in class, their learning about structural racism and classism might challenge their single-story narrative.

The Children's Community School (2018) has put together a helpful graphic that outlines the stages of child development and the types of conversations that might be appropriate for those ages (visit https://bit.ly/3FuwEC1). This graphic highlights development steps and identifies resources for talking about race with children from birth through to age six plus.

When I'm asked, "When is the right time to talk about race?" I typically answer, "Every time is a good time to talk about race." Talking about race teaches students how

Talking about race teaches students how to engage in conversations about race, helps them explore and understand their racial identities, and supports healthy social development.

to engage in conversations about race, helps them explore and understand their racial identities, and supports healthy social development. Part of building skills for racial conversations means not waiting for a major moment to have the conversation. To put it another way, teachers are proactively preparing students by equipping them with the tools to have effective dialogues.

For example, in discussing a book with the class, a teacher might ask,

- "What do you notice about the characters? How would you describe them? Using words about skin color, race, gender, and age, how would you add to those descriptions?"

- "The character in this book was treated differently because of their race. What are some examples where the character was treated differently?"

- "What advantages or privileges (or lack thereof) did characters hold? What connections do you make between race and how characters were treated in this book?"

If teachers learned from early messages they received that race is not a safe topic of conversation, it makes sense that they might feel uncomfortable or unprepared to talk about it with students. Through the lens of identity-conscious practice, teachers can shift from avoidance to invitation. By developing the skills needed to engage in difficult conversations about race, teachers no longer need to fear opening the door to discussion in the classroom.

Noticing How Race Intersects With Other Identities

While race is a salient factor in the identity-conscious practice, it is also important to acknowledge that other aspects of identity contribute to how a person experiences the world. Race can also be informed by other identities such as class, gender, disability, and sexual orientation. In other words, how does a person's race intersect with other identities they hold? In an interview with Katy Steinmetz (2020) for *TIME*, lawyer and scholar Kimberlé Crenshaw explains the term *intersectionality*, which she coined in 1989.

It's basically a lens, a prism, for seeing the way in which various forms of inequality often operate together and exacerbate each other. We tend to talk about race inequality as separate from inequality based on gender, class, sexuality or immigrant status. What's often missing is how some people are subject to all of these, and the experience is not just the sum of its parts.

For example, we know that school discipline reports demonstrate disparities in the rates of discipline for Black boys versus White boys (Riddle & Sinclair, 2019). But, what happens when we also look at the intersection of gender and race? Researchers Edward Morris and Brea Perry (2017) studied the racial disparities in the discipline process of Black girls. Morris and Perry (2017) noted:

> troubling and significant disparities in the punishment of African American girls. Controlling for background variables, black girls are three times more likely than white girls to receive an office referral; this difference is substantially wider than the gap between black boys and white boys. Moreover, black girls receive disproportionate referrals for infractions such as disruptive behavior, dress code violations, disobedience, and aggressive behavior. We argue that these infractions are subjective and influenced by gendered interpretations. Using the framework of intersectionality, we propose that school discipline penalizes African American girls for behaviors perceived to transgress normative standards of femininity. (p. 127)

Given these two studies, it is not enough to simply look at race, although race is a significant factor in discipline outcomes. Morris and Perry's (2017) research illustrates that the intersection of being both Black and female results in specific outcomes.

What does this have to do with teachers' identity-conscious practice? Researchers Valentina Migliarini and Subini Ancy Annamma (2020) explain: "When teachers understand (1) ways students are systemically oppressed, (2) how oppressions are (re)produced in classrooms, and (3) what they can do to resist those oppressions in terms of pedagogy, curriculum, and relationships, they can build solidarity and resistance with students and communities" (p. 2). Examining the role of identity and the ways in which identities intersect provides teachers with a more robust understanding of students and their lives. This perspective is an essential part of creating a more inclusive school and classroom community.

Activities for Building Awareness of Race

What do K–12 educators need to know, do, and demonstrate in order to incorporate race into their identity-conscious practice? The three activities in this chapter guide you to reflect on your relationship with race, identify gaps in your learning, and notice how race intersects with other identities.

Activity 1: Engaging in Reflection

In this work of building identity consciousness around race, it is important to think about the first and early messages you received that inform and impact your approach to race. Read the following reflection questions, and record your thoughts and experiences in the space provided.

1. What were the earliest messages you received about race? What did you see, learn, or notice about race? Were these messages positive? Were they negative?

    _____

    _____

    _____

    _____

2. How have your earliest messages about race informed or impacted who you are or what you do today? How do those first messages show up in your teaching, your curriculum, or your interactions with students and families?

    _____

    _____

    _____

    _____

3. What messages, if any, did you receive about race while you were in school?

    _____

    _____

    _____

    _____

4. What, if anything, would have been different if you learned positive messages about other racial groups in your schooling and education?

_____

_____

_____

_____

Activity 2: Identifying Gaps in Your Learning

In addition to receiving messages about race in their homes and families, people receive messages about race through their schools and learning experiences. For this activity, choose one racial group and answer the following questions to determine strengths and gaps in your understanding of that group. To gain further insight, repeat this exercise, considering a different race each time.

- What were your earliest messages from school about this group?

- What positive contributions by this group did you learn about in school?

- What challenges have you learned about related to this group?

- What gaps exist in your learning about this group?

- Where might you go to seek information about this specific group?

- What tools would you bring in to make sure you teach lessons from the perspective of this racial group?

- What available resources or partnerships can you connect with to give your students an accurate and appropriate learning experience about this group?

_____

_____

_____

_____

_____

_____

_____

_____

_____

After completing the activity, reflect on the following questions.

- What do you notice about your responses to the questions?

- Which questions were difficult to answer? Which questions were easy to answer?

- Why do you think schools leave out information about certain groups? Why do you think schools include information about certain groups?

- How were certain groups included in your own formal schooling? How were certain groups left out of your own formal schooling?

- What steps would you take to make sure you are engaging with culturally responsible content?

Activity 3: Building Your Identity-Conscious Practice

Race intersects with other identities, such as class, gender, sexual orientation, immigration status, education, disability, and geographic location. What do you notice or wonder about how race is informed and impacted by other aspects of your identity? In the space provided, write about how your experiences with race might show up in your teaching, leading, and learning.

_____

_____

_____

_____

Discussion

This guide provides structures for you to think deeply about identity and difficult conversations. To advance this beneficial work, engage in conversations with others using the following discussion prompts.

1. Have a conversation with a partner or a small group of three to four people. Go through each activity in this chapter together. Leave enough time to engage in conversation that does not rush learning. Be sure to create intentions for the conversation and expectations for participation. See Bringing People Together on page 8 to help set expectations.

2. In a larger group, engage with the following questions.

   ○ What did you experience as you did the activities in this chapter?

   ○ What did you notice about yourself as you completed these activities?

   ○ What do you believe is your next step as you continue this learning process?

CHAPTER 4

Class

Every summer since 2015, I have taught in the Department of Leadership in Education at the University of Massachusetts Boston. The program is a three-week intensive summer residency where teachers and administrators come together five days a week, eight hours a day, and dive deep into issues of equity in education.

One day, I stood at the front of the class discussing a reading about social class and identity. To extend beyond the academic material, I shared that, growing up, I experienced a lot of tension around the issue of class. My parents immigrated to the United States from the Philippines in the mid-1970s and came from humble beginnings. But, because of their academic, social, and cultural privilege, they were able to secure jobs in the medical field and quickly build a financial foundation for our family. While we had all the comforts of financial stability, my parents never let my siblings and me forget that life had not always been like this for them.

In telling this story, I was trying to highlight for the students how my socioeconomic status often conflicted with the values my dad had instilled in me. I went on to say, "When my dad, who is a doctor at a hospital, goes to eat lunch in the cafeteria, he doesn't sit with the other doctors. He often feels really uncomfortable with them and prefers to go have lunch with people who are just maintenance workers and cleaners."

At that moment, a student uttered a noise of disgust. This startled me. I said, "Oh, I heard a reaction. Would someone like to say more?" A student replied, "*Just* the maintenance workers and cleaners, Dr. Talusan? Well, my dad is one of those people who are *just* the maintenance workers."

I felt my body responding faster than my mind. My heartbeat quickened. My face went hot. Anger rose from the pit of my stomach all the way to the top of my head. I started sweating. My first response was defensive and angry. I thought, *How dare he embarrass me in this moment! Of course, I didn't mean it that way! Of course, I'm not classist! I'm a good person!*

My second response, after I took a very deep breath, was humble and grateful. I said, "Thank you. You are right. What I just said—the words I chose, the story I was telling, and my lack of awareness—was incredibly offensive. I have a lot of work to do here. Thank you."

Confronting biases around class identity can be uncomfortable, emotional, and sometimes even embarrassing. And yet, to avoid or resist that work keeps you stuck, allows your prejudice to go unchallenged, and perpetuates your disconnection from your students and peers.

In this chapter, I'll identify some of the ways class shows up in school. I'll define the term *class*, share how class identities have informed my experiences with students, and invite you to reflect on your class identity. You'll explore how becoming aware of class can support you in cultivating equitable practices for all students. During their education, teachers rarely learn how to discuss class identity with their students. As a result, they must develop these skills through an identity-conscious practice. As you grow your understanding of how class affects your life and work, you'll be better equipped to facilitate student conversations on that topic. Finally, you'll have a chance to explore how class intersects with other identities. In the activities at the end of the chapter, you'll reflect on early messages you received about class and create action plans for engaging in difficult conversations.

ESSENTIAL QUESTIONS

- What were some of the earliest messages I received about class, money, status, and wealth?

- Is class a fixed identity, or can it change and shift with different experiences?

- How do issues of class or classism show up in my personal life and professional life?

Identifying How Class Shows Up in School

Outside of an identity-conscious practice, a teacher might be unaware of how differences in socioeconomic status show up in the classroom. I must begin an exploration of this identity category by defining what I mean by *class*. Social scientists find it difficult to agree on the criteria and definitions for determining class because societies are constantly in a state of change (Bird & Newport, 2017). For the scope of the discussion in this chapter, I'll reference researchers Laura Smith, Susan Mao, and Anita Deshpande (2016), who note that *social class* tends to "refer to one of the ways that society is stratified with the result that different groups have characteristic sets of advantages and disadvantages" (p. 129). They provide the following typology, acknowledging that these descriptions are not absolute.

- **Poverty:** Predominantly describes working-class people who, because of unemployment, low-wage jobs, health problems, or other crises are without enough income to support their families' basic needs.

- **Working class:** People who have little power or authority in the workplace, little control over the availability or content of jobs, and little say in the decisions that affect their access to health care, education, and housing. They tend to have lower levels of income, net worth, and formal education than more powerful classes.

- **Middle class:** Professionals, managers, small business owners, often college educated and salaried. Middle-class people have more autonomy and control in the workplace and economic world than do working-class people, and often more economic security; however, they rely upon earnings from work to support themselves.

- **Owning class:** People who own enough wealth and property that they do not need to work to support themselves (though they may choose to); people who own and control the resources by which other people earn a living. As a result of their economic power, people in this class frequently also have significant social, cultural, and political power relative to other classes. (p. 129)

Having read those descriptions, pause for a moment. Given your life experiences, how connected or disconnected do you feel to any of these classifications or the language used to describe them? Why? Next, consider the following questions.

- As you reviewed the definitions that Smith and colleagues (2016) provide, where did you locate your social class growing up? Where do you locate yourself now?

- What examples have you seen in your school, community, or town that are evidence of these different social class groups?

- In examining inequities in education through the lens of class, do you think schooling is a source of social mobility for the working class, or does it remain a means of maintaining upper- and middle-class advantages? What evidence do you have of this?

As I've said, students are not identity neutral. These social classes are not definitive of every student's experiences, but such class descriptions offer a way for them to identify their experiences and their interactions with others. How might class show up in school and affect the way students and teachers interact with one another?

I'll share an example from my own experience. As a teacher, I had the duty to sit at a lunch table with students in grades 1–5. Teachers had assigned seating each month as a way to build community across the grades, and my job was to get conversation going at the table. I was teaching at an independent school—where the yearly tuition cost three times the yearly tuition at the local state university. As we had just returned from a long break, I had an icebreaker ready: "So, did everyone have a nice vacation?"

A third grader responded, "It was fun. We went skiing every single day. It eventually got boring, but I really like staying at our ski house." Another student mentioned she flew to Florida for the vacation. At first, I was confused by the way she was describing the flight. I soon realized she was talking about her family's private jet. Conversation quickly shifted to what people had received as holiday gifts—new iPads, Apple watches—and where they had gathered with friends—in a private restaurant, at a theater rented out for a few families, and a friend's house with a state-of-the-art movie theater.

Students are keenly aware of differences in access, material, and opportunities based on class. In addition, parents and caregivers are aware of the ways in which class privilege provides greater access to opportunities such as leadership, networking, and creativity that might not be available in schools. Researchers Kaisa Snellman, Jennifer M. Silva, and Robert D. Putnam (2015) found that:

> While public schools theoretically provide equal access to afterschool activities to all enrolled students, the reality is that access has become increasingly limited to children from middle- and upper-class families. We examined trends in extracurricular participation from the 1970s to today. Our findings are alarming: while upper-middle-class students have become more active in school clubs and sports teams since the 1970s, working class students have become increasingly disengaged and disconnected, their participation rates plummeting in the 1990s and remaining low ever since. (p. 7)

In the above example of winter vacation, the students who lived an upper-class and owning-class lifestyle had greater access to opportunities during the vacation, while other students who did not have access were home for the winter break and may not have had access to the same types of enrichment. If I were to replay that moment at the lunch table, I would not have asked if the students had a nice vacation. I would have asked, "What was one thing that was important or memorable for you?" This would have widened the pathway for students to talk about meaningful moments. If I were in class, I might simply ask for the students to write about an experience instead of reporting it aloud to others. This way, we could have exchanged meaningful feedback without putting it on display for others to hear.

Class issues show up in parents' and guardians' involvement in school, too. Research demonstrates that parental involvement is an empirically validated predictor of school success (LeFevre & Shaw, 2012). Yet, socioeconomic privilege affects who can volunteer to be a class parent and dedicate hours during the school day to help out with field trips, art projects, and lunch duty. Parent council meetings are often held on weeknights and are adults only, excluding participants who cannot access childcare or arrange dinner for their families. Class identity shows up in teacher appreciation gifts, annual galas, silent auctions, and fundraising events. Parents, guardians, and caring adults also experience class differences through relationships at school.

As teachers aim to build strong connections with family, they should incorporate issues of class, access, and opportunity into this identity-conscious practice. How does class serve as a barrier to parent or guardian involvement? In many ways, class can serve as a barrier to scheduling conferences or ensuring students complete complicated projects that require independently purchased materials. We, as teachers, might also hold deep assumptions about what involvement looks like. Ask yourself what judgments you might be making about parents or guardians who are unable to come in for a conference, respond to your requests, or assist their students with projects. It is important for us to remember that some students might leave school and go to music lessons, dance class, athletic practice, test preparation, tutoring sessions, or other extracurricular and academic activities while others might go directly home to take care of a younger sibling or other family member.

Educators cannot flatten the structures of socioeconomic privilege, but we should pay attention to how class privilege shows up in the lives of our students. Teaching about classism may seem overwhelming and a bit scary, but it is important. The gap between America's richest and poorest families is growing, creating opportunities for issues of classism to show up in our classrooms (Institute for Policy Studies, n.d.). We have opportunities to build the habits and skills for noticing, addressing, and dialoguing about class and the impact of class in our communities.

Cultivating Equitable Practices

The impact of social class is also evidenced in your teaching practices. When you're unaware of your own biases, you perpetuate them in your interactions with students (Dhaliwal, Chin, Lovison, & Quinn, 2020). For example, during the prekindergarten years, educators sometimes subtly steer students from higher-income families toward academic play that promotes school readiness more so than students from lower-income families (Stirrup, Evans, & Davies, 2017).

Associate professor of sociology Jessica McCrory Calarco (2011) shares a story from her research that illustrates this point well. Sadie and Carter were students from working-class backgrounds paired together to work on a mathematics problem. The teacher asked if students had any questions. Sadie and Carter did not raise their hands. The teacher proceeded to work with and support a group of students from middle-class backgrounds who had requested her assistance. Sadie and Carter struggled through the activity but did not ask for help. Fifteen minutes later, Sadie and Carter were the only ones who did not finish and were reprimanded for not finishing. According to Calarco (2011), "This kind of silence seemed to reflect working-class students' limited sense of entitlement to assistance from teachers. It also hindered teachers' awareness of working-class students' needs, preventing teachers from stepping in to help" (p. 870). One lesson teachers can draw from this study is to move from group to group instead of waiting for students from working-class backgrounds to ask for help. Calarco's (2011) research illuminates how students from middle-class backgrounds create privileges in the form of assistance seeking, which may contribute to inequity in the classroom.

This is a tricky line for teachers to walk: recognizing class-based barriers to student success while resisting the tendency to buy into class-based stereotypes. Education researchers Carolyn S. Hunt and Machele Seiver (2018) suggest that "educators recognize and resist deficit views of economically disadvantaged students and families [and] support teachers in identifying and changing elements of school culture and curriculum that may marginalize and pathologize class differences" (p. 353). A helpful guideline is noticing whether your view of a student's abilities is rooted in the deficit view Hunt and Seiver (2018) point to. Do you interpret assessments differently based on your assumptions about class? Do you make judgments about a struggling reader's home life or feel pity for them?

A teacher's willingness and ability to examine and interrupt personal bias have consequences for students. How can teachers address the impact of class on teaching and curricula? First, teachers can examine early messages they received about class and understand how class serves as a lens for their own curriculum choices. Take inventory of your books, lessons, and assisting behaviors, and critically examine whether they're rooted in a deficit model or asset model. Second, be aware of how class and stereotypes about class shape narratives you have of students and families. Is a student and family's class background informing assessment, placement, and engagement? In particular, examine whether your discipline practices and language are informed by class. Third, get to know students and their families beyond the classroom. How do their own stories shape their experiences in and out of school? How do these stories disrupt singular and perhaps stereotypical messages you have about class? Finally, diversify text and classroom discussions about class, drawing from multiple viewpoints and multiple representations of class in texts.

Talking to Students About Class

There are a number of reasons why people find it difficult to talk about social class. In some families, talking about money and social class is considered rude or distasteful. Some may find talking about class difficult because of the stereotypes that accompany different social-class experiences. Others avoid the conversation to keep their social class hidden.

When working with schools, I like to observe the types of workshops they ask me to present. As expected, most of the workshops are on issues of race, parenting, diversity, and inclusion. When I ask the teachers, "What is a topic that is really difficult to talk about in your community?" the topic of class always comes up, yet no one wants to talk about it.

But even if teachers avoid explicitly talking about class, it's natural for students to comment on the differences they notice among their peers. Consider the following scenarios.

- During the first week of school, it becomes clear that the parents and guardians of four of your students are unable to furnish the required supplies.

- Many students in class carry fancy stainless-steel water bottles promising to make their water taste crisp, cold, and refreshing even after a full day. A handful of other students carries disposable plastic water bottles, which they refill and reuse every day, or no bottles, being relegated to using unhygienic water fountains.

- Students returning from holiday break are eager to share about the parties they hosted, gifts they received, and vacations they took. As these conversations unfold, it's evident that not all students experience the same financial, class, and wealth privileges.

How might you respond to conversations arising among students in response to these scenarios? Would you shut them down? Would you let them play out? Your own comfort with talking about class informs and impacts your approach. In response to the first example, I might send a note home with the school supplies list inviting families to provide one extra item on the list for classroom supplies. Once families provide the supplies, I might also consider structuring them as collective classroom resources so that students share all supplies provided in the classroom. Take a moment to think about how you might respond to the second and third examples. How could you use restructuring resources, shifting focus, or dialoguing with students and families to resolve the challenges presented in these scenarios?

It makes sense that teachers come to school unprepared to talk about class identity, especially if their education didn't provide them with skills for engaging in difficult conversations. The field of education does not adequately address social class (Stirrup et al., 2017), and educators need greater preparation on teaching diverse students. The issue might even be rooted in those who teach preparation courses. For example, teacher educators Christopher C. Jett and Stephanie Behm Cross (2016) find that teacher educators who prepare preK–12 teachers do not feel equipped to teach these teachers about social class. Those who teach teachers might be leaving out critical experiences, lessons, and reflections about class, which then fails to prepare teachers to teach K–12 students. For these reasons, it is important that we disrupt the cycle and address class as identity-conscious educators.

> The field of education does not adequately address social class (Stirrup et al., 2017), and educators need greater preparation on teaching diverse students.

While teacher preparation programs may not have prepared educators to talk openly about class, teachers can take steps to build an identity-conscious practice in this area.

- **Build habits and skills for having difficult conversations:** The more teachers engage with the discomfort of talking about class, the more familiar the discomfort becomes, and the more agile they become in navigating these conversations. The activities at the end of this chapter are intended to be a starting point to building competency.

- **Engage in reflection:** Teachers can reflect on moments in which class affects how they teach, the books they select, and assumptions they make about families from different class backgrounds.

- **Mentor new teachers:** Teachers in leadership positions can mentor new teachers. Mentor relationships offer powerful opportunities for leaders to have conversations with novice teachers about the impact of class. This type of vulnerable practice creates learning and builds competency over time.

- **Access personal development:** Schools can provide robust professional development to create structures for teachers to discuss, address, and remedy issues of class inequality in the schools.

Through the lens of identity-conscious practice, teachers can shift from avoidance to invitation. By developing the skills needed to engage in difficult conversations about class, teachers can support their students in learning about and engaging with issues of social class.

Noticing How Class Intersects With Other Identities

How does class intersect with other identities in ways that shape a person's experience in the world? Researcher Rhonda Soto (2008) writes, "Discussing race without including class analysis is like watching a bird fly without looking at the sky: it's possible, but it misses the larger context" (p. 1). The identity-conscious practice calls teachers to understand this wider context of how class intersects with other identities.

Research illustrates how the intersection of class and gender shows up in school. Researchers Richard V. Reeves and Sarah Nzau (2021) found that boys from low-income families do worse (by measures such as income, marriage, college attainment, incarceration, and upward mobility) than girls raised in low-income families. "Most strikingly, boys raised in families in the bottom fifth of the income distribution are less likely than girls either to be employed or to move up the income ladder once they become adults" (Reeves & Nzau, 2021). Think about the intergenerational effect this can have on families over time. In addition, boys are most strongly influenced by family environment, the quality of the school, and neighborhood poverty.

Teachers in the K–12 classroom play a role in this dynamic. As teachers become aware of intersectionality and recognize the resulting barriers and challenges students face, they can provide opportunities for them to solve problems, think critically, and use the strengths of their intersections. "Taking into account intersectionality enables educators to focus on the systemic barriers that contribute to problematic outcomes associated with particular students or student groups" (Lazzell, Jackson, & Skelton, 2018, p. 3). Practice becoming aware of how academic preparation, success, and pathways to higher education affect boys from low socioeconomic backgrounds. Then seek to provide opportunities for them in the classroom by crafting culturally competent instruction, curricula, and assessment.

Class can be the lens through which teachers make choices about curricula, projects, discipline, and interactions with students. I hope that all you've learned in this chapter will support you in incorporating class into your identity-conscious practice. Make sure to extend your learning about class to include its intersections with other identities and become aware of where it shows up in your classroom.

Activities for Building Awareness of Class

What do K–12 educators need to know, do, and demonstrate in order to incorporate class into their identity-conscious practice? The five activities in this chapter will guide you to reflect on your relationship with class, notice class interactions in your school community, examine class privilege, write about your experience with class, and notice how class intersects with other identities.

Activity 1: Engaging in Reflection

In this work of building identity consciousness around class, it is important to think about the first and early messages you received that inform and impact your approach to class. Read the following reflection questions, and record your thoughts and experiences in the space provided.

1. What were the earliest messages you received about social class? What did you see, learn, or notice about class? Were these messages positive? Were they negative?

    _____

    _____

    _____

    _____

2. What do you believe is the impact of *not* talking openly about social class?

    _____

    _____

    _____

    _____

3. In your experience, how, if at all, are people rewarded for talking about social class? In your experience, how, if at all, are people penalized for talking about social class?

    _____

    _____

    _____

    _____

4. At the beginning of this chapter (page 51), I shared a story of my first response (defensive and angry) and second response (humble and grateful) when a student reacted to my class bias. How would you have responded in this situation? What informs that response?

_____

_____

_____

_____

Activity 2: Making Connections to Your School Community

As I demonstrated earlier in the chapter, class distinctions are prevalent not only in the student community but also in the adult community. While you focus on the impact of class in your teaching and learning, you should also focus on how class can impact your interactions with your peers. In order to create a more identity-conscious school community, teachers have to pay attention to all members of the community. The graphic for this activity illustrates interaction of social-class evidence between the adult and student communities.

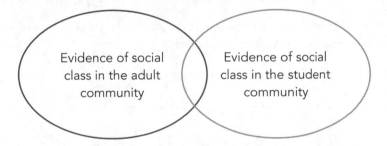

Read the following reflection questions, and record your thoughts and experiences in the space provided.

*   What do you notice about social class in the adult community at your school (among parents, caregivers, teachers, and administrators)? List evidence of where you see class issues among your peers.

_____

_____

_____

_____

- What do you notice about social class in the student community at your school? List evidence of where you see class issues among students.

  _____

  _____

  _____

  _____

- What class issues impact both students and adults at your school? Where do you see commonalities in these two populations? What do you believe is the impact of those commonalities?

  _____

  _____

  _____

  _____

- What would be different about your teaching or leading if you were able to have open and difficult conversations about class?

  _____

  _____

  _____

  _____

- What steps can you take to create a more inclusive environment where class issues are openly discussed and the impact of class distinction is minimized?

  _____

  _____

  _____

  _____

Activity 3: Examining Class Privilege

Read the statements for examining class privilege in the table for this activity. Then write about the experience of considering the statements and your class privileges by answering the reflection questions.

My debt, if I have any, is manageable, and I can pay it off reliably.	I can choose what times and days I go to work.	I am required to wear a uniform at my place of work.	I have shared a bedroom with a sibling or a family member.
The neighborhood around my home is safe.	My school has plenty of resources, such as books, technology, or sports equipment.	My family or I utilize government assistance to pay for food.	I have access to good hospital and medical care.
If I break or lose something, I can easily replace it.	My family or I have hired help for tasks that we do not want to do.	I have avoided going to the doctor out of concern for how to pay the medical bill.	I have had to rely on walking or public transportation as a primary means of travel.
I have friends or family members who could bail me out of most financial situations.	I did not have to wait for a sale in order to purchase something I wanted.	One of my parents or caregivers was laid off from work or unemployed (not by choice).	I attended private school (not on scholarship).
I attended a summer camp or enrichment program (not on scholarship).	I received free or reduced lunch at my school.	My family or I own the home we live in.	Growing up, I had to work to financially contribute to paying my family's bills.

- Which of the statements felt familiar to you? Which felt unfamiliar to you?

_____

_____

_____

_____

- Which statements were clear and to the point for you? Which statements made you pause and think about particular situations or examples?

_____

_____

_____

_____

- If you were to consider the perspectives of others, how might someone interpret a statement differently than you did because of their experiences with class or class privilege?

_____

_____

_____

_____

Activity 4: Writing Your Autobiography

Writing an autobiographical story related to social class allows you to reflect on an incident or experience and provide transparency about the experience. The purpose of this activity is to help you explore the impact of class on your own life, teaching, and leadership. The next section provides direction and space for your autobiography. The section that follows provides an example you can use as a model.

Your Autobiography

Take the following two steps to draft your story.

1. Recall an experience you had as a teacher, student, or leader related to social class. You may also want to connect your story about class with other identities discussed in this book (race, sexual orientation, gender, and disability), but resist the urge to move away from focusing on class itself.

2. Reflect on the following questions.

    ○ What does the event reveal about class, money, privilege, and opportunity?

    ○ How does writing about this make you feel? What emotions come up as you write this autobiography?

    ○ What, if any, action items come from this story that you are telling? How might these action items inform and impact your teaching?

The Identity-Conscious Educator © 2022 Solution Tree Press • SolutionTree.com
Visit **go.SolutionTree.com/diversityandequity** to download this free reproducible.

_____

_____

_____

_____

Jorge's Story

The following is a real-world example from Jorge Vega, a Puerto Rican, AfroLatinx teacher who grew up in a working-class home. As a new teacher, Jorge still toggled between the experiences of having money, due to his weekly paycheck, but also feeling deeply connected to working-class culture, values, and challenges. As a teacher in an independent school, Jorge mostly worked with students whose families came from upper-middle-class backgrounds. Use Jorge's story as a model for crafting your autobiography:

> I was the director of theater at a prestigious private school. They poured money into the arts and, as a young educator, I felt like I'd found my golden ticket early. I didn't make much money, but I was given a great deal of autonomy by both the school leadership and the families of my students. I got to pick plays and musicals that mattered and was allowed to tell stories in ways that I imagined expanded the thinking of the community. In short, I thought I was a big deal.
>
> One day, while giving post-rehearsal notes to the cast of that year's musical, I discovered how much I wasn't.
>
> "Mr. Vega," a student said. "Where did you get that shirt?" I was wearing a T-shirt. It wasn't anything fancy. I'd picked it because of the logo on the pocket. It was a cool-looking logo.
>
> "I don't remember. I've had it for a while. Let's get back to notes."
>
> "You've had it for a while?" she asked.
>
> The shirt wasn't something I'd had "for a while." At the end of the previous school year, just before unclaimed clothing was sent to the donation center, I looked through the bin for anything that I could wear. I was a young teacher on a budget and was always amazed by how much was just left behind every single year by students: brand-name clothing, shoes, jackets, and bags. They never even looked for the items; they simply bought new ones.
>
> "That's weird," the student replied. "Because that's my dad's company on the shirt."
>
> Other students were whispering, some giggling as they put two and two together.
>
> She looked at me, looked at the shirt, and then looked back at me before she said, "But, _where_ did you get that, Mr. Vega? Because those shirts weren't sold or anything. He made them just for family and employees." This student was not particularly happy with the role she was playing in the musical, and the look on her face was a celebratory smirk. She turned, walked away, and whispered to the rest of the cast.

page 6 of 7

And suddenly, the students knew that I, their teacher and director, was wearing a student hand-me-down.

In that moment, while watching kids laugh and shake their heads, I realized just how fragile my influence and status were. How easy it was for a sixteen-year-old to eclipse that status and remind everyone, but mostly me, what real influence looked like.

Even more than two decades since that took place, I feel small when I retell that story. I realize that, even as I have achieved so much in my teaching career in terms of social, cultural, and financial capital, class issues can quickly put me back in my place.

As a teacher, I am very sensitive to class issues not only within the student community but also among my peers. As a school leader, I am so close to these issues of class and classism, and this proximity drives my advocacy for equity and opportunity, especially in places where class disparity is so obvious. (J. Vega, personal communication, January 4, 2021)

Activity 5: Building Your Identity-Conscious Practice

Class also intersects with other identities, such as race, gender, immigration status, education, disability, and geographic location. What do you notice or wonder about how class is informed and impacted by other aspects of your identity? In the space provided, write about how your experiences with class might show up in your teaching, leading, and learning.

_____

_____

_____

_____

Discussion

This guide provides structures for you to think deeply about identity and difficult conversations. To advance this beneficial work, engage in conversations with others using the following discussion prompts.

1. Have a conversation with a partner or a small group of three to four people. Go through each activity in this chapter together. Leave enough time to engage in conversation that does not rush learning. Be sure to create intentions for the conversation and expectations for participation. See Bringing People Together on page 8 to help set expectations.

2. In a larger group, engage with the following questions.

   ○ What did you experience as you did the activities in this chapter?

   ○ What did you notice about yourself as you completed these activities?

   ○ What do you believe is your next step as you continue this learning process?

CHAPTER 5

Sexual Orientation

I have always had a complicated relationship with sexual orientation. I did not grow up with many people in my life who were openly gay. But I knew about people in my extended family who were lesbian or gay; our family often talked about relatives having "roommates" or "close friends" of the same sex instead of stating the obvious: they were in same-sex partnerships or relationships.

Growing up, I heard a story about a distant male relative who "liked to wear high heels" and "was very feminine." But the story never mentioned that relative's talents, habits, or kind heart. He was essentialized by his "desire to dress as a woman." Such stories about my family members were never told with anger or animosity, but they were certainly never told with affection or kindness, nor did they recognize the whole of their humanity.

First and early messages people receive about sexual orientation inform and impact their ability to engage in difficult conversations about sexual identity. For some, talking about sexual orientation was off-limits. For others, conversations about sexual orientation were a vital part of dialogues with family and friends. In North America, the collective conversation about sexual orientation has shifted dramatically since the early 2000s. The laws and policies enacted to grant rights and protections to lesbian, gay, bisexual, transgender, and queer (LGBTQ) people have affected not only the general population but also students and families, shaping how schools function (Movement Advancement Project, n.d.). Conversations and actions related to the inclusion of LGBTQ students, faculty, and families—such as Genders and Sexualities Alliance (GSA) clubs, Diverse Families clubs, Safe Space trainings, and updated nondiscrimination policies—are part of school communities.

In this chapter, I'll define sexual orientation while also acknowledging that labels are subject to change and are most helpful when used with respect. Students of diverse sexual orientation overwhelmingly report feeling unsafe in school. As an educator, you are positioned to ensure a safe environment for all students by creating a positive and inclusive classroom. Through the lens of identity-conscious practice, you can build the skills you need to engage in conversations about sexual orientation. Finally, you'll have a chance to explore how sexual orientation intersects with other identities. In the activities at the end of the chapter, you'll reflect on early messages you received about sexual orientation and create action plans for engaging in difficult conversations.

ESSENTIAL QUESTIONS

- — What were the earliest messages I received about sexual orientation?

- — What aspects of this topic might be difficult for me to discuss?

- — What role, if any, do I have in addressing issues of sexual orientation as an educator?

Defining Sexual Orientation

One reason conversations about sexual orientation can be difficult is that the language is fluid and changing. While the following might be the accepted description at the time of this writing, you may find that people are using different words, definitions, and descriptors to identify themselves.

The American Psychological Association and the National Association of School Psychologists (2015) provide this definition of *sexual orientation*:

Sexual orientation refers to the sex of those to whom one is sexually and romantically attracted. Categories of sexual orientation typically have included attraction to members of one's own sex (gay men or lesbians), attraction to members of the other sex (heterosexuals), and attraction to members of both sexes (bisexuals). Some people identify as pansexual or queer in terms of their sexual orientation, which means they define their sexual orientation outside of the gender binary of "male" and "female" only. While these categories continue to be widely used, research has suggested that sexual orientation does not always appear in such definable categories and instead occurs on a continuum. (p. 6)

It is important for teachers to recognize the diversity of sexual orientation represented among students and to respect students' preferences for how they talk about their identity. Please be mindful, make adjustments, and correct your language as needed.

"What happens if I say the wrong thing or use the wrong term?" you might ask. Take a deep breath. This will likely happen. If you say the wrong thing or use the wrong term, do and say the following.

1. **Apologize:** "I'm sorry."

2. **Express gratitude:** "Thank you for correcting me."

3. **Commit to doing better:** "I will continue to work on this."

That's all. There is no need to make it about you or how you feel. If you did something wrong—even if it was unintentional—simply apologize, express gratitude, and commit to doing better.

Even the LGBTQ acronym is evolving. You've likely seen it listed as *LGBTQ+*, the plus sign serving to acknowledge that the acronym can express many more identities and experiences that are included in the community. You may also see inclusion of individuals and communities who identify as Two-Spirit, as in *LGBTQ2*. Rooted in Indigenous communities, the term refers to gender-variant members and the social and spiritual roles they fulfill. As you build your identity-conscious practice, remember that hundreds of Native and Indigenous cultures have different attitudes about sex and gender. According to the Indian Health Service (n.d.), "Even with the modern adoption of pan-Indian terms like Two-Spirit, not all cultures will perceive Two-Spirit people the same way, or welcome a pan-Indian term to replace the terms already in use by their cultures." What further complicates labels, naming, and acronyms is that the addition of Two-Spirit in the broader LGBTQ acronym may also contribute to the conflation of sexual orientation and gender. As you continue on your personal and professional journey of building skills for greater inclusion, note that there may be words, phrases, and acronyms that are ever evolving. It is important that we are both knowledgeable and flexible in this learning.

Further, it's important to note that some people do not like the idea of labels at all and reject the use of labels to self-identify. Other people feel comfortable with certain labels and not others. Educators must respect all people's decisions about how they want to identify. This is an essential practice for making school a safe place for all students.

Ensuring a Safe Environment for All Students

I remember a game going around my schoolyard, back in the mid-1980s, called the "Are you gay?" test. It was exactly as offensive as it sounds. A student would repeatedly run knuckles across the back of your hand to see if the skin would rub off. (Of course it did: it's called *friction*.) If you got a scar, you were not gay. If you didn't, you were gay. If you didn't take the test, it meant one of two things: (1) you were too afraid to do the test or (2) gay.

I never took the test. I was too afraid. And, of course, there was a rumor going around school that I was gay.

As children, my classmates and I were choosing to engage in harm, in violence, and in fear. Though I haven't seen evidence of that game going around during my decades-long teaching career, I've seen other games evolve that create equally powerful social learning and shaming. Social media, text messaging, and other forms of technology are the 21st century's tools for victimizing students who are different. As educators, we have heard about peer-taken photos and videos of students distributed and proliferated without the subject's permission. Schools hold disciplinary meetings—and some colleges even rescind offers of admission—based on social media posts that either target social identities or bully other students. Sexually diverse students are frequently victimized in school settings.

In 2021, the Trevor Project conducted a survey of over thirty-four thousand LGBTQ youths across the United States to provide a critical understanding of the experiences and mental health impacting youth ages 13–24 (www.thetrevorproject.org/survey-2021). Consider the following statistics (The Trevor Project, 2021):

- "94% of LGBTQ youth reported that recent politics negatively impacted their mental health."

- "75% of LGBTQ youth reported that they had experienced discrimination based on their sexual orientation or gender identity at least once in their lifetime."

- "48% of LGBTQ youth reported they wanted counseling from a mental health professional but were unable to receive it in the past year."

- "LGBTQ youth who had access to spaces that affirmed their sexual orientation and gender identity reported lower rates of attempting suicide."

Educators have a responsibility to meet the needs of LGBTQ students, and that means intervening when they witness bullying, teasing, or exclusion of LGBTQ identities or experiences. The American Psychological Association and the National Association of School Psychologists (2015) find that gender-diverse and sexual orientation–diverse students who are bullied or targeted in school are "at increased risk for mental health problems, suicidal ideation and attempts, substance use, high-risk sexual activity, and poor academic outcomes," such as high levels of absenteeism, low grade point averages, and low interest in the pursuit of postsecondary education (Kosciw, Greytak, Diaz, & Bartkiewicz, 2010; Kosciw, Palmer, & Kull, 2015; Russell, Ryan, Toomey, Diaz, & Sanchez, 2011; Toomey, Ryan, Diaz, & Russell, 2011). Given that educators interact closely with students in classrooms, in advisory, in clubs and organizations, and in hallways and on athletic fields, they have a responsibility to provide an environment free of bullying and harassment so that all students can thrive.

Research supports the idea that positive environments are a key factor in helping youth thrive. According to the American Psychological Association and the National Association of School Psychologists (2015), studies demonstrate that students of diverse gender and sexual orientation report increased connectedness and safety when school personnel intervene in four ways:

> (1) addressing and stopping bullying and harassment, (2) developing administrative policies that prohibit discrimination based on sexual orientation, gender identity and gender expression, (3) supporting the use of affirming classroom activities and the establishment of gender and sexual orientation diverse-affirming student groups, and (4) valuing education and training for students and staff on the needs of gender and sexual orientation–diverse students (Case & Meier, 2014; Kosciw et al., 2010; McGuire, Anderson, Toomey, & Russell, 2010).

When students feel affirmed and safe in the classroom, they learn better, create deeper connections, and engage in the daily life of the school. Education lecturers Mandie Shean and David Mander (2020) further find, "In schools, emotional safety is developed through supportive relationships; being valued and treated with respect; and clear boundaries and support for students to achieve their potential academically, socially and personally" (p. 225).

Too often, students who identify as LGBTQ do not experience that sense of safety, support, and respect. Teachers can change that by providing inclusive curricula and positive class discussions. As teachers and school leaders, we can lean on research that affirms these conversations to create a deeper sense of safety. For example, when researchers Shannon D. Snapp, Jenifer K. McGuire, Katarina O. Sinclair, Karlee Gabrion, and Stephen T. Russell (2015) studied the effects of curricula that include LGBTQ people on students' perceptions of personal safety and school climate safety, they found that:

> When students feel affirmed and safe in the classroom, they learn better, create deeper connections, and engage in the daily life of the school.

> LGBTQ-inclusive curricula were associated with higher reports of safety at the individual and school levels, and lower levels of bullying at the school level. The amount of support also mattered: supportive curricula were related to feeling safer and awareness of bullying at the individual and school levels. (p. 580)

You've seen that the identity-conscious educator has to build safety in the classroom for students who identify as LGBTQ. But how do teachers prepare for difficult conversations around this identity? One way is by incorporating LGBTQ-inclusive curricula and discussions in the class. LGBTQ students who attend schools with a curriculum that is inclusive of LGBTQ identities experience a better school climate and, therefore, more positive outcomes (GLSEN, n.d.). Teachers can provide positive representations of LGBTQ people, history, or events in schools. Consider GLSEN's (n.d.) "Developing

LGBTQ-Inclusive Classroom Resources" (www.glsen.org/activity/inclusive-curriculum
-guide) for support in expanding your curriculum.

Teachers don't have to do this work in isolation; they can seek support from their colleagues too. Libraries and resource centers can make LGBTQ resources available to students. School administration can support these efforts by providing professional development to teachers, staff, and school leaders about how to support LGBTQ students. In addition, schools need to create policies that support LGBTQ students and ensure their safety and belonging at school.

Talking to Students About Sexual Orientation

Conversations about sexual orientation can be difficult for several reasons. People often consider sexual orientation, like many other topics about identity, a taboo or impolite discussion topic. Some people have experienced that engaging in conversation about sexual orientation puts them at risk of bullying or isolation by family or friends. Still others have found they could not talk about sexual orientation because of culture, religion, or ideology. Schools sometimes discourage conversations about sexual orientation for fear of backlash from parents or worry that children are too young to talk about such issues. The challenge of talking about this topic is especially strong when teachers aren't able to show up with a personal awareness of sexual orientation. Teachers come to school carrying their own complex histories around sexuality, and the first messages they received on the subject likely impact their interactions with students.

Here are six great ways to start effective conversations about sexual orientation in your classroom. These approaches are effective because they invite community voice and contribution. You may feel overwhelmed by the amount of information available about sexual orientation, and you may have questions about what is appropriate. By connecting with LGBTQ communities, families, and resources, you open your network of possibilities, viewpoints, and conversations. For example, while some teachers may not have extensive experience talking about LGBTQ issues, parents and caregivers in your classroom or school may have a wealth of experience to share. You are not alone in this work. Consider the following six helpful ways to get started.

1. Prepare yourself to answer questions that students may bring up out of curiosity. The Welcoming Schools (n.d.c) website lists several topics that will allow you to get ready in advance (https://welcomingschools.org/resources /responding-to-questions).

2. Connect your conversation to larger goals within your classroom. If, for example, your goals include respecting LGBTQ people, honoring diverse families, and being kind, then connect the conversation to those goals and behaviors toward others.

3. If appropriate, reach out to parents and caregivers in your class who identify as LGBTQ, and invite them to share recommendations for books, discussion topics, or language they use within their homes.

4. Provide opportunities for students to read about or explore different types of families and experiences. The Welcoming Schools (n.d.a) website has a list of helpful books (https://welcomingschools.org/resources/books).

5. Work with your team leaders or school leaders for support as you lean into this topic. If your school declares it is a welcoming space for all, then encourage your school to support you as you include diverse families, experiences, and identities in your classroom conversations.

6. Take care not to approach identity work from a deficit model. While you may lean on books to help you get the conversation started, make sure your resources do not overly focus on the struggles and challenges of certain identities; they should also include joys, successes, and celebrations of those identities and experiences. In addition, there are books available that simply depict people from diverse backgrounds as characters without emphasizing identity. To get started, check out the following resources: Social Justice Books (https://socialjusticebooks.org/booklists/lgbtq), the Rainbow Book List (https://glbtrt.ala.org/rainbowbooks), and the New York Public Library (www.nypl.org/blog/2020/06/01/reading-trans-literary-landscape). Be sure to provide healthy representation in your class.

> To create environments where students can thrive, teachers must engage in identity-conscious practice, understanding that who they are informs and impacts how they act and interact with others.

To create environments where students can thrive, teachers must engage in identity-conscious practice, understanding that who they are informs and impacts how they act and interact with others. As they grow their understanding and become more comfortable, they can support students to talk about sexual orientation and make the classroom inclusive for all students.

Noticing How Sexual Orientation Intersects With Other Identities

As teachers incorporate sexual orientation into their identity-conscious practice, they should also make it a priority to notice how sexuality intersects with other identities. Consider the role of intersectionality in the following statistics reported by The Trevor Project (2021):

- "Half of all LGBTQ youth of color reported discrimination based on their race/ethnicity in the past year, including 67% of Black LGBTQ youth and 60% of Asian/Pacific Islander LGBTQ youth."

- "12% of white youth attempted suicide compared to 31% of Native/Indigenous youth, 21% of Black youth, 21% of multiracial youth, 18% of Latinx youth, and 12% of Asian/Pacific Islander youth."

- "30% of LGBTQ youth experienced food insecurity in the past month, including half of all Native/Indigenous LGBTQ youth."

- "Nearly 60% of transgender and nonbinary youth said that COVID-19 impacted their ability to express their gender identity."

Where do you notice intersectionality in your classroom? How do students' intersectional identities inform their experience in your classroom? In your school? And how might seeing your students through the lens of intersectionality create opportunities for understanding, connection, and respect in your classroom?

Teachers and school leaders who engage in identity-conscious practices can contribute to the growing number of LGBTQ students who thrive in schools. The work that teachers and school leaders do to create safe and affirming environments across all aspects of identity improves outcomes for students, safety and well-being, and opportunities for thriving.

Activities for Building Awareness of Sexual Orientation

What do K–12 educators need to know, do, and demonstrate in order to incorporate sexual orientation into their identity-conscious practice? The five activities in this chapter will guide you to reflect on your relationship with sexual orientation, imagine how you would respond to students' identities, examine your school's level of acceptance of LGBTQ students and policies that influence those attitudes, and notice how sexual orientation intersects with other identities.

Activity 1: Engaging in Reflection

In this work of building identity consciousness around sexual orientation, it is important to think about the first and early messages you received that inform and impact your approach to sexual orientation. Read the following reflection questions, and record your thoughts and experiences in the space provided.

1. Given the different definitions of sexual orientation categories provided earlier in the chapter (page 68), which definitions feel most familiar to you? Which feel unfamiliar to you? If you were to locate your identity in a category, where would you self-identify?

   _____

   _____

   _____

2. What were the earliest messages you received about people who have the same sexual orientation as you do? What did you see, learn, or notice about sexual orientation? Where did you learn those messages? Were these messages positive? Were they negative?

   _____

   _____

   _____

   _____

3. What were the earliest messages you received about people who have a different sexual orientation than you do? Where did you learn those messages? Were they positive or negative messages?

   _____

   _____

   _____

   _____

The Identity-Conscious Educator © 2022 Solution Tree Press • SolutionTree.com
Visit **go.SolutionTree.com/diversityandequity** to download this free reproducible.

4. When, if at all, have you been challenged about your beliefs and attitudes regarding different sexual identities? What did you experience? What did that feel like for you?

_____

_____

_____

_____

Activity 2: Imagining How You Would Feel

Read the following prompts, and for each one, write a short response in the space provided. Make note of your words and also your emotions, your responses, and your reactions to the statements.

- As a parent or caregiver, if I found out my child was gay or lesbian, I would _____

_____

_____.

- If a coworker of mine, who I assumed was heterosexual, told me they were gay, I would feel _____

_____.

- As a parent or caregiver, if I learned my child was heterosexual, I would _____

_____

_____.

- As a parent or caregiver, if I learned my child was bisexual, I would _____

_____

_____.

- If I were attending an overnight conference and found out my roommate was gay, lesbian, or bisexual, I would _____

_____.

- When I think about children who are being raised by lesbian or gay couples, I feel

_____

_____.

- When I think about children who are being raised by heterosexual couples, I feel

  _____

  _____.

- If I learned a student in my class was lesbian, gay, or bisexual, I would _____

  _____

  _____.

Take a minute to reflect on the following questions. Write your responses in the space provided.

- Which of the preceding prompts were difficult to answer?

- Which ones were easier to answer?

- Which statements brought up feelings you had in activity 1 (page 75)?

- Were most of your answers a negative response, positive response, or neutral response?

- What meaning, if any, would you make of those responses?

_____

_____

_____

_____

Activity 3: Considering School Culture

Educators are working not only with their own experiences and beliefs but also within the parameters of their school's culture or beliefs. Use the following two scenarios to think through some challenges you might face as an educator and school leader. Read each scenario, and answer the reflection questions in the space provided.

Scenario 1: Dana's Breakup

Dana is a student in your class who typically engages in class discussions, does her homework in a timely manner, and is generally sociable with other students. This week, however, you notice a change in Dana's behavior. She comes into class quietly with her head down, keeps to herself during discussions, and turns in late or incomplete assignments. You ask her to stay after class so you can chat. You let her know that you've noticed a difference in her and ask if there is anything she wants to talk about with you. She tells you she had been dating someone and felt so happy, but she got dumped last week without any explanation. She has been so sad, has had a tough time concentrating, and hasn't really been able to turn to anyone. In an effort to cheer her up, you say, "Well, I'm so sorry to hear this. Dating can be so hard, and boys can sometimes be so insensitive." She looks at you and says, "Yeah, well, I wasn't dating a boy."

- What emotions or reactions came up for you as you read the scenario?

_____

_____

_____

_____

- How would you like to react in this scenario?

_____

_____

_____

_____

- What about school culture, rules, or expectations supports your reaction? What factors serve as a barrier to your reacting to or addressing this situation?

_____

_____

_____

_____

- What do you do next?

_____

_____

_____

_____

Scenario 2: Celebrations

During a faculty meeting at school, the principal asks if people have any good news to share in their community. A colleague raises her hand to say that her child got accepted into college. Another teacher shares that he just became a grandfather this weekend. A teaching intern shares that she and a few other teachers ran a big road race in town together. Each of these celebrations receives enthusiastic applause. Your colleague Alex raises his hand and shares that he got engaged this weekend to his longtime partner. The principal says, "Congratulations to you and your lucky bride!" You know that Alex is gay and that his partner is a man.

- What emotions or reactions came up for you as you read the scenario?

_____

_____

_____

_____

- How would you like to react in this scenario?

_____

_____

_____

_____

- What about school culture, rules, or expectations supports your reaction? What factors serve as a barrier to your reacting to or addressing this situation?

_____

_____

_____

_____

- What do you do next?

_____

_____

_____

_____

page 5 of 7

Activity 4: Examining School Policy

For this activity, think about the policies, practices, programs, and procedures that might impact inclusion of LGBTQ students and community members at your school.

- What practices in your school support or encourage talking about diverse sexual orientations? What practices prevent you or discourage you from having these conversations?

  _____

  _____

  _____

  _____

- What messages in your school community might contribute to homophobia among your students? What messages might contribute to homophobia among adults on campus?

  _____

  _____

  _____

  _____

- What would be different if your school community was more inclusive of LGBTQ students and adults? What would need to happen for your community to be more inclusive? What first step could you take to make this happen?

  _____

  _____

  _____

  _____

- How do the activities in this chapter inform and impact your attitudes, beliefs, and actions in the classroom?

  _____

  _____

  _____

  _____

Activity 5: Building Your Identity-Conscious Practice

Sexual orientation also intersects with other identities, such as race, class, gender, immigration status, education, disability, and geographic location. What do you notice or wonder about how sexual orientation is informed and impacted by other aspects of your identity? In the space provided, write about how your experiences with sexual orientation might show up in your teaching, leading, and learning.

_____

_____

_____

_____

Discussion

This guide provides structures for you to think deeply about identity and difficult conversations. To advance this beneficial work, engage in conversations with others using the following discussion prompts.

1. Have a conversation with a partner or a small group of three to four people. Go through each activity in this chapter together. Leave enough time to engage in conversation that does not rush learning. Be sure to create intentions for the conversation and expectations for participation. See Bringing People Together on page 8 to help set expectations.

2. In a larger group, engage with the following questions.

    ○ What did you experience as you did the activities in this chapter?

    ○ What did you notice about yourself as you completed these activities?

    ○ What do you believe is your next step as you continue this learning process?

CHAPTER 6

Gender

I grew up in a community where gender was only acknowledged in a binary: a person was either male or female, man or woman, boy or girl, masculine or feminine. Anyone who expressed an identity in any way outside this binary was teased or labeled *different*, *weird*, and *strange*. I remember that my classmates and I called one girl named Maxine "Max" throughout junior high and high school because she self-identified as a tomboy. She was athletic and rugged, and she never wore a dress or skirt. I remember another person in my small town who was singled out for their differences, a young clerk at the local grocery store. I didn't realize until I was an adult that this person was transgender. Customers would stare and snicker at the clerk, move checkout lines to avoid them, or gawk at them from two lanes away to satisfy their curiosity.

To live outside the gender binary during my upbringing in a small, religious community near Boston was, in many spaces, unfamiliar, unknown, or unaccepted; people had to conform or risk being bullied, targeted, or whispered about. During that time, I learned some of the most hurtful and hateful words to describe people who do not conform to gender norms. Now, too many years later, I recognize the pain my peers might have suffered knowing there were negative consequences to being their whole, authentic selves in and outside of school.

As an adult, I still find myself fighting problematic gender stereotypes in my thinking, writing, parenting, and work; they have been so present and pervasive in my life. I have decades of socialization to unlearn. To challenge these stereotypes, I try to place myself in spaces where people are talking about gender, disrupting gender norms, and engaging in gender-expansive dialogues. I attend conferences, workshops, online lectures, and book groups about gender. I follow people on Twitter who write about gender and gender identity. Every time I am in those learning spaces, I realize I have so much to (un)learn.

A particular challenge for me is examining subtle gender stereotypes in my life. As a girl in my family of seven, I helped with kitchen tasks like washing the dishes and setting the table. Yet, I was also responsible for shoveling our long driveway during New England snowstorms, taking out the garbage, and learning how to fix broken items in the house (this part was mostly informed by my dad's do-it-yourself upbringing). While our household chores were not assigned strictly along gender lines, boys and girls in my family were certainly treated differently. As a girl, I had more restrictions on where I could go, who I could be with, and how I could dress. My brothers had much more freedom in what they could do and the choices they could make. They could stay out later at night and had fewer restrictions on their experiences. My brothers were encouraged to be risky; I was taught to stay safe. Despite the work I've done to expand my understanding of gender identity, I still carry those early messages with me, and they inform the way I act and interact with others.

In this chapter, I'll start by defining the terms *sex*, *gender*, *gender binary*, and *gender nonbinary* before recognizing how the gender binary shows up in school. The language students hear, the examples they encounter, and the expectations set for "boys and girls" all can reinforce that a person's gender must exist along a binary; research shows that such messages alienate gender-nonconforming students and compromise their ability to thrive. Educators must take responsibility for designing gender-inclusive classrooms and communities where all students are welcome. For many educators, though, talking about gender is challenging given the early messages they received. Through the lens of identity-conscious practice, you can build the skills you need to engage in conversations about gender. Finally, you'll have a chance to explore how gender intersects with other identities. In the activities at the end of the chapter, you'll reflect on early messages you received about gender and create action plans for engaging in difficult conversations.

ESSENTIAL QUESTIONS

- How have definitions of gender changed or shifted since I first learned about gender?

- What issues related to gender show up in my classroom and in my interactions with others?

- How do I empower and support my students regarding their gender identity? In what ways do I negatively impact my students regarding their gender identity?

Recognizing the Gender Binary in Schools

Before we talk about gender in schools, it will be helpful to define our terms. First, sex and gender are different. *Sex* often refers to the physical differences between people who identify as male, female, or intersex. You might hear the term "sex assigned at birth" to refer to these physical differences. *Gender* is defined as a broad spectrum informed by different sociocultural constructs, including roles, norms, and attitudes that may determine what is considered acceptable or appropriate (World Health Organization, n.d.). *Gender binary* is defined as the "core belief that there are two discrete categories into which all individuals can be sorted" (Hyde, Bigler, Joel, Tate, & van Anders, 2019, p. 171). It is important to note that many cultures recognize and embrace third genders, which do not align along a gender binary. *Gender nonbinary* refers to the broad range of gender identity that does not fall within the binary genders of man or woman (Harbin, 2016). Research in neuroscience and psychological science alongside transgender and intersex activist movements has refuted society's limited understanding of a gender binary and challenges the gender binary from multiple lenses (Hyde et al., 2019).

Building on the early messages they receive about gender from their home, community, and culture, students in North America learn about the gender binary throughout elementary and secondary school (GLSEN, 2013a; Woolley, 2015). Adrienne B. Dessel (2010), lecturer at the University of Michigan's School of Social Work, finds that teachers and administrators often reinforce gender norms rather than actively work to fight against them. So, it's not surprising that this binary is evident in classroom procedures, activities, and curricula. Consider the following examples of how the gender binary shows up in the classroom.

- A teacher hands out a homework assignment to second graders, directing them to color the drawing that is just like them: a gingerbread boy or a gingerbread girl.

- Before taking them to recess, an elementary teacher says to students, "OK, boys and girls, let's get in line. Boys on the left, girls on the right."

- A school's dress code specifies that all students must look "neat and tidy," and it provides clear rules: all bottoms must be khaki colored, and all tops must have a collar. Boys are instructed to wear pants, while girls are given a choice between pants and skirts. Boys are not permitted to wear skirts.

- Elementary students are expected to adhere to standards of behavior. When a boy pushes or shoves another boy, his teacher gives him a warning against such "rough play." When a girl engages in the same behavior, pushing or shoving another girl, her teacher rebukes her for her "shocking" and "unkind" behavior. When a boy is assertive as a line leader or classroom helper, his teacher rewards him for being a "good leader." When a girl is assertive in the same manner, her teacher calls her "bossy."

As you read through the scenarios, was the gender binary obvious to you? Did it feel familiar? Did it seem problematic? Your early messages and life experiences about gender likely shaped your response. Gender constructs and societal messages perpetuated about gender roles affect how a teacher perceives students' behavior in the classroom and how the teacher responds to students. Table 6.1 features a list of observable behaviors. Notice how teachers might interpret those behaviors through gendered responses, and then compare those responses to the gender-inclusive approach described in the right-most column. Take a moment to reflect on the reactions that arise for you.

Colgate University associate professor of educational studies and LGBTQ studies Susan W. Woolley (2019) notes that a significant challenge in implementing a more gender-expansive approach is that not all people believe nonbinary, transgender, gender-fluid, and gender-nonconforming students exist. In examining the gaps between gender-expansive policies and their implementation (or lack thereof) in classrooms and school culture, Woolley (2019) found that "administrators' and teachers' beliefs that trans"

TABLE 6.1: Examples of Observable Behaviors and Gendered and Gender-Inclusive Responses

Observable Behavior	Gendered Interpretation for Boys	Gendered Interpretation for Girls	Gender-Inclusive Approach
Pushing and shoving	These are seen as playful behaviors among boys. Physical play is encouraged. Boys are told to "be careful" and to "not be too rough."	These are seen as aggressive or unladylike behaviors among girls. Physical play is discouraged. Girls are told to "be nice" and to "be kind."	Offer a wide range of opportunities for students to engage in dramatic play, physical play, nurturing play, and creative play that do not limit their choices to gender stereotypes. Be mindful of how you draw attention to different types of play.
Crying	When boys cry, it's seen as a weakness. They are often told to "stop crying" or "be strong."	When girls cry, it's seen as a mark of sensitivity. They are comforted and given room to express their feelings.	Affirm that crying is a natural response to having big feelings. Create space for students to share or discuss how they are feeling.
Speaking out of turn	This behavior is seen as a mark of leadership or assertiveness in boys.	This behavior is interpreted as a mark of rudeness or impoliteness in girls. They're told, "Wait your turn."	Provide wait time between asking a question and receiving an answer. Be mindful of how often you are calling on boys first and the ratio of boys to girls you choose to answer questions.

students did not exist in their schools structured ways in which such students were not seen, advocated for, or imagined" (p. 25). The notion that some people are transgender remains a new concept to many Americans, even though transgender individuals have been documented across cultural contexts for centuries (Stryker, 2017). Despite the diversity of understanding about transgender identity, educators have a responsibility to create classrooms and communities that are welcoming to gender-nonconforming students.

Designing Gender-Inclusive Classrooms and Communities

> The notion that some people are transgender remains a new concept to many Americans, even though transgender individuals have been documented across cultural contexts for centuries (Stryker, 2017).

From a young age, children receive implicit messages about gender stereotypes in their homes and through books and media; those messages continue throughout their school years in classrooms and through textbooks and activities (Steffens, Jelenec, & Noack, 2010). The constructs become so ingrained that by the time students reach adulthood, they find it hard to break free from those constraints and imagine a new way, much less act outside the scripts they've relied on for so many years. I'll share one experience from my life where this was especially clear.

My sister sent me a photo of her first-grade daughter, my niece, taken in front of her school on Halloween. The photo showed a row of seven children. Six of the children were dressed as princesses in large, flowing dresses with lace and frill. Each princess had her hair tied up in a high bun or released to flow in large, springy curls. One child at the end was dressed as a street fighter covered head to toe in a red-and-black spandex costume, including a mask that obscured the child's face. While the other children brandished princess wands, this child held a bō staff, a common martial arts weapon used in close combat. I knew in an instant that the child dressed as a street fighter was my niece. In a row of princesses with their bright smiles and glittery makeup, my niece looked like she was ready to take on the villain. As the photo made its way through a family text-message thread, the responses came in: "Oh my gosh! Look at her! Of course, she didn't dress up as a princess!" "Yup, leave it to her to be different from the rest." Others responded with some version of "Why can't she just be like the other girls?"

I was reminded how difficult it is for adults to dismantle their reactions to gender, gender expectations, and gender expression. While my family will tell you that we believe in gender equity and that many of us have disrupted gender norms, we still had much to say about my niece's costume choice. Had we secretly wished she had just chosen a princess costume? What was that reaction saying about us? How would you have responded as a teacher if a similar scenario happened in your classroom?

With the perpetuation of such reactions in students' homes and in their schools, individual educators must disrupt gender-binary attitudes in classrooms to support gender-nonconforming students to thrive. In 2021, the National Council of Teachers of English issued a statement about the importance of providing greater representation and inclusion for gender diverse and gender expansive stories, affirming that students of all gender identities and expressions—those who demonstrate those identities visibly while they are in our classes *and* those who may live their gender more expansively after they leave our classrooms—deserve to see themselves in books and other curricular materials and confirm the wide spectrum of identities that do not exist in a vacuum, but are a part of an ever-growing and changing world.

Cisgender students—those whose assigned sex at birth aligns with their gender identity—also benefit from reading about and learning from stories that include gender expansive characters. Encountering diversity in literature offers new perspectives and supports critical thinking about complex issues. Gender Spectrum (https://genderspectrum.org/articles/integrating-gender-diversity) provides a wealth of resources for integrating gender diversity into the classroom and curriculum.

In 2016, the U.S. Department of Education, Office for Civil Rights, and Department of Justice, Civil Rights Division published the Dear Colleague Letter on Transgender Students to focus on how preK–12 schools could meet their obligations to fulfill the needs of transgender and gender-nonconforming students (Croteau & Lewis, 2016). In a press release about the letter, Principal Deputy Assistant Attorney General Vanita Gupta commented:

> Every child deserves to attend school in a safe, supportive environment that allows them to thrive and grow. . . . Our guidance sends a clear message to transgender students across the country: here in America, you are safe, you are protected and you belong—just as you are. (U.S. Department of Justice, 2016)

Educators can help lead this shift away from a gender-binary approach and advocate for transgender and gender-nonconforming students (Simons, Beck, Asplund, Chan, & Byrd, 2018). In their journal article "Transgender and Gender-Creative Students in PK–12 Schools," researchers Elizabeth J. Meyer, Anika Tilland-Stafford, and Lee Airton (2016) provide six recommendations for teachers working to create a more gender-inclusive environment.

1. **Develop a more student-centered, flexible curriculum:** Formal, printed curricula might not be reflective of gender issues as we know them in the 21st century. Provide spaces for students to lead these inquiries and bring information about what they know or experience into the classroom.

2. **Promote interdisciplinary and project-based learning:** Talking about gender is not limited to the social sciences or humanities; explore how you can work across disciplines to talk about, read about, or research issues informed and impacted by gender.

3. **Model and promote creativity:** Gender-binary thinking is very limiting, so be sure to bring in different examples in your writing, projects, and dialogues that might include different pronouns, family structures, and relationships. In addition to using word problem examples that feature *she/her* or *he/him* pronouns, add *they/them* to describe individuals, give examples of stories including same-sex parenting and partnerships, or assign creative writing that does not assume gender or gender roles but rather invites a more expansive narrative.

4. **Establish restorative justice programs:** Provide opportunities for students to learn, to heal, and to correct wrongdoing or injustice in place of punitive zero-tolerance policies that fail to take into account diverse student identities.

5. **Reduce or entirely remove sex-segregated activities and spaces:** For example, find creative ways for students to line up. Instead of saying, "Boys on one side and girls on the other," say, "Let's line up with ten students on one side and ten on the other," "Line up by birthday month," or "Line up alphabetically."

    Disrupt the idea that there is information just for boys or just for girls; rather, all students can benefit from information, such as in desegregated health education classes or activities. Note that some spaces and programs may be geared toward sex-segregated populations (for example, Girls Who Code or Boys Who Cook). While these are intended to disrupt stereotypes, be mindful of their impact in your school or grade level and how they could exclude students who identify as nonbinary or as transgender.

6. **Integrate discussions of gender diversity as a social justice issue throughout the curriculum:** There are many ways to engage with the identity of gender, so provide representation and advocacy in your readings, writing prompts, and projects. For example, when doing a biography project or presentation, provide a range of options that students can choose from, and do not limit them to picking a subject of their own gender. Encourage them to research a person who has different identities and experiences than they do. For example, girls can present a biography project on Jackie Robinson, and boys can present a biography project on Rosa Parks. They do not have to align with the gender of their subject.

Social scientist Umut Ozkaleli (2011) notes additional ways that teachers can address gender in the classroom, like replacing groupings by sex and gender with more flexible and fluid choices for students; creating opportunities for dialogue in the classroom; and making note of how gender stereotypes show up in activity books, lessons, and readings. Teachers can challenge gender stereotypes by designing lessons that include issues about gender-related topics, including bullying and being an ally (Gonzalez & McNulty, 2010). Elementary, middle, and high school counselors can use exercises from GLSEN's (2013a) No Name-Calling Week, which promotes advocacy and support for every student. In addition, teachers can create more inclusive classrooms by engaging with these strategies: (1) providing students with an opportunity to share their preferred names before reading aloud an official list for attendance, (2) setting a tone of respect by letting students know policies and practices are focused on gender inclusion, (3) making sure that teachers have consent from the student to use certain names in different spaces, and (4) reminding and correcting other students if they use the wrong name or pronoun to refer to a classmate.

School administrators also have a vital part to play in creating gender-inclusive environments. The Dear Colleague Letter (U.S. Department of Justice, & U.S. Department of Education, 2016) emphasizes the role of school leaders in upholding policies that protect students. Rutgers University associate professor of education Melinda M. Mangin (2020) finds that principals play a key role in creating an inclusive environment: "To create gender-inclusive schools, principals need to facilitate extended learning that interrogates the ways in which rigid gender norms facilitate heteronormative and cisnormative school environments" (p. 279). School leaders provide the guidance and support that classroom teachers need in order to feel confident sharing more diverse representations of gender, gender roles, and gender expression in discussions, lessons, and examples.

Talking to Students About Gender

Teachers who are becoming aware of gender constructs for the first time or are new to the identity-conscious practice may feel unprepared to talk with students about gender. As you've seen throughout this book, engaging in difficult conversations is a process. By building the skills you need to join in the discussion, you'll be better prepared to support your students in their dialogues. You can also gain support in talking to students about gender by leaning on available resources.

Sometimes, confusion arises about what it means to be transgender due to the conflation of sex, gender, and sexual orientation (Mangin, 2020). Sam Killermann (2017), an artist and activist who focuses on gender, sexuality, and global justice, created a very helpful resource, the Genderbread Person, that describes terms such as *identity*, *expression*, *sex*, *gender*, and *sexual orientation* in ways that support a nuanced understanding and application of them. The Genderbread Person may be a helpful visual to bring in when talking to students about the differences between *sex* (the physical traits a person is born with or develops), *gender* (the cultural roles, behaviors, activities, and attributes expected of people based on their sex), and *sexual orientation* (a person's sexual and emotional attraction to another person and the behavior that may result from this attraction). You can download a free, printable poster version of this resource online (www.genderbread.org /resource/genderbread-person-v4-0-poster).

Teachers can sometimes rely on students as a helpful resource for opening the door to difficult conversations. Kids are curious and observant; sometimes, they catch on faster to changing norms than their adult counterparts do. This was highlighted for me when a relative asked to stop using *she/her* pronouns and instead use *they/them*. Because I lived in environments and worked in school cultures that perpetuated the gender binary, I initially struggled with transgender and gender-nonconforming pronouns. When I received the request from my relative, I was eager to support them in this way. "Of course, we will use *they/them* pronouns," I immediately responded. In reality, though, following through with it was difficult. I unintentionally misgendered my loved one, and I unfairly put the burden on them to correct me. Interestingly, while the adults in this young person's life struggled to use *they/them* pronouns for them, the youngest family members (ages six and eight at the time) seamlessly made the switch and frequently corrected the adults time and again, saying, "They do not use *she/her* pronouns. They use *they/them*."

So, what do you do if you're not sure of someone's pronouns? I've learned two ways of engaging with a person in that scenario. First, I simply come right out and say, "Hi, my name is Liza, and I use *she/her* pronouns." That introduction leaves space for the person I'm meeting to do the same, if they would like. Second, if I don't know what pronouns a person uses, I simply refer to them using the gender-neutral pronoun *they*. This way, I do not assume the person uses *he* or *she*. For example, I might say, "What I heard Joan say is that they really enjoy helping out with homework and learning alongside their third grader during the online lessons." Joan could correct me and tell me they use *she/her* pronouns or *he/him* pronouns, if they wanted to, but by using the gender-inclusive pronoun *they*, you're not making assumptions.

If educators are going to design gender-inclusive classrooms and communities where people of all gender identities can thrive, they must remember that who they are informs and impacts how they act and interact with others. Through an identity-conscious lens, teachers can shift from avoidance to invitation and rely on the skills they're building to engage in difficult conversations about gender.

Noticing How Gender Intersects With Other Identities

As you incorporate gender into your identity-conscious practice, remember to notice how gender intersects with other identities. One way this shows up in school is in the current state of teacher diversity. According to the Albert Shanker Institute (2015), "At the national level, progress is being made toward a more diverse teaching force, but at a relatively modest pace" (p. 1). Drawing from 3.5 million full- and part-time public school teachers in the U.S., the National Center for Education Statistics (2021) reported the following data for the 2017–2018 school year:

- 76 percent identified as female

- 24 percent identified as male

- the largest gap occurred in the elementary levels, where 89 percent identified as female and 11 percent identified as male

- no data was collected about transgender and gender nonbinary teachers.

Given racial distribution for the same data (National Center for Education Statistics, 2021):

- 79 percent of teachers identified as White

- 7 percent identified as Black

- 9 percent identified as Hispanic

- 2 percent identified as Asian

- 1 percent identified as American Indian or Native Alaskan

- less than 1 percent identified as Pacific Islander.

Take a moment to consider the data in the preceding lists. What do you notice about the identities represented there? Now consider the identities of students enrolled in public school in the United States during the same school year (National Center for Education Statistics, 2021):

- 47 percent of students identified as White

- 15 percent identified as Black

- 27 percent identified as Hispanic

- 5 percent identified as Asian

- 1 percent identified as American Indian or Native Alaskan

- 4 percent identified as two or more races

- and less than 1 percent identified as Pacific Islander

How does a largely homogenous teaching force impact the experiences of students who hold multiple historically marginalized identities? Assistant professor Travis Bristol explains the need for representation: "There's a growing body of research on the qualitative end that suggests that teachers of color actually understand the lived experiences of their students of color better, because they have lived them—or similar ones—themselves" (as cited in Beach, 2021). If you're teaching in a school that does not have a diverse faculty and staff, your identity-conscious practice should take this into account, perhaps by imagining other ways to provide representation for students who hold traditionally marginalized identities.

A collaborative report from the National Women's Law Center and the Education Trust (n.d.) highlights inequity at the intersection of gender and race. "Embedded within school discipline policies, dress codes, or codes of conduct are gender and racial biases that manifest in exclusionary punishments that have more to do with who girls are rather than what they do" (National Women's Law Center, & the Education Trust, n.d.). Teachers and school leaders must reform policies to create a positive school climate where students holding multiple historically marginalized identities are ensured safety and belonging. And schools must invest in recruiting, retaining, and mentoring diverse teachers and leaders who can bring their lived experience into that process of reform.

Activities for Building Awareness of Gender

What do K–12 educators need to know, do, and demonstrate in order to incorporate gender into their identity-conscious practice? The three activities in this chapter will guide you to reflect on your relationship with gender, imagine how you would respond to uncomfortable situations involving gender identity, and notice how gender intersects with other identities.

Activity 1: Engaging in Reflection

In this work of building identity consciousness around gender, it is important to think about the first and early messages you received that inform and impact your approach to gender. Read the following reflection questions, and record your thoughts and experiences in the space provided.

1. What were the earliest messages you received about gender? What did you see, learn, or notice about gender? Were these messages positive? Were they negative?

    _____

    _____

    _____

    _____

2. Educators have a responsibility to create an affirming and safe environment for all students. Yet, many of us learned that gender was a binary option only: boy or girl, man or woman, masculinity or femininity. What are some examples of how the gender binary is perpetuated in your classroom community? What steps can you take to create a more fluid, expansive, and inclusive environment for all gender identities?

    _____

    _____

    _____

    _____

3. Complete the following sentences as you reflect on your learning about gender identity.

    ○ In thinking about gender, I wonder _____

    _____.

    ○ In thinking about gender, I hope _____

    _____.

○ In thinking about gender, I am looking forward to _____

_____.

What do your answers in the sentences tell you about the first messages you received about gender? What impact have these first messages had on your own approach to gender and gender identity?

_____

_____

_____

_____

Activity 2: Imagining What You Would Do

Part of the discomfort in working with identity is people's natural tendency to get stuck when they aren't sure what to do next. In this activity, you'll read about four scenarios involving gender identity and, in the space provided, write about how you might respond.

- **Scenario 1:** You are meeting a parent of one of your students. When the parent introduces themself as Morgan, you're not sure what pronouns to use. What do you do?

_____

_____

_____

_____

- **Scenario 2:** A staff member shares at a meeting that they identify as transgender and, from now on, they will no longer be using the name Ellen and instead will use the name Ian. While everyone at the staff meeting is very positive and affirming in the moment, some colleagues still refer to Ian using their former name. What do you do?

_____

_____

_____

_____

- **Scenario 3:** You are on a committee that is writing recommendations for students. As members begin discussing the recommendation for a girl applying to a competitive college, one faculty member states that the girl is often "difficult to get along with" because she "is so driven and can be too focused" and "during group projects in class, she just takes over the project." The faculty member gives her a mediocre recommendation rating on the college application. What do you do?

_____

_____

_____

_____

- **Scenario 4:** The same committee from scenario 3 is discussing the recommendation for a male student. The committee is discussing that this student is a true leader who takes initiative. In class, he often leads group projects, picking up his classmates' slack. He is described as driven and laser focused when it comes to his future. He does not often rely on classmates to move things forward but instead shows leadership by making decisions even when his classmates do not agree. The committee decides to give him a glowing recommendation for his college application. What do you do?

_____

_____

_____

_____

Activity 3: Building Your Identity-Conscious Practice

Gender also intersects with other identities, such as race, immigration status, education, disability, and geographic location. What do you notice or wonder about how gender is informed and impacted by other aspects of your identity? In the space provided, write about how your experiences with gender might show up in your teaching, leading, and learning.

_____

_____

_____

_____

Discussion

This guide provides structures for you to think deeply about identity and difficult conversations. To advance this beneficial work, engage in conversations with others using the following discussion prompts.

1. Have a conversation with a partner or a small group of three to four people. Go through each activity in this chapter together. Leave enough time to engage in conversation that does not rush learning. Be sure to create intentions for the conversation and expectations for participation. See Bringing People Together on page 8 to help set expectations.

2. In a larger group, engage with the following questions.

   ○ What did you experience as you did the activities in this chapter?

   ○ What did you notice about yourself as you completed these activities?

   ○ What do you believe is your next step as you continue this learning process?

CHAPTER 7

Disability

In 2005, just after my daughter's second birthday, I noticed that one of her eyes started to look a bit off center. It didn't look this way all the time, but on occasion, her eyes didn't focus in the same direction. As first-time parents, my husband and I created worst-case scenarios: she would have to wear an eye patch, or she would need glasses for the rest of her life. The fear and anxiety I'd felt during her birth, when her preterm delivery almost landed her in the neonatal intensive care unit, shot through my body again.

In the doctor's office, my two-year-old looked so tiny in that big vinyl chair as she waited to have her vision tested. The pediatric ophthalmologist handed her a plastic device, showed her how to place it over one eye, and instructed her to look at the pictures projected on the wall ahead of her and name what she saw. She reported, "I see a car, a phone, a book, and a puppy." The ophthalmologist praised her and instructed her to switch the device to her other eye. "OK, Naomi, now what do you see?"

Silence.

"Naomi, what pictures do you see on the wall now?"

Silence.

I chimed in. "Honey, look at the wall. What are the pictures that you see?"

The doctor took the device from Naomi (not her real name) and told her how smart she was and what a great patient she was being. Naomi flashed a big smile and clapped for herself. Then the doctor showed her a tiny little flashlight and explained he needed to look into her eyes. Naomi flinched when the light flashed into her left eye; when the doctor flashed the light into her right eye, she gave no response.

What started as a visit to the pediatric ophthalmologist ended with us in an operating room eighteen hours later, where my toddler's eye was removed. She had been diagnosed with retinoblastoma, cancer of the eye, and the tumor had grown so large that her retina had detached. Weeks after surgery, she began a six-month course of systemic chemotherapy. In addition to observing the milestones of a toddler—learning to count, identifying colors, developing gross motor skills—my husband and I were checking off boxes of white blood cell counts, weeks until our next hospital visit, and the healing process of a prosthetic eye. We took great care to physically protect Naomi, and we struggled with the emotional support of being parents in a time of uncertainty. We sought out support groups for children with retinoblastoma and got advice about how to best support Naomi in school through individualized education plans and conversations with teachers. Together, we brainstormed compassionate responses to children's curious questions and prepared for some of the assumptions people would make of her abilities and her actual limits.

As much as we loved and cared for Naomi in our family, we worried about the time she was away from us and in school. In school, we could not protect her. We were not there to guide her, to address stereotypes people had of her, and to keep her from being teased or bullied. We relied on teachers, aides, and other children to be kind and to step in if she was being hurt. We advocated for teachers to both be sensitive to her disability and not limit her because of her disability.

Some teachers were so helpful, communicating with us about how Naomi experienced school and sharing both successes and challenges. Some teachers guided other children and taught lessons about difference and kindness toward each other. But many teachers struggled with walking that fine line of not treating Naomi special because of her disability but also having awareness of the real challenges she faces. One teacher told me, "Liza, I treat all of my students the same, and Naomi is no different. If she needs to make adjustments or changes, she can do that on her own." I believe the teacher meant well, advocating an equality-focused mindset that Naomi knew her body and her limits. But I believe this situation called for an equity-focused mindset. I kept thinking, *That's not enough. We need real structures to keep her safe. That's our job as adults.*

As I talked about these challenges with teachers and educators, I noticed that people often responded with how they were raised to think about disabilities or examples of people with disabilities from their own lives. They based how they treated my child on what they knew, who they knew, what they read, or what they saw on television. It was this life experience that helped me build the identity-conscious approach: What is it about *me* that informs and impacts my approach to disabilities? And how does that approach impact students? I knew my own fears about keeping Naomi safe weren't about Naomi; rather, they were about how I saw other children with disabilities treated when I was a child. I saw how classmates were bullied, made fun of, or excluded from everyday activities, and I didn't want that to happen to my daughter.

We live in a time when schools, students, and families have become more transparent about disabilities. Campaigns to destigmatize disabilities, such as Spread the Word to End the Word (www.spreadtheword.global), the Body Is Not an Apology (https://thebodyisnotanapology.com), and #SeeMe (www.stompoutbullying.org/see-me -campaign), are engaging a broader audience about disabilities. And yet, there is still more work to do; schools can take the lead in raising awareness of disabilities. Educators should be at the forefront of ensuring that students of all abilities have equal access to learn and thrive.

In this chapter, you'll read about accommodating for and including disability in the classroom, starting with the federal policies that have shaped protections and opportunities for people with disabilities in public schools. I'll discuss what teachers need to consider when creating an inclusive classroom for students of all abilities, drawing from multicultural education to construct a helpful framework. Engaging in dialogue about disabilities can be challenging as the definitions and terms evolve, especially when teachers come into the classroom without adequate training in supporting students with disabilities. However, through identity-conscious practice, teachers can build the skills they need to engage in conversations about disability. Finally, you'll have a chance to explore how disability intersects with other identities. While it's not possible to cover all types of disabilities within the scope of this chapter, the activities at the end will help you build awareness and create action plans for engaging in difficult conversations.

ESSENTIAL QUESTIONS

- How have collective understandings about disability changed and shifted given our understanding of and inclusion of disability in schools?

- What do I notice related to disability in my classroom, my school, and my community?

- How might difficult conversations about disability show up in my personal life and professional life?

Accommodating for Disability in the Classroom

People with disabilities have been subjected to biased assumptions and harmful stereotypes and prejudices held by those who are unfamiliar or uneducated about disabilities. According to the Anti-Defamation League (n.d.), people with disabilities in the 1800s were viewed as "abnormal and feeble minded" and were often sent away to institutions to be separated from society. After World War II, veterans with disabilities pressured the government to provide training, support, and rehabilitation services. Structural changes ensured that people with disabilities had greater access to transportation, bathrooms, and telephones. This shift allowed the disability civil rights movement to emerge alongside the racial civil rights movement in the 1960s. People with disabilities demanded equal treatment, equal access, and equal opportunities. Parents of children with disabilities were at the forefront of local advocacy as they fought for their children's right to attend community schools.

In 1975, the U.S. Congress enacted the Education for All Handicapped Children Act (Public Law 94–142) to "support states and localities in protecting the rights of, meeting the individual needs of, and improving the results for . . . infants, toddlers, children, and youth with disabilities and their families" (U.S. Office of Special Education Programs, 2007, p. 1). Over the next twenty-five years, Congress provided amendments, eventually resulting in what we know as the Individuals with Disabilities Education Act (IDEA; 1990).

The disability civil rights movement shifted national attention from disabilities as an individual issue to examining how collective factors like legislation, medical studies, and sociocultural influences created particular barriers to equity for people with disabilities. In response to these structural and systemic issues, scholars and practitioners advocated for a comprehensive approach to addressing inequity. Remedying existing barriers to full access for people with disabilities meant including different disciplines, understandings, and frameworks for building capacity and advocacy; Disability Studies emerged (Mullaney, 2019). In his book *An Introduction to Disability Studies*, David Johnstone (2001) notes:

> The study of disability crosses academic boundaries and draws from a variety of disciplines, including philosophy, sociology, psychology, and history in order to analyze issues concerning the relationship between disability, social justice, and political understanding . . . Disability Studies forms a basis for understanding both disability culture and social justice. (p. 5)

"Disability Studies forms a basis for understanding both disability culture and social justice" (Johnstone, 2001, p. 5).

Because the identity-conscious practice requires building habits and skills across disciplines, Disability Studies is an important link to the broader context of how educators can work toward greater accessibility in classrooms and schools. Disability Studies offers teachers and school leaders a lens to analyze current practices in schools that may limit the success of students with disabilities and construct policies, practices, programs, and procedures that remove structural and institutional barriers to success. As Johnstone (2001) notes, there is a relationship between disability, social justice, and political understanding; building an identity-conscious practice is a framework for seeing and addressing these intersections.

Teachers and school leaders must collaborate to develop action plans for change. For example, teachers can help destigmatize disabilities by engaging students in learning and dialogue about the different factors that influence definitions of disability. Some of those factors may include culture, politics, economics, and social norms. Teachers can facilitate learning through the lens of historical and global contexts, identifying that society's approach to disabilities has changed over time and is informed by culture. Students can examine policies, media, art, literature, history, and cultural approaches that shape international perspectives about disability.

Unfortunately, teacher preparation programs do not adequately prepare preservice teachers for working with students with disabilities (Tristani & Bassett-Gunter, 2020). In order to gain this necessary experience, a teacher has to pursue licensure or additional courses of study in special education. Many teachers have expressed that accommodating for disabilities can be taxing in the classroom precisely because of this gap in their teacher preparation (Hernandez, Hueck, & Charley, 2016). Education professors Roben W. Taylor and Ravic P. Ringlaben (2012) find that "teachers continue to have mixed feelings about their own preparedness to educate students with disabilities in the general education setting" (p. 16).

What do teachers need to be better prepared for their role in this work? Research suggests that teachers need more specialized training in how to support students with disabilities. Teachers who receive opportunities to work and interact with different types of students and who receive training in strategies for working with students with disabilities "are more likely to exhibit greater confidence and positive attitudes toward inclusion" (Taylor & Ringlaben, 2012, p. 17). Think back to your teacher training. What did you learn about disabilities? What did you learn about students with disabilities? What did you experience in your practicum or field training?

If your responses to the preceding questions included answers like, "I only had one class that addressed students with disabilities" or "I didn't have any field-training experiences working with students with disabilities," then is it possible you hold negative or neutral biases toward students with disabilities? Training during the preservice teaching period that includes Disability Studies can significantly reduce negative attitudes teachers might have toward students with disabilities by increasing positive contact, developing confidence in their training, and providing opportunities to connect classroom and field-based practice (McCrimmon, 2015; Shani & Hebel, 2016).

In order to build the knowledge and skills they need, teachers in the preservice classroom must have opportunities to engage with academic and experiential learning. However, preparation programs must provide diverse learning rooted in an asset model rather than a deficit model of disability or one that does not consider multiple intersections of identity. For example, professor Christine Ashby (2012) shares that students in teacher preparation programs often start with readings that:

> address the overrepresentation of students of color in special education and the ways in which labeling, special education, and tracking have been used to resegregate students of color in public schools. We also consider the intersection of disability and poverty and the role of economic privilege in assessing services and supports for students with disabilities. (p. 94)

Special education professor Paul M. Ajuwon and colleagues (2012) find that the following preservice training recommendations can help teachers develop positive attitudes toward students with disabilities and confidence in teaching students with disabilities.

- Embed knowledge of working with students with disabilities in all courses, and not just in an isolated course during training.

- Provide field-based experiences where preservice teachers can observe and teach students with disabilities and can receive feedback about their teaching from mentor teachers.

- Invite teachers with disabilities to participate in the training of preservice teachers through guest lectures, through supervision, or as co-instructors of courses. This provides firsthand experience and knowledge that can benefit students beyond just theoretical learning.

- Provide opportunities to combine field-based experiences with students with disabilities, so that preservice teachers are proximate to students, as well as academic assignments, reflections, and research topics to deepen their understanding about disabilities.

If you are no longer in your preservice training, what opportunities can you pursue to build positive approaches to students with disabilities and confidence in teaching? How might your school implement Ajuwon and colleagues' (2012) recommendations?

If you are no longer in your preservice training, what opportunities can you pursue to build positive approaches to students with disabilities and confidence in teaching? How might your school implement the preceding recommendations? Although it's not a replacement for specialized training or professional development, the identity-conscious practice can support teachers to access the tools and competencies they need to become more inclusive of students with disabilities and to engage in difficult conversations on the topic.

Welcoming Students of All Abilities

A central tenet of IDEA is the *least restrictive environment* principle, which means that students with disabilities should receive the individualized support they need to be able to learn alongside their peers in the general education classroom. While federal mandates do secure disabled students' place in the classroom, they don't yet ensure that teachers are prepared to create equitable learning opportunities for all students. If they are not prepared, then it is difficult to create measures of accountability. Because IDEA functions to hold educators and campuses accountable for ensuring that all students have equal access to learning in the general education classroom, it is important to identify what accountability looks like. What are some examples of standards and accountability you see enacted at your school? Likely, your school has a process in place for evaluating teachers and their connection to student success. In your experience, have your school's accountability practices successfully achieved the intended goal? Reflect for a moment on the benefits and drawbacks of these initiatives.

At the national level, laws such as No Child Left Behind (2002) "extended the reach of Washington into American classrooms with a national system for evaluating schools based on math and reading test scores and required schools to raise scores every year or endure intensifying consequences" (Valle & Connor, 2019, p. 13). In 2015, President Obama signed the Every Student Succeeds Act (2015) into law, which shifted responsibility for school accountability from the federal government to the states. Here again, these mandates are meaningful, but they can only do so much; on their own, they can't ensure classrooms are inclusive for all students. As Jan W. Valle and David J. Connor (2019) note in their book *Rethinking Disability: A Disability Studies Approach to Inclusive Practices*, "We can legislate policy, but we can't legislate attitude" (p. 12).

Identity-conscious practice can help educators work to close the gap between federal policies and educators' attitudes about implementing them. By examining their thoughts, attitudes, behaviors, and beliefs toward disability, teachers can become aware of the dynamics that inform and impact their relationship to disability in the classroom. When it comes to working toward inclusion for students of all abilities, multicultural education offers a helpful framework. Multicultural education seeks to "ensure educational equity for members of diverse racial, ethnic, cultural, and socioeconomic groups, and to facilitate their participation as critical and reflective citizens in an inclusive national civic culture" (Education Encyclopedia, n.d.). James A. Banks (1993), the father of multicultural education, identifies five dimensions of multicultural education: (1) content integration, (2) the knowledge construction process, (3) prejudice reduction, (4) an equity pedagogy, and (5) an empowering school culture and social structure. Table 7.1 (page 106) offers an example of how teachers might use Banks's five dimensions to create an inclusive environment for all students, identifying helpful resources to consult within each dimension.

What came up for you as you read through Banks's five dimensions and the suggestions in the table? Take a moment to examine your reactions as you think about your relationship to disability in the classroom. From that place of awareness, you can begin to build skills for engaging in difficult conversations about disability.

Talking to Students About Disability

A challenge to talking about disability, which we've seen with other identities, is the fluid nature of definitions of this identity and its related terminology. Educators, scholars, and researchers employ different ways of writing, speaking, and researching

TABLE 7.1: Banks's Five Dimensions of Multicultural Education

Dimension	Example	Action Items and Resources
Diversification of the canon	Don't overly rely on White voices or dominant voices; include stories and examples of people of color, people with disabilities, women, and others.	Include children's books that address disabilities. See Margaret Kingsbury's (2019) blog post "Representation Matters: 10 Children's Books With Disabled Characters" (www.thinkinclusive.us/10-childrens-books-with-disabled-characters). Include texts for older students and adults that address disabilities. See Grace Lapointe's (2019) blog post "6 Powerful Books by Disabled Authors" (https://bookriot.com/books-by-disabled-authors).
Understanding of the impact of perspective, knowledge, and value and what is presented as perspective, knowledge, and value	Address that history is often told from an ableist perspective and reinforces a dominant narrative—historically and currently—that excludes people with disabilities as contributors.	Provide multiple ways to access information: print, digital readers, text-to-speech, audiobooks, text enlargement, screen color, captioning, and so on. If students cannot access the information, they have a barrier to learning. Visit the website of the Kennedy Center, which provides lesson plans that celebrate arts and education with opportunities for people of all abilities (www.kennedy-center.org/education; Kennedy Center, n.d.).
Reduction of prejudice and assumptions	Provide multiple accounts and perspectives of an event or a view, and challenge stereotypes about people of color or people with disabilities.	Visit the Disability Visibility Project's (n.d.) website to read stories by disabled people of color (https://disabilityvisibilityproject.com/tag/disabled-people-of-color).
Application of equity-based pedagogies	Address biases in grading, assessment, participation in class, and discipline that may privilege White students, White students, or able-bodied students.	Prioritize content and assignments that reflect the skills learned instead of prioritizing busywork. This way, students spend more time on assignments that count toward their grade in more meaningful ways. Structure grades to include student effort, improvement, and progress versus the final product. Diversify the options for outcomes, such as demonstrating content knowledge via writing, podcasts, blogs, videos, graphic arts, and other outcomes that show understanding of content but in ways that privilege the learning process. Change weights of grades, knowing that some students do well on homework while others do well on tests; vary this percentage weighting to reflect a more inclusive structure. Provide flexible workspaces in the classroom: a quiet area and large-group, small-group, and group instruction spaces. Have options for headphone usage during independent work.
Support of school culture that empowers students	Integrate diverse voices, experiences, and viewpoints not just in one area of the school but embedded as a critical practice in the life of the school. Give students voice and choice in their learning and expression.	Implement a cross-age program where students have partnerships designed to build community, develop and support self-esteem and social skills, and foster meaningful relationships within the school. Create service-learning projects where students can work together on different initiatives that benefit the classroom, school community, and local community. Provide choices and options, and center the needs and interests of students with disabilities in the decision-making process. Support the inclusion of students with disabilities in clubs and organizations designed to engage students in leadership and learning.

Source for dimensions: Banks, 1993.

about disabilities. Some prefer people-first language and use terminology such as "people with disabilities" or "people living with disabilities." Others use the term *dis/ability* to emphasize the presence of ability and an asset-based approach to the community. Others, preferring identity-first language, state that using the term *disabled person* is a more accurate way to include disabilities because it centers the identity of being disabled in a system that has privileged ableism. Special education and inclusive education professors Subini Ancy Annamma, David Connor, and Beth Ferri (2013) write that *dis/ability* is:

> an elastic category because it expands and contracts over time and throughout cultures. What is considered a dis/ability today may or may not have been seen as a dis/ability 100, 50, or even 10 years ago. Because dis/ability is socially and historically contingent, dis/ability is always shifting and moving as a category of difference. (p. 24)

It is important to honor how individuals choose to identify and to use the terminology they want you to use. It is also important to know that words or phrases that may have gained popularity in some communities are considered offensive and condescending in others. For example, for a period of time, words such as *differently abled, challenged,* and *handicapable* were common to hear, yet the Americans With Disabilities Act National Network (n.d.) makes clear these terms are condescending. An identity-conscious approach honors how people wish to self-identify and adopts the language and terms of their choice.

In addition, not all disabilities are immediately apparent or easily recognizable. And yet, that makes them no less valid. For example, consider the case of an *invisible disability*, which the Invisible Disabilities Association (n.d.) defines as "a physical, mental, or neurological condition that is not visible from the outside, yet can limit or challenge a person's movements, senses, or activities." Invisible disability can refer to "debilitating pain, fatigue, dizziness, cognitive dysfunctions, brain injuries, learning differences and mental health disorders, as well as hearing and vision impairments," and symptoms can range from mild to severe (Invisible Disabilities Association, n.d.). To learn more about invisible disabilities, visit the Invisible Disabilities Association's website (https://invisibledisabilities.org). Teachers may unintentionally make assumptions and judgments about people based on their perceptions that perpetuate barriers for students with disabilities. The identity-conscious practice is a powerful tool for helping educators obtain accurate information about students and create supportive environments to meet their needs.

By reflecting on first messages, pervasive stereotypes, and existing beliefs with the goal of interrupting or disrupting problematic behaviors, teachers can build a process for examining identity and developing skills to engage in the conversations they encounter.

It is not possible to cover all categories, identities, experiences, and aspects of disability within the scope of this book. But by reflecting on first messages, pervasive stereotypes, and existing beliefs with the goal of interrupting or disrupting problematic behaviors, teachers can build a process for examining identity and developing skills to engage in the conversations they encounter.

What do teachers need to consider when engaging in difficult dialogues about disabilities? The Americans With Disabilities Act National Network shares some helpful suggestions for talking and writing about individuals with disabilities (Americans With Disabilities Act Knowledge Translation Center, 2018).

- **Do not assume people want to disclose their disability:** Ask the person first and then follow their lead. It is good practice to ask and not assume. Do not assume students want everyone to know. While some students may be very open about disability, others may choose to be more private in and outside of class. In addition, if the disability is not relevant to the dialogue, do not include the disability unless the individual wants you to do so.

- **Emphasize ability:** Instead of saying, "That person is wheelchair bound," say, "That person uses a wheelchair." Instead of saying, "That person can't talk," say, "That person uses a communication device." We teachers must also remember to honor how people choose to identify or describe themselves and align our language with how they want us to refer to them. While some individuals may prefer people-first language, others prefer identity-first language. If you are unsure how a student or family uses terms to describe themselves, you can say, "Before we go further in our conversation, I hear you using the phrase 'child with autism,' and I want to make sure I'm using language that you and your family use. Is this the phrase you would like me to use when we talk with and about Christopher?"

- **Use language that emphasizes the need for accessibility:** This includes using language like "accessible bathroom" instead of "handicapped stall" or "accessible parking" instead of "handicapped parking." At school, be mindful of how you refer to bathroom spaces or parking spaces in this way.

- **Be mindful of using language like "normal" as a comparison against people with disabilities:** You can use phrases like "child without disabilities" in place of the term "normal child" since the latter implies a negative stereotype of those with disabilities. It is important to model this with children and to be open to their learning stages and processes. Children often like to point out differences, and sometimes, they compare what they believe to be or name as "regular" or "normal" with anything that is different. In addition, while you may be using this language at school, your students may be hearing different messages or uses of language at home. You can explain to students why you use this language as a way for them to understand context and content.

- **Do not use language that perpetuates negative stereotypes about psychiatric disabilities:** I often hear adults and young people use words that refer to psychiatric disabilities or mental health conditions in very casual ways that perpetuate stereotypes. Phrases that have found their way into common use, such as "mental case," "crazy person," and "committed suicide," reinforce mental stigma. Instead, use language such as "person receiving mental health services," "person with a mental health condition," and "died by suicide." Our society has a long way to go to disrupt stereotypes in our own thoughts, attitudes, behaviors, and beliefs related to mental health and psychiatric disabilities. Some campaigns (for example, Spread the Word to End the Word) are making an impact in our changing language and negative associations.

- **Portray successful people with disabilities in a balanced way:** Too often, people with disabilities are called "courageous" or "brave" simply for living their lives. While some human-interest stories certainly are examples of people addressing obstacles, these stories sometimes are told in a way that elicits pity and perpetuates negative stereotypes.

- **Honor the ways that individuals may or may not want to talk about their disabilities:** Openness and willingness to talk about one's disability might shift from day to day, context to context, or moment to moment. Honor and respect that just because students shared information about their disability one day, that does not mean they are open to or willing to talk about it all the time. Check in, ask permission, and honor their choices.

Openings for challenging conversations will likely arise naturally in the classroom and within your school community. By continuing their identity-conscious practice through building knowledge, engaging in reflection, and moving to action, teachers can acquire the skills they need to join the conversations.

Noticing How Disability Intersects With Other Identities

As part of developing an identity-conscious practice around disability, it's important to notice how disability intersects with other identities. Because students, families, and peers are complex, teachers must approach their work in disabilities as being informed by multiple influences. Disability Studies is helpful here, as it emphasizes the social model of disability informed and impacted by political, economic, social, historical, and cultural factors (Pearson, 2016). The social model of disability acknowledges that disability rights are deeply connected to other issues such as citizenship rights, equal opportunity, inclusion, and social justice. This means that when educators work with disabilities in the school community through a critical and social model of disability, they're examining how family, education, income, financial support, employment, housing, transportation, and the built environment impact people with disabilities (Barnes & Mercer, 2010; Pearson, 2016). Teachers and school leaders working with an identity-conscious lens acknowledge the many factors that influence experiences in the classroom and use that understanding to support students.

IDEA has supported the development and validation of culturally relevant assessment and intervention practices. As the U.S. Office of Special Education Programs (2007) notes, there are four key culturally relevant instructional principles that lead to improved learning and higher achievement:

- Link assessments of student progress directly to the instructional curricula rather than to abstract norms for standardized tests.

- Examine not only the individual child but also his or her instructional environment, using direct observational data.

- Create classroom environments that reflect different cultural heritages and accommodate different styles of communication and learning.

- Develop and implement family-friendly practices to establish collaborative partnerships with parents and other caregivers, including those who do not speak English. (p. 6)

While Disability Studies is a helpful framework for teachers and school leaders to increase their knowledge and skills to create more inclusive classrooms, Dis/Ability Critical Race Studies, or *DisCrit*, provides a framework for examining the more specific intersections of disability and race. Researchers Annamma et al. (2013) state that teachers and school leaders must examine the relationship between disability and race in order to address oppression and marginalization in classrooms and schools:

Given the racial gap in graduation, incidents of discipline, and incarceration rates, along with vast over-representation of students of color in special education and the lackluster achievement rates within many of these special education programs, we must critically examine why so many students labeled with a dis/ability, partic-ularly students of color, are either experiencing failure or being perceived as failing and on what grounds. (p. 6)

There is evidence that the existing system of education reinforces racial hierarchies. For example, Annamma et al. (2013) summarize the ways in which racial groups are examined and discussed in the discourse on disabilities.

- Asian Americans are underrepresented in special education, which allows them to be seen as a homogenized "model" minority (Lee, 2009) and reinforces that Asian Americans do not need support. This leads to the needs of Asian Americans being overlooked or ignored.

- Native Americans are often excluded in the discourse on education even though they are overrepresented in many categories of special education, particularly in states with large numbers of Native American students (Brayboy, 2005; Fierros & Conroy, 2002). This systemic erasure perpetuates inequities for Native American students.

- Latino, Latina, Latine, and Latinx students are overrepresented in special education in some regions of the United States where their population is high and where teachers, who do not know how to accommodate English learners, overly refer students to special education programs. While not all Latino/a/e/x students speak Spanish nor are English learners, there exists a deficit-oriented approach to Latino/a/e/x rooted in stereotypes and biases (Luelmo & Bindreiff, 2021).

- Emerging bilinguals are more likely to be overrepresented in special education in middle and high school (Artiles, Rueda, Salazar, & Higareda, 2005).

- The overrepresentation of African Americans in special education across the United States, regardless of social class, continues to be a problem rooted in existing structural inequities in American education (Erevelles, Kanga, & Middleton, 2006; as cited in Annamma et al., 2013).

This examination of race and the intersection of dis/ability demonstrates that educators must understand the impact and consequences of race and dis/ability. Classroom teachers are often the first ones to recommend students for evaluation, assessment, and services for disabilities (Hayes, Dombrowski, Shefcyk, & Bulat, 2018). Yet, how often is this decision informed by biases and stereotypes? How are referrals informed and impacted by awareness of race, class, gender, and other identities? By engaging in the frameworks of DisCrit, and more broadly Disability Studies, teachers can better understand these dynamics.

Understanding that social justice movements have not historically included disability, teachers' identity-conscious practice must include disability and accessibility. As educators build the habits and skills for an identity-conscious practice, they may seek out opportunities to learn about, reflect upon, and be more inclusive in their work. Building an identity-conscious practice means constantly noticing when identity is present and also when it is missing. That awareness gives rise to action that seeks to create greater inclusion for all students.

Activities for Building Awareness of Disability

What do K–12 educators need to know, do, and demonstrate in order to incorporate disability into their identity-conscious practice? The five activities in this chapter will guide you to reflect on your relationship with disability, brainstorm ways to accommodate for disability in the classroom, imagine responding to uncomfortable situations, write about your experience with disability, and notice how disability intersects with other identities.

Activity 1: Engaging in Reflection

In this work of building identity consciousness around disability, it is important to think about the first and early messages you received that inform and impact your approach to disability. Read the following reflection questions, and record your thoughts and experiences in the space provided.

1. What were the earliest messages you received about disabilities or people with disabilities? What did you see, learn, or notice about disability? Were these messages positive? Were they negative?

   _____

   _____

   _____

   _____

2. How, if at all, have those messages changed since you became a teacher or school leader? What messages are similar to those you grew up with? What messages are different from those you grew up with?

   _____

   _____

   _____

   _____

3. What do you notice about other people and their relationship to disabilities? What do you hear people say? What do you observe in their actions? What expectations do others have related to disabilities?

   _____

   _____

   _____

   _____

4. What challenges related to disabilities have you faced in your teaching? What opportunities related to disabilities have you faced in your teaching?

_____

_____

_____

_____

Activity 2: Creating a More Inclusive Environment

Inclusion requires teachers to think about multiple experiences, barriers, and approaches to widen pathways of participation. In this activity, you'll consider a week of lessons in your classroom, reflect on the needs of students with disabilities, and identify ways you would improve the classroom environment to meet students' needs.

The chart for this activity provides an example of a teacher's reflections on adapting the classroom environment to meet the needs of a student with a prosthetic eye. In the space provided in the chart, list the disabilities represented in your classroom, and record your thoughts about the following.

- **Biology:** How does the medical or biological condition inform and impact how you engage with a student with this disability in your classroom?

- **Culture:** How do cultural expectations, conditions, and experiences inform and impact how you engage with a student with this disability in your classroom?

- **Design:** How does the design of your classroom inform and impact how you engage with a student with this disability in your classroom?

- **Curriculum:** How do your choices of literature, science, art, mathematics, and other content areas inform and impact how you engage with a student with this disability in your classroom?

- **Policies:** How do policies and practices of your classroom, your school, or your community inform and impact how you engage with a student with this disability in your classroom?

Disability	Sample: Student with a prosthetic eye		
Biology	Sample: I tend to notice this student's prosthetic eye. I notice myself not knowing where to look when I'm talking with the student.		
Culture	Sample: I notice this child often uses her hair to cover her prosthetic eye. I'm wondering if she feels she needs to hide herself to avoid interactions or if she just likes wearing her hair this way.		
Design	Sample: This student does not have peripheral vision on her right side. Are there spaces in my classroom that could unintentionally hurt or poke her if she cannot see from the peripheral view? Can she see me if I'm standing on the side of her prosthetic eye? How can I be more inclusive in my physical awareness of where I am in the room?		

Curriculum	Sample: I do not have any books, stories, or examples of people who have prosthetics, who have gone through cancer, or who have a disability related to vision and seeing.		
Policies	Sample: I've never thought about this. I need to explore this further and come back to this box. As a first step, I'll look at our student handbook and see if there are policies specific to vision or disabilities related to vision.		

Read the following reflection questions, and record your thoughts and experiences in the space provided.

- As you completed the chart, which questions were easy for you to answer? Which were more difficult?

- List a few action items that result from completing the chart. What might you need to do to create a more inclusive environment for your students?

_____

_____

_____

_____

Activity 3: Answering, "What Would You Do?"

Educators are working not only with their experiences and beliefs but also within the parameters of school policies, school beliefs, and actions that districts and school leaders are willing to support. As you read the following scenarios, think through some challenges you might face if you found yourself in each situation, and identify areas you would need to address. After each scenario, take a moment to reflect on the listed questions.

Michelle's Story

Michelle is a first-year high school student who was a star athlete. In an accident during an ice hockey game in the winter of her ninth-grade year, Michelle hit the boards headfirst and was unable to move. Michelle was paralyzed from the neck down.

After over a year of rehabilitation, Michelle planned to return to school in the fall of eleventh grade. But the building, classrooms, and structures did not allow for unobstructed access for individuals using wheelchairs. The school also lacked effective technology for Michelle to gain access to accessible lessons, opportunities, and assignments. In addition, the faculty did not have adequate training in how to effectively work with students with disabilities in general, nor how to best support Michelle in particular.

Knowing that Michelle was preparing to return to school, the school leadership team, with support from the school district, made significant changes to a few classrooms. Class locations were reassigned so that Michelle could access her classes on the first floor. The school upgraded the main doors to have an automatic electronic entry, and it installed a new lift for navigating the few steps in a previously inaccessible first-floor hallway. While structural changes were made to provide greater accessibility, faculty and staff received little training to help them expand their thoughts, attitudes, behaviors, and beliefs in response to Michelle's experience.

Two weeks before school starts in September, you learn that Michelle is going to be a student in your eleventh-grade English class this year. You have been told that Michelle has limited movement of her legs and arms. And you are aware that Michelle did not lose the ability to think, feel, learn, or connect. While you know about Michelle's ability, you find yourself challenging existing stereotypes you have learned about people with disabilities. You have never worked with a student who experienced a spinal cord injury. To create conditions so Michelle can fully access your class and the experiences within your class, you need to make significant changes to your teaching and facilitation.

- What emotions or reactions came up for you as you read the scenario?

_____

_____

_____

_____

- How would you like to react in this scenario?

_____

_____

_____

_____

- What aspects of school culture or structures keep you from being inclusive? What opportunities exist for you to create an inclusive classroom experience?

_____

_____

_____

_____

- What is your first step to building a more inclusive classroom experience? What do you need to do? Whom do you need to learn from? Whom do you need to collaborate with?

_____

_____

_____

_____

Cherie and Mayra's Story

Cherie (not her real name) is a friend of mine who has been vocal about her experiences as a parent advocate of a child with a disability. Despite the fact that she is highly educated and understands how to navigate complicated educational systems, she found herself frustrated when advocating for her child, Mayra (not her real name). In the following personal communication, Cherie provides a helpful narrative from a parent's perspective.

> My name is Cherie, and I am the White adoptive parent to an internationally adopted child of color, Mayra. Mayra was born in Guatemala and was in a loving foster family in her home country until she came home as my daughter at 7.5 months old.
>
> I knew early on that my daughter was approaching life differently than her neurotypical peers; she didn't play with toys and much of her play was repetitive. At the time, I did not understand that Mayra's repetitive pattern was a form of trauma-informed play.
>
> As a parent, I felt like I knew both everything and nothing at the same time; I felt like I knew my child so well and yet had no formal training to help me articulate what

I saw. For example, when Mayra was in preschool, I received a progress report that said Mayra was able to name all her colors and shapes. I was surprised to hear this because Mayra was never able to do this at home. I followed up with the day care, asking if I should be concerned about the discrepancy in behavior between day care and home. The teacher clarified, "Oh, Mayra doesn't say the colors out loud, but if I put the colors or shapes on the floor and ask her to 'stand near yellow' or 'stand near a square,' she can do it. So, I know she knows them." I believed that at four years old, Mayra should be able to verbally name her colors or shapes. The teacher responded, "Don't worry. She is in the range for development."

While the teacher had come up with a creative way to assess Mayra's learning, this process unfortunately masked some real needs and failed to provide support that would have helped Mayra, delaying the necessary services. I now know that my daughter has a rapid naming deficit, which is why she could not verbally name her colors and shapes. While I appreciated the creativity to assess in this way, the process did not help us understand that Mayra needed a different type of support.

Over the course of a few years, I kept hearing that phrase, "She's in the range," again and again. I came to abhor that phrase from teachers. While I think it was supposed to bring me comfort, it always felt condescending and dismissive, especially as I did not see that Mayra's progress was in the range of anything. As a parent, I struggled with trying to figure out what was best for my child. In navigating this journey, I wish teachers and school leaders would admit when they don't know. My child needed help, and being told that "she's in the range" made me feel like people didn't want to admit she needed support.

I know there are budget implications to calling in experts and adding academic specials to a child's schedule. Yet this is my child, my daughter. As her parent, it is my job to advocate for her. I have gone to the school superintendent and committee meetings, and I've voted on issues supporting funding for education. I believe in supporting teachers who are supporting my child. I wish teachers and school leaders would understand that I come from a place of deep love for my child and an uneducated understanding of how my child is navigating her world. I need their help navigating what to request or even advocate for. As a parent, I often feel lost in the woods with an injured child, and teachers are my only guide to safe harbor (Cherie, personal communication, January 20, 2021).

- What emotions or reactions came up for you as you read Cherie and Mayra's story?

_____

_____

_____

_____

- How would you like to react in this scenario? How would you react to Cherie? To Mayra?

_____

_____

_____

_____

- What aspects of school culture or structures keep you from being inclusive of Cherie (as a parent) and Mayra (as a student)? What opportunities exist for you to create an inclusive classroom experience?

_____

_____

_____

_____

- What is your first step to building a more inclusive classroom experience? What do you need to do? Whom do you need to learn from? Whom do you need to collaborate with?

_____

_____

_____

_____

Jaleesa's Story

Jaleesa is a former elementary school teacher who currently serves as a school administrator for diversity, equity, and inclusion initiatives. In this personal communication, Jaleesa shares about her experiences with chronic illness and how school colleagues can be supportive and inclusive of her and others with disabilities.

> This chapter holds a lot of personal significance for me. As someone with both a chronic illness and a diagnosed disability (some people do not see my diagnosis as a disability), it is important for me to share my experience. My diagnosis of Ehlers-Danlos syndrome—a rare genetic connective tissue disorder that impacts my joints—changed my life but not in the ways one might expect. It validated the symptoms that I exhibited for years that doctors and other medical personnel dismissed as being psychosomatic. Invisible illnesses can be so difficult to navigate

because when people can't see something, they struggle to accept its validity. This is especially true for someone like me who has a dramatically different presentation of symptoms depending on the day. On a given day, I can appear to be able bodied and "look normal." However, on another day, I can have multiple joints dislocate simultaneously and repeatedly, resulting in being bedridden. It is often hard to explain to others what it feels like to live in my body or to get them to believe me when I describe it.

As a person navigating this world with a disability, I have developed such empathy for others. I have always been someone who cares deeply for others. However, having an invisible illness has really helped me to understand that we have no idea what is going on in someone else's life. I often joke that I look my best on my worst days, but it's true. For me, it also highlights that just because someone may not "look" like they need an accommodation like disabled parking (even though they have a placard), we have no right to judge anyone else's journey.

Most people don't realize how exhausting it is for me as a teacher to spend the day giving 100 percent to students and faculty who absolutely deserve it. My students get 100 percent of me every day, the effects of which can start to add up. It isn't a slight to them, but it does mean that by the end of the day, both my body and my mind are beyond exhausted. Many days, I go home and collapse into bed because I am literally, not just figuratively, holding my body together. In chronic illness circles, we often talk about spoon theory to help people understand our experiences. In any kitchen, you have a finite number of spoons, and once they have all been used, there is some time needed before you've got more to use. Well, my body is that way. If I use up all my spoons, I need to replenish them, and that takes time.

I need colleagues, parents and caregivers, and school leaders to understand that my students come first, which means if I set a firm boundary around my time, it is essential. It means that I either am right at my breaking point or likely have already passed it. Please respect the boundary that I have set, and know that when I have been restored, you'll get 100 percent of me again. The 100 percent is worth the short wait (Jaleesa, personal communication, January 19, 2021).

- What emotions or reactions came up for you as you read Jaleesa's story?

_____

_____

_____

_____

- What are some takeaways you, as a peer, draw from Jaleesa's story? What do teachers often miss about the needs of other teachers and coworkers?

_____

_____

_____

_____

- What aspects of school culture or structures serve as barriers to Jaleesa? What opportunities exist to be supportive of Jaleesa or to make structures more inclusive?

_____

_____

_____

_____

- How might supervisors perceive Jaleesa's day-to-day experience, and how might these observations or critiques perpetuate implicit bias?

_____

_____

_____

_____

Craig's Story

Craig's story is an aggregate of a few personal stories I've heard from young people in high school. When I worked as a grade-level dean for ninth- and tenth-graders, students often talked about their struggles with focus and attention, as well as the pressure to perform academically. Teachers frequently sent students to my office for "acting out" or "distracting" the class. Craig's story represents a number of different narratives of students who have experienced this and have internalized messages of failure or burden.

> I was a good student when I was younger. I loved school. I loved elementary school, reading time, and creative writing. I felt like I was always the student who had the answers. By middle school, my attitude toward school began to change. I know that work is supposed to get harder the older we are, but I felt like the transition from elementary school to middle school was impossible. I spent more and more time reading but not really understanding what was going on. When we had timed reading

assignments in class, I was always the last one done. Most times, I didn't even finish, while the other kids were already done way before I was. I had to read every sentence two or three times just to understand it. I was embarrassed, and instead of asking for help in middle school, I used to say things like, "This reading is dumb anyway," or say something to draw attention away from the fact that I hadn't completed the work. I tried being funny as a way to distract the teacher, but I just ended up getting in trouble a lot and was asked to leave the room. I felt even more embarrassed.

When high school started, I got really frustrated with the fact that I couldn't read quickly. And, when I did try to read quickly, I was lost and confused. My grades started to really slip, and I didn't like going to school anymore. But I felt like something wasn't right. I wanted to learn. I wanted to read. I wanted to like school. It just felt like something was keeping me from it.

I did an internet search for some of the things I was feeling, and there was a recommendation to get tested for a learning disability. I felt so relieved that maybe there was really something to all of this, but I also felt so embarrassed. No one in my family has a learning disability. My older siblings all loved school, did very well, and went off to great colleges.

I also don't want to burden my family because I think that this kind of treatment for learning disabilities is expensive, and my family is already struggling financially. My parents are really stressed out, and I don't want to have to add something else on their plates to worry about. I think school was easy for them, and I don't think they'll understand what it is I'm going through. I have a feeling they'll just ground me, tell me to work harder, and tell me to stop spending so much time on my video games. So, if I bring this up, it may mean that I get some privileges taken away, too.

- What emotions or reactions came up for you as you read Craig's story?

_____

_____

_____

_____

- What aspects of identity show up in Craig's story? How do those identities inform and impact Craig's experiences?

_____

_____

_____

_____

- What aspects of school culture or structures serve as barriers to Craig? What opportunities exist to be supportive of Craig or to make structures more inclusive?

_____

_____

_____

_____

- How might your approach to this story be informed by identity?

_____

_____

_____

_____

Activity 4: Writing Your Autobiography

Writing an autobiographical story related to disability allows you to reflect on an incident or experience and provide transparency about the experience. The purpose of this activity is to help you explore the impact of disabilities on your own life, teaching, and leadership. Take the following two steps to draft your story.

1. Recall an experience you had as a teacher, student, or leader related to disability. You may also want to connect your story about disability with other identities discussed in this book (race, class, sexual orientation, and gender), but resist the urge to move away from focusing on disability itself.

2. Reflect on the following questions.

   ○ What does the event reveal about ability, disability, and your biases?

   ○ How does writing about this make you feel? What emotions come up as you write this autobiography?

   ○ What, if any, action items come from this story that you are telling? How might these action items inform and impact your teaching?

_____

_____

_____

_____

Activity 5: Building Your Identity-Conscious Practice

Disability also intersects with other identities, such as race, gender, immigration status, education, and geographic location. What do you notice or wonder about how disability is informed and impacted by other aspects of your identity? In the space provided, write about how your experiences with disability might show up in your teaching, leading, and learning.

_____

_____

_____

_____

_____

Discussion

This guide provides structures for you to think deeply about identity and difficult conversations. To advance this beneficial work, engage in conversations with others using the following discussion prompts.

1. Have a conversation with a partner or a small group of three to four people. Go through each activity in this chapter together. Leave enough time to engage in conversation that does not rush learning. Be sure to create intentions for the conversation and expectations for participation. See Bringing People Together on page 8 to help set expectations.

2. In a larger group, engage with the following questions.

   ○ What did you experience as you did the activities in this chapter?

   ○ What did you notice about yourself as you completed these activities?

   ○ What do you believe is your next step as you continue this learning process?

Part III
TURNING PLANNING INTO ACTION

In part II (page 37), you learned about, reflected on, and built action items related to five core identities: (1) race, (2) class, (3) sexual orientation, (4) gender, and (5) disability. Now that you have a process for incorporating identity work into your life, part III turns your focus toward action. You will examine the different ways that action—or, in some cases, inaction—occurs in your journey to being an identity-conscious teacher. I will cover topics such as becoming an ally and beyond (chapter 8, page 127), responding when you fail (chapter 9, page 147), engaging in ongoing learning (chapter 10, page 169), and facilitating conversations about identity (chapter 11, page 185). Because I could not cover every identity within the scope of this book, I've included a chapter to recap the three-part model for thinking about identity and experience: (1) build knowledge, (2) engage in reflection, and (3) move to action. In chapter 12 (page 203), you'll practice adapting the model for identities you want to explore in the future.

I want to acknowledge that the chapters in this part of the book may be challenging to read, and I'd like to validate any feelings that come up for you. By now, you understand that this work of identity-conscious practice is difficult because of the way it asks us to critically examine our attitudes, beliefs, and behaviors. As educators, we like to believe ourselves to be good people. Of course, if you have made it this far in the book, you know that being a good person is a start, but it's not enough to create inclusive environments. We must build the habits and skills for seeing where inequity lives, interrupting it, and creating more inclusive schools for all students.

CHAPTER 8

From Ally to Abolitionist

OK, let's pause. I hope you've had the opportunity to work through the previous chapters before diving into this one. If you are reading this as an isolated chapter and you have not spent considerable time building knowledge, engaging in reflection, and moving toward action, the following content might feel overly critical of your work. This chapter discusses pitfalls of the journey from ally to abolitionist, noting how failure can be a barrier or a catalyst for growth, depending on how we choose to respond. I admit, I have faced my share of failures within my identity-conscious practice, one of which I share with you in chapter 9.

If you encounter strong feelings as you work through this content, notice where those feelings are located in your body. Are your shoulders tensing? Are you feeling defensive? Are you saying to yourself, "She can't be talking about me, right?" Those feelings are all natural and understandable. And yet, they can serve as barriers to an identity-conscious practice. I hope the practice you've built thus far will support you to reflect on your ally behaviors, where you are in your journey along the spectrum from ally to abolitionist, and how you wish to continue to grow.

During a particularly difficult time in my life, I was experiencing very traumatic racism, institutional oppression, and an attack on my character while working at a school. I turned to a colleague—who held multiple privileged identities and could be helpful to me—and let her know what I was experiencing. She wanted to know how she could help me, what she could do, and how she could be an ally. Through my tears, I told her, "I feel like I'm on fire. Help me by picking up a bucket of water, and start putting out this fire that is burning me." She replied, "But what if I don't even know where to find a bucket of water?" Though I believe her reply was sincere, I felt only heartbroken anger. I was heartbroken to hear her response. I was angered by her lack of action.

While I was burning, my ally was asking me to help her find the bucket of water. Though I acknowledge her desire to help, I couldn't stop thinking about her response.

So, I have to experience the problem and provide the solution? Even if I did manage to find the bucket of water to help put out this fire, would she take action? I could see it in her response—she was calculating the risk to herself of going to find the bucket of water, of using the bucket of water, and of keeping me from burning.

As you've seen in this book's three-part model, the natural progression of the identity-conscious journey is to ultimately be compelled to action. But when people who are new to ally work hold unrealistic expectations about what that work entails, they can fail to be effective in their role as allies. To borrow from my metaphor, they may find that bucket of water—that strategy to be helpful—but they might spend more time thinking about their own comfort than taking action to put out the fire and help those being harmed. They might check to see if the water is the right kind of water. They might measure to see if it's the right temperature. They might assess whether the bucket handle is ergonomically correct so as not to strain their hand. They might ask if the water has been naturally sourced. They might wonder if, while walking to the fire, the water might splash on their new shoes.

As you feel compelled to move into action, this chapter asks you to pause and consider a few questions: What exactly is the role of an ally? If you are committing to be an ally, what does that mean? What does that require of you?

In this chapter, I'll discuss how the identity-conscious practice compels people to move into action. It starts with awakening to inequity. As people recognize injustice, they want to do something about it; they feel called to become allies. But when educators hold unrealistic expectations about that role, they struggle to assume the responsibilities and commitments required of an ally and can fail to take effective action. It's also important to acknowledge that becoming an ally is not an end goal but a first step. Beyond allies exist accomplices, co-conspirators, and abolitionists. Ultimately, educators engaging with the identity-conscious practice strive for abolitionist teaching—moving beyond reform to remove oppression at the root and reinvent educational spaces that are loving, valuing, and caring of all students. Activities at the end of the chapter will help you build awareness and create plans for moving into action.

ESSENTIAL QUESTIONS

- What does it look like to be an ally?

- What are the risks to being an accomplice and co-conspirator?

- What does it mean to engage in abolitionist teaching in the classroom?

Awakening to Inequity

As teachers and school leaders, we have ample opportunities to witness the reality that education is an inequitable system. While our daily work is about building knowledge and skills for young people, we do this in different ways, with different resources, and with different challenges. For example, some teachers work in schools that are well resourced while others work in schools that have not had structural updates since the 1970s. These inequities have long existed, and the global pandemic only amplified them.

When the pandemic hit, many of the private and independent schools I partner with easily moved to remote learning. Their students and teachers had access to technology in their homes and classrooms and had daily practice with navigating online platforms. The well-resourced schools I partner with already had a 1:1 device program implemented as early as elementary school. Students at those schools had a distinct advantage over students attending some of the public and charter schools I partner with. Those students share technology carts and have limited internet access in their homes. When schools moved to remote learning, it took months to provide digital access to students in districts that did not have adequate resources.

Once we got through those final months of the school year, I saw firsthand how some of my client schools spent hundreds of thousands of dollars to update their HVAC systems over the summer so that the buildings were ready for students to return in person by the fall of 2020. In contrast, many public schools spent nearly three months trying to get internet availability in student homes; they struggled to get technology in the hands of students and teachers. Many students, displaced to different homes, were difficult to locate. When the fall 2020 semester started, many students continued remote learning; my own children didn't return in person until April 2021—over thirteen months after their school buildings closed. In their case, this was due to lack of proper ventilation and the inability to socially distance in an already overcrowded school, an ongoing health concern that disproportionately affected lower-income and predominantly Black and Brown communities.

I was navigating both worlds. I saw up close how disparities were playing out each day. While the global pandemic exacerbated these inequities, it didn't create them; the education system has never been fair, it has never been equally distributed, and it has not provided common outcomes.

In addition, K–12 schools tend to adopt curricula that are rooted in Whiteness and continue to perpetuate only one type of excellence—White excellence—in books, history lessons (Utt, 2018), science knowledge (Higgins, 2016), and mathematics problems (Kokka, 2020). It has left out Black and Brown people, LGBTQ people, people with disabilities, and people who identify as gender nonconforming or gender fluid, and it tells single stories about those who have wealth and those who experience poverty.

So, as concerned educators, how do we respond to these examples of inequity? We can simply say to ourselves, "That's too bad," and continue on with our teaching and leading, allowing the system to continue unchallenged. Or we can be curious about what has kept us from seeing inequities in the classroom, school, and community. By leaning into an identity-conscious practice, we can use our tools to individually and collectively create more equitable structures. We can be active in shaping more inclusive classrooms and communities. We can use our voices to amplify the inequity, to create structural changes, and to advocate for solidarity with those who are most marginalized.

Becoming an Ally

So you're ready to be an ally, but what does that actually mean? What does becoming an ally entail? And what kind of commitment are you taking on when you self-identify as an ally? The term *ally* has historically been used to describe a relationship, an association, or a friendship with another (Washington & Evans, 1991). When we think about allies in a political sense (for example, the United States and Canada are allies), we often think about countries that have a positive relationship or have signed agreements for international support or trade. Political allies commit to standing by one another in the event of a global conflict.

When used in an identity-conscious context, the term *ally* is focused on the acts of people who are not like you, who do not have identities in common with you, and who do not have the same experiences with oppression as you do. Its first uses in justice-based movements are often traced back to the multicultural initiatives of the 1980s when community activists drew support across identity groups and experiences (Washington & Evans, 1991).

> When used in an identity-conscious context, the term *ally* is focused on the acts of people who are not like you, who do not have identities in common with you, and who do not have the same experiences with oppression as you do.

The first printed occurrence of the term appears in *Beyond Tolerance: Gays, Lesbians and Bisexuals on Campus*, a 1991 resource manual published by the American College Personnel Association; Jamie Washington and Nancy Evans (1991) include it in their chapter, titled "Becoming an Ally." For many years, *ally* referred mostly to examples of heterosexual, cisgender people who stood with LGBTQ people advocating for equal rights and access. The term has evolved and is used more broadly to describe a person who does not share an identity category or experience and who speaks and acts in service to equality and access (for example, a White person who engages in ally behaviors toward people of color).

But the work of an ally must go deeper than actions and words. Becoming an ally requires a fundamental shift, an understanding of one's privilege and a commitment to using it in service of those without access to the benefits of that privilege. Writing in the foundational text *Beyond Tolerance*, and referring to heterosexual allies for the LGBTQ community, Washington and Evans (1991) state:

> the individual who decides to undertake the ally role must recognize and understand the power and privileges that one receives, accepts, and experiences as a heterosexual person. Developing this awareness is often the most painful part of the process of becoming an ally. (p. 196)

People who engage in ally behavior understand that they must no longer be willing to protect their privileges for their own sake; rather, allies speak up, refuse to stay silent, and stand with those who experience marginalization. This is sometimes easier said than done. Legal scholar and civil rights lawyer Derrick A. Bell Jr. (1980) poses a theory that identifies why this is so hard. The theory, called *interest convergence*, stipulates that White people will accommodate the interests of people of color striving to achieve racial equality only when those interests converge with their own (Bell, 1980). What does that mean? It means that White people, when engaging in ally behavior, are less likely to be compelled by moral reasons and more likely to engage for reasons that also benefit their own interests.

Professors of education H. Richard Milner IV, F. Alvin Pearman III, and Ebony O. McGee (2013) point to a prime example of this: the U.S. Supreme Court's ruling for desegregation in *Brown v. Board of Education* (1954). Milner and colleagues (2013) state the ruling was not based on moral reasoning but rather guided by economic and political reasons:

> The Brown v. Board of Education (1954) decision, in which the Supreme Court outlawed de jure segregation of public schools, was not the result of a moral breakthrough of the high court but rather a decision that was necessary: (1) to advance American Cold War objectives in which the United States was competing with the Soviet Union for loyalties in the third world; (2) to quell the threat of domestic disruption that was a legitimate concern with Black veterans, who now saw continued discrimination as a direct affront to their service during WWII; and (3) to facilitate desegregation in the South, which was now viewed as a barrier to the economic development of the region. (p. 339)

In my role as a strategic partner for diversity, equity, and inclusion, I interact daily with teachers, school leaders, committee members, and peers who call themselves allies but who aren't sure how to take action. I often receive questions from such allies about how they can do better, do more, and move beyond just showing up. They watched the events of 2020. They have witnessed the killing of Black people (Chughtai, 2021). They have heard the cries to address systemic racism and violence (The White House, 2021). They have learned of the murders of transgender people (Sonoma, 2021), the deaths of people at the southern U.S. border (Reznick, 2021), and the missing Indigenous women whose deaths have not been accounted for (Bezucha, 2021). They have read about the racial disparities in COVID-19 diagnoses, treatments, and survival rates (Mude, Oguoma, Nyanhanda, Mwanri, & Njue, 2021). They have done lots of self-work, and they see all the holes, implicit assumptions, early messages, and problematic stereotypes. They are outraged, angry, and frustrated by the injustices and inequities in the world. They're compelled to do something. They say things like, "I just can't stand by and watch anymore," or "I just need to do something—anything, but something."

I've heard those same sentiments from allies I've met in workshops: they feel the pain both empathetically and sympathetically. Their faces get hot with anger when I bring up examples of injustice in their communities. They clutch their hands and shake their heads. They grab the hair at their temples and say things like, "I'm so angry I could just pull my hair out!" Rage vibrates through their bones. And again, these allies ask, "What do I do?" Too often, well-meaning people rush to call themselves allies without thinking through the impact of their action or inaction.

> Some people who call themselves allies will only help if it doesn't hurt them.

They are ready to act . . . except there are conditions to their actions. Some people who call themselves allies will only help if it doesn't hurt them. This is a critical aspect of the way the ally role has evolved—allies' willingness to only go so far as to benefit their own needs and agenda. In your journey to becoming an ally, examine this tendency within yourself. Do you use your privilege in service of others, or do you hold back if your privilege is threatened?

What could it look like for you to act as an ally in your personal life and in your professional life as a teacher and a leader? What does it mean for you to recognize privilege in your life and use it in service of those without access to such privilege? In what ways will you move beyond words to taking action? Consider the four basic levels of becoming an ally outlined by Washington and Evans (1991): (1) awareness, (2) knowledge, (3) skills, and (4) action. Table 8.1 provides descriptions of these levels and action items for reaching these levels in the classroom.

In light of how this role of an ally is sometimes limited, new terms such as *accomplice* and *co-conspirator* began to make their way into the language to emphasize that *action* is needed to create real change. Engaging in ally behavior is just the beginning. As you continue along your identity-conscious journey, understand that becoming an ally is not the end goal—it's a starting point for moving to action.

TABLE 8.1: Action Items for Allyship

Level	Description	Classroom Action Items
Awareness	Build your knowledge through books, blogs, documentaries, interviews, and (if others are willing to speak with you) conversation.	Have diverse books in your classroom that build awareness of different identities and experiences. Structure time to read, reflect on, and discuss the books as a class.
Knowledge	Learn about policies, programs, practices, and procedures that might oppress certain groups or privilege your own identities. Look at advocacy websites discussing policies that limit access in schools.	Examine policies, programs, practices, and procedures in your school and classroom. Determine which of them privilege some identities while limiting access to others. Dismantle those and implement more inclusive and equitable practices.
Skills	Develop skills to communicate the knowledge you have gained. Strive to become comfortable talking about these issues even when others are not supportive.	Participate in dialogue groups. Create a peer community with other teachers and school leaders. Engage in experiential activities to practice what you would say or do in challenging situations. Use this book and the discussion prompts to support your learning and build your skills.
Action	Allyship is action; therefore, the work you do must engage your behaviors. You cannot simply think of yourself as an ally—you have to make that role visible and actionable.	Gather support from others in your school and community to speak out against bias, bullying, or injustice. Join advocacy groups; be vocal about changes that need to be made at your school or district level. Do not rely on the labor of those most impacted by oppression; as someone who allies with communities, take direction from those most impacted, and speak up.

Source for levels: Washington & Evans, 1991.

Acting as an Accomplice and Co-Conspirator

So, how are allies, accomplices, and co-conspirators different? Why do these designa
tions exist, why do they matter, and what do they have to do with the identity-conscious
journey? Kutztown University director of women's and gender studies Colleen Clemens
(2017) provides a helpful distinction between allies and accomplices in the article "Ally
or Accomplice? The Language of Activism." When a person calls someone else an ally,
it tends to mean, "You stand with me; you stand by me," and it is an important role in

social justice work. But allies tend to wait patiently to be called upon to assist or respond to a given situation, whereas accomplices proactively engage and anticipate when their voices and action are needed. Accomplices speak up in advance.

The role of co-conspirator goes beyond that of accomplice, intending to dismantle oppressive systems. Alicia Garza, a cofounder of the Black Lives Matter movement, describes co-conspirators as "people who are ready and willing to dismantle White supremacy and in particular to reject the benefits they receive from it" (as cited in Bell & Kondabolu, 2017). Co-conspirators place themselves in harm's way and accept the risks of acting alongside those who experience oppression.

As an example of these differences, imagine your colleague is speaking up at a faculty meeting about racial injustice. You notice other team members remain somewhat quiet in the room, choosing not to engage with the discussion. Acting as an ally, you text your colleague after the meeting is over, "Great job. Keep up the good work!" Though affirming, the behavior does little to change the meeting, reinforce the topic, or support your colleague. Now imagine that, instead, you speak up in support of your colleague during the meeting, highlighting the inequities and proposing action steps. You refer back to what your colleague said, affirm and validate their points, give them credit for saying them, and insist that this topic stay on the agenda. This approach reflects accomplice behavior.

Accomplices stand publicly with others, and together, they push an idea or action forward. Renée Graham (2019), a columnist for *The Boston Globe*, wrote a favorite line of mine about being an accomplice: "An ally thinks the system is merely broken; an accomplice learns to recognize not a broken system, but one operating exactly as it was intended—and works to dismantle its scaffolding, piece by piece." Have you witnessed accomplice behavior? What did it look like? And how did it ignite change?

What does co-conspirator behavior look like? Bettina Love (2019), author of *We Want to Do More Than Survive: Abolitionist Teaching and the Pursuit of Educational Freedom*, tells a story that highlights the difference between an ally (someone who knows all the right words) and a co-conspirator (someone who puts something on the line to take a risk for somebody). Love speaks about the day in 2015 when activist Bree Newsome, a Black woman, climbed the flagpole at the South Carolina State House and took down the Confederate flag (C-SPAN, 2019). The movement was largely organized by a number of activists, but in the end, Newsome was the one who climbed the pole and who risked the most. Love shares that James Tyson, a White man, saw that police were getting ready to tase the flagpole to forcefully and violently remove Bree Newsome from it. Tyson placed his hand on the pole, knowing that these police officers would not dare harm him. He used his White, male, and familiar privilege and risked his own safety to protect Newsome by putting himself in harm's way. By doing so, he allowed Newsome to complete her task. You can view the full interview with Bettina Love on the C-SPAN (2019) website (www.c-span.org/video/?458837-1/we-survive).

Striving for Abolitionist Teaching

I, too, am on this journey of recognizing my own shortcomings as an ally, accomplice, and co-conspirator. I am far from perfect in achieving what Love (2019) refers to as *abolitionist teaching*, the practice of pursuing educational freedom for all students by eradicating racism in all forms in schools. I choose readings that center the narratives of scholars, practitioners, and students of color. I speak the difficult truth that many of us as educators tend to uphold structures of racism rather than dismantle them. And I ask my students to think about the challenges and risks of engaging in such bold work. Consider the following story, which I shared in a blog post on my website (Talusan, 2018):

> This morning, while driving into work, I was listening to NPR and the testimonies of the women (many who were girls at the time) who had been sexual[ly] assaulted by the doctor who was hired by the National Gymnastics Association. Over and over again, the women stated that people knew, and they did nothing. One woman stated that "people knew what he was doing, and they still made me go back to see him again and again." Many women stated that they didn't have to convince people it was happening—everyone already knew. People were disgusted. People were angry. People were horrified. And yet, people made women continue to see this doctor.

News and social media are full of stories about people who have experienced abuse and trauma while friends, family members, colleagues, and peers knew it was happening and said nothing. What types of educational trauma do educators witness lesson after lesson, unit after unit, term after term, year after year without speaking up? In 2021, a video of a high school math teacher dancing around a classroom in a fake feathered headdress went viral (Downey & Escobar, 2021). The teacher continued the spectacle while playfully teaching a mnemonic device for remembering trigonometric functions. In 2020, the New York Attorney General's Office investigated an incident in which a fourth-grade teacher held a mock slave auction where White students placed bids on two Black classmates (McMahon, 2020). In 2018, a group of school teachers dressed up as Mexicans and as a border wall (Goldstein, 2018).

While these examples may seem extreme, schools across the United States exhibit everyday instances of educators engaging in culturally offensive practices in the classroom. These range from mispronouncing names (Rice, 2017) to misgendering students in class (Buterman, 2015). Students are not immune to these microaggressions. Students are traumatized by repeated exposure to a range of dehumanizing behavior (Gray, 2019). Crosby, Howell, and Thomas (2018) argue that teachers are responsible for reckoning with trauma in educational practices, and that they should: "acknowledge the ways in which a young adolescent's life course is subsequently affected by trauma, and [use] trauma-sensitive strategies in place of the traditional, punitive, and trauma-blind school practice that has historically compounded the effects of students' trauma" (p. 17).

Students may also experience educational trauma as a result of curriculum violence. Assistant professor Stephanie P. Jones (2020) explains: "*curriculum violence* occurs when educators and curriculum writers have constructed a set of lessons that damage or otherwise adversely affect students intellectually and emotionally." Curriculum trauma can occur as a result of classroom activities. For example, Jones (2020) writes about the time a teacher instructed the class to pick cotton as a way to demonstrate how difficult this task was for enslaved people; it was Jones's first exposure to chattel slavery. Teachers must bring a critical eye to their curriculum as part of the identity-conscious practice. Consider the following steps teachers can take to address curriculum violence:

- Critically examine the curriculum and scope and sequence for potentially distressing or insensitive content. Name any identities that may be impacted directly. Revise the curriculum to remove the problematic content and replace it with culturally competent material.

- Identify areas of growth and development that teachers and departments may need to engage in with additional professional learning.

- Embrace the struggle that comes with naming, owning, and interrupting curriculum violence and educational trauma. This work is not easy, especially for teachers in contexts with a longstanding history of using particular books or frameworks.

- Expand beyond deficit approaches. For example, Black history should not tell a single story of enslavement but should also include Black people's contributions and successes.

Critically examining a curriculum is just the first step. If educators wish to create culturally sustaining communities, they must commit to engaging in abolitionist teaching. Love (2020) encourages educators to move beyond reform and into abolitionist work: "Abolitionists want to eliminate what is oppressive, not reform it, not reimagine it, but remove oppression by its roots." What might it look like for you to take Love's call to heart?

Let's consider an example. Imagine a teacher is working through a unit on Pilgrims arriving and creating communities in North America. The teacher starts by sharing stories of early Pilgrims and then includes perspectives of Native, First Nations, and Indigenous people. If this teacher were engaging in abolitionist teaching, they would start with the narratives of Native, First Nations, and Indigenous people as thriving communities with a rich heritage of ancestral lands and vibrant culture. The arrival of the Pilgrims and other Europeans would build on that foundational knowledge, and learners would be challenged to see them through the perspective of Indigenous people. In this scenario, abolitionist teaching calls educators to center the narratives of Native, First Nations, and Indigenous people, and reform how they teach the arrival of Europeans.

As you can imagine, this work will not be easy! In fact, Love (2019) states:

> I know as an educator that this task seems daunting and overwhelming in an already taxing mission, but courage and vision are required. Abolitionist teaching is choosing to engage in the struggle for educational justice knowing that you have the ability and human right to refuse oppression and refuse to oppress others, mainly your students. (p. 11)

Abolitionist teaching in the classroom looks different in every school, in every subject, and for every teacher. But at the core of abolitionist teaching is applying a critical lens; engaging in actions such as protests or boycotts; and using one's voice and privilege to name, own, and interrupt policies, practices, programs, and procedures that are racist, homophobic, ableist, classist, and sexist, among others. As teachers, we must build skills to talk about issues of identity and lead the way for students to understand how harmful these oppressions are, not only to those most impacted but also to our society.

Love (2020) reminds us that abolitionist teaching focuses on care, love, and compassion rooted in dismantling systems that cause violence and trauma. For example, a school or classroom committed to abolitionist teaching is focused on processes that engage learning, develop critical thinking skills, and create spaces for learners to challenge systems. Abolitionist teaching helps educators create environments where students feel seen, loved, valued, and cared for—not surveyed, punished, and disciplined through an unfair power structure. Through this lens, teachers and school leaders are part of the community, and they understand where their students live, learn, and gather because they, too, are part of that community.

> But at the core of abolitionist teaching is applying a critical lens; engaging in actions such as protests or boycotts; and using one's voice and privilege to name, own, and interrupt policies, practices, programs, and procedures that are racist, homophobic, ableist, classist, and sexist, among others.

As part of adopting abolitionist teaching, educators must be committed to the social-emotional health of students. It is important to note, though, that some social-emotional learning privileges Whiteness and Eurocentric approaches while others place social and racial justice at the center. In particular, many of the behaviors that are set as markers of emotional well-being are rooted in regulation of the mind and body: self-awareness, self-management, social awareness, relationship skills, and responsible decision making (CASEL, n.d.). Yet, some behaviors exhibited by Black and Brown students that don't fit the model may actually be responses to experiencing educational trauma: "Educators and students could learn about how certain emotions are exhibited, like anger, when there is a perception of danger and it triggers a person's flight or fight response. Threats, like racism, sexism, homophobia, xenophobia, and the continued violence against Black and Brown people, build up" (Kaler-Jones, 2020). To incorporate social-emotional learning without understanding the cultural context oversimplifies the experiences of students holding traditionally marginalized identities.

The Abolitionist Teaching Network's website (https://abolitionistteachingnetwork .org) is an excellent place where those striving for abolitionist teaching can find community, connection, and resources such as the *Guide for Racial Justice and Abolitionist Social and Emotional Learning* (Abolitionist Teaching Network, 2020). Table 8.2 outlines some key practices the Abolitionist Teaching Network shares in its *Guide for Racial Justice and Abolitionist Social and Emotional Learning* and some actions teachers can take to implement the practices in their classroom and school.

What might this look like in practice in the classroom? I'll share an example from my own experience. I currently teach courses on socially just educational leadership, and the majority of my students is classroom teachers. At the start of every class, I center students' emotional, academic, and psychological needs. I tell them that this is not a simple icebreaker but, rather, a way for us to bring our humanity into the classroom space, to

TABLE 8.2: Social-Emotional Learning and Abolitionist Teaching

Abolitionist Approach	Action to Take
Abolitionist social-emotional learning is healing centered, transformative, and dialogic.	Cultivate an ongoing practice of dialogue and conversation with peers and students.
Abolitionist social-emotional learning resists punitive disciplinary approaches.	Remove punitive practices that harm, embarrass, shame, or are violent toward Black, Brown, and Indigenous students.
Abolitionist social-emotional learning is not a one-time event but rather an ongoing learning and unlearning process.	Create structures for ongoing learning that are embedded in your professional development, your class lessons, and your approach to your teaching and learning.
Abolitionist social-emotional learning models vulnerability.	Center the full humanity of students and build relationships; provide opportunities for a full range of emotions to be present.
Interrogate how SEL frameworks may be harmful to Black and Brown students.	Create classroom environments that center the beauty, joy, and variety of Black, Brown, and Indigenous stories and experiences to provide a broader range of possibilities.

Source: Adapted from Abolitionist Teaching Network, 2020.

provide pathways for checking in with each other, and to create structures for advocacy. Once students settle into class, I ask them five questions:

1. On a scale of 1 (not very) to 10 (extremely), how present are you for class today?

2. On a scale of 1 (not very) to 10 (extremely), how prepared are you for class today?

3. On a scale of 1 (not very) to 10 (extremely), how comfortable are you with our topic for today?

4. On a scale of 1 (not very) to 10 (extremely), how prepared do you feel to have this discussion with your peers?

5. Given the numbers you wrote on your paper, what would you need to create in order for you to move your number up by one?

This activity allows students to locate their own emotional experience as we engage in the challenging content that makes up the course, and together we've created structures for them to advocate for their needs. Many of my students have adopted this practice with their students. They often report that their students look forward to the check-in because it allows them to talk about their feelings, their needs, their challenges, and their relationships.

Abolitionist teaching calls educators to center student needs, reform how we teach, and dismantle structures that require students to be performative. It is a model that prioritizes the collaboration between teacher and students so that all students thrive.

Committing to Action

It's been years since the experience I shared at the beginning of this chapter, yet I still carry emotional scars. I lost faith, for a time, in allies. I wondered if this work of writing and reflecting on identity-conscious practice would even matter. When I think back on what happened, I can feel that burning sensation; my face gets hot, I start to sweat, and my heart races. Years later, I still feel like I am on fire.

I continue to work through the lingering pain of that experience. Yet, each time I meet teachers, leaders, and friends who are deeply committed to action, the disappointment and hurt of the past ease a bit. I remind myself that I, too, have failed as an ally to others. I honor that uncomfortable truth and recommit to taking action. I can do better. I can move forward. I can continue to grow.

As an ally committing to grow toward abolitionist teaching, you'll need tools to help you on your way. Consider the following actions you can take in moments when you feel stuck in emotion, self-doubt, or failure (Talusan, 2018). You will face challenges along this journey. Expect them and cultivate the tools you need to keep showing up and taking action. Here are actions you can take, which I (Talusan, 2018) share on my website.

- **Speak up:** If you see something burning, sound the alarm. That is, if you see someone who is being taken advantage of, who is being overrun by power, who is being unfairly and unjustly treated—speak up. Use your voice. Is there someone you know who wants to use gender non-binary pronouns but is being shut out or told to "wait until the organization is ready"? Well, speak up!

- **Point to the fire:** In situations where there is injustice, the oppressor often tries to misdirect you. It's the old, "Look! No, don't look here—look over *there*! *Way* over *there*!" That's a tool used to distract you. Point to the fire. Point to the place where injustice is happening. Point to the person who is setting the fire. Remember your CPR training? Look someone in the eye and say, "You, yes, you, go call 9-1-1 and get help." Calling into a crowd will yield you nothing. Be specific. Be direct.

- **Use data:** While we know that stories and storytelling are compelling, you need data to make your case. If someone says your job performance is poor, require data. Require metrics. Require deliverables. . . . Use data about participation rates or engagement or family metrics. . . .

- **Speak with your feet and your wallet:** People who are compelled to go to protests often believe that their presence matters. Well, it does. If you are committed to a situation, experience, or organization, show up. Or, if you are protesting, don't show up. Walk out. . . . Use your own feet, your own presence, and your own wallet (the absence of donation or participation speaks loudly!) to take action. There are a number of companies that I do not do business with because of their historic or present-day exclusion or oppression of certain types of people and issues. . . .

- **Reach out to stakeholders:** In situations of injustice and oppression, there is a reliance on secrecy. It's the old, "If people knew about this, we'd have to be accountable." Okay, well, let people know about it, and hold them accountable. [Not] maintaining secrecy on behalf of the oppressors will usually result in some sort of intimidation, threat, fear, and leaning on relationships. . . . How might you engage stakeholders, even knowing that this will upset those in power?

Injustice should make you angry. Allow that anger to fuel your work in support of marginalized identities and against oppressive systems. Along the journey from ally to accomplice to co-conspirator to abolitionist, some ideas and situations might feel confusing. Don't let that confusion stop you from taking action.

Grab the bucket and get to work.

Activities for Moving From Ally to Abolitionist

What do K–12 educators need to know, do, and demonstrate in order to become allies, accomplices, co-conspirators, and abolitionists? The four activities in this chapter will guide you to reflect on early messages you received about ally behavior, consider experiences you've had with accomplice behavior, determine your risk threshold, and consider adopting an abolitionist approach to teaching.

Activity 1: Considering First Messages

An important aspect of allyship is understanding how early messages you received inform and impact your approach to action. Reflect on the following questions to take a deep dive into your beliefs about allyship.

1. To engage in ally behavior often means to engage in conflict. What were the earliest messages you received about conflict in social justice work? Were they positive or negative messages?

    _____

    _____

    _____

    _____

2. How, if at all, did you see conflict resolved in your life? In what ways do those resolutions affect how you show up today?

    _____

    _____

    _____

    _____

3. What are your earliest memories of someone standing up for another person? What impact does that memory have on you today?

    _____

    _____

    _____

    _____

The Identity-Conscious Educator © 2022 Solution Tree Press • SolutionTree.com
Visit **go.SolutionTree.com/diversityandequity** to download this free reproducible.

4. What have you been told (either explicitly or implicitly) about getting involved in issues of injustice?

_____

_____

_____

_____

Activity 2: Moving From Ally to Accomplice

An ally stands with and alongside someone, whereas an accomplice takes part in the planning and joins in the action. An accomplice recognizes the risks and conflicts that come with speaking up and speaking out. Consider the following questions, and think about the kinds of actions (and inaction) that might impact your transition from ally to accomplice.

1. Write about a time when someone intervened on your behalf. What did you experience in that moment? What risks—real or perceived—did that person face?

_____

_____

_____

_____

2. Write about a time when you intervened on someone's behalf. What did you experience in that moment? What risks—real or perceived—did you face?

_____

_____

_____

_____

3. Write about a time when you failed to show up or engage in ally behaviors. What kept you from engaging? What risks—real or perceived—did you face? What would need to be different in order for you to engage in that situation?

_____

_____

_____

_____

page 2 of 6

Activity 3: Determining Your Risk Threshold

As you have read about in this chapter, engaging in accomplice behavior requires taking some risk and moving outside your sphere of comfort. However, this is not easy, nor is it always possible. In this activity, you'll identify your risk threshold. Note that identifying your risk threshold is not about making judgments regarding what you are willing to do or not do; instead, it is about identifying your capacity or ability to do it. The chart for this activity provides an example of a teacher's writing about their risk threshold given their low capacity for conflict, their financial instability, and their available support systems. In the space provided in the chart, write about your own risk threshold, considering things you are willing and unwilling to risk and things you would find helpful on your journey.

Things I Can or Am Willing to Risk in My Actions	Things I Cannot or Am Not Willing to Risk	Things I Would Find Helpful on My Journey
Sample: I am willing to risk being called a troublemaker. This would be hard for me because I do not like conflict, but I think this is something I am willing to risk.	Sample: Right now, I am struggling financially. My spouse lost their job, and we are supporting not only our children but also my mother financially. So, I cannot risk doing anything that will put my own employment at risk. That's hard to write, but if I'm being honest with myself, this is true.	Sample: I guess it would be helpful to know if some of these risks are real or if I just assume they are. For example, I wrote that I might lose my job. But, honestly, I wonder if that's true. I have worked there for fifteen years. I am well respected by my peers. And I have the support of families who have known me to be fair, kind, and compassionate over the many years. So, I have to really face this fact: Would I actually lose my job if I spoke up? I think it would also be helpful to have others who are willing to take these risks with me. I also have to answer the question, "If I am alone, will I still continue the fight?" I don't know if I have an answer to that yet, so I need to reflect on what else keeps me from moving forward.

Things I Can or Am Willing to Risk in My Actions	Things I Cannot or Am Not Willing to Risk	Things I Would Find Helpful on My Journey

Read the following reflection questions, and record your thoughts and experiences in the space provided.

- How true are these risks for you?

- How realistic are these risks for you?

- How might others be impacted by your ability or willingness to take risks?

- How might others be impacted by your inability or unwillingness to take risks?

_____

_____

_____

_____

Activity 4: Taking Abolitionist Approaches to Teaching

The following questions are adapted from the Abolitionist Teaching Network (2020). Consider changes to your own classroom, teaching, and learning that may align with an abolitionist approach to teaching. Write your responses to the following questions in the space provided.

1. What long-term changes can you make in your curriculum to center the beauty, joy, and resilience of Black, Brown, and Indigenous people?

_____

_____

_____

_____

2. What current school policies and practices are harmful and oppressive to students of color?

_____

_____

_____

_____

3. What does healing from racial trauma or other identity-oppressive trauma look like in your classroom for students? For your colleagues?

_____

_____

_____

_____

Discussion

This guide provides structures for you to think deeply about identity and difficult conversations. To advance this beneficial work, engage in conversations with others using the following discussion prompts.

1. Have a conversation with a partner or a small group of three to four people. Go through each activity in this chapter together. Leave enough time to engage in conversation that does not rush learning. Be sure to create intentions for the conversation and expectations for participation. See Bringing People Together on page 8 to help set expectations.

2. In a larger group, engage with the following questions.

    ○ What did you experience as you did the activities in this chapter?

    ○ What did you notice about yourself as you completed these activities?

    ○ What do you believe is your next step as you continue this learning process?

Source: Adapted from Abolitionist Teaching Network. (2020, August). Guide for racial justice and abolitionist social and emotional learning. Accessed at https://abolitionistteachingnetwork.org/guide on June 8, 2021.

CHAPTER 9

The Role of Failure in Identity Work

One summer day, I was passing through a local park on my morning walk. It's one of the few green spaces in my busy city, crowded with tall buildings, concrete, and fast roadways. In order to make the park safe for pedestrians, the city closes the cut-through roadway overnight and designates it as a one-way street after 9:30 a.m. On occasion, a rogue car does get onto the roadway early in the morning—by accident, because of faulty GPS directions or an open gate. There is little signage that the road is closed, and you only know about it if you happen to be in the know.

As I approached the roadway that day, I came upon an argument between a White man and two Black teenagers. The two Black teenagers, who were probably seventeen years old, were driving a car slowly and carefully along the roadway during the time when cars are not allowed. It was obvious that they were lost and had happened upon this road unintentionally, as they appeared panicked and scared. The White man was banging on the hood of their car and yelling at the Black teenagers, demanding that they drive *backward* down the one-way street and return to the park entrance, approximately three-quarters of a mile from where they were. Not only was it illegal to drive backward down the one-way road, but the pathway was filled with pedestrians who, not expecting to have a car drive in reverse ahead of them, could be in real danger.

The White man was loud, demanding, and aggressive. The Black youth pleaded with him, "Please just let us drive forward to the exit. I don't feel safe driving backward. Please just let us go forward, sir. We didn't know this road was closed."

The White man stood in front of their car and continued to yell at these young men. "No, I will not let you go forward. No!"

I'd like to tell you that I did the right thing at that moment. I'd like to tell you that I intervened, that I distracted the White man from his anger, or that I connected with the young Black teens in the car to let them know I was there for them. I'd like to tell you that I promised the White man I would make sure the young people got to the exit ahead of them. I'd like to tell you that I took responsibility, engaged in risk, and did what was right.

But I can't tell you any of that.

I walked toward the White man, keeping a safe distance from him. I raised my voice and told him to leave the kids alone. "They made an innocent mistake," I said. "Just let them drive to the exit. It's safer for everyone if they just drive forward."

The White man turned his body toward me, and his eyes pierced right through me. His face was contorted with anger. I felt so aware of my body, my proximity to his anger, and my identity as an Asian American woman. I was alone. I felt physically vulnerable in my shorts and tank top. My body began to shake with fear.

I'd like to tell you that I channeled my vulnerability and fear into strength. I'd like to tell you that I took a deep breath, puffed out my chest, and stood toe to toe with the man. I'd like to tell you that I told him to back off. I'd like to tell you that my vulnerability connected me to the teenagers in the car and moved me to act.

But I can't tell you any of that.

I shook my head, turned away from the White man, and quickened my pace away from him—away from the young Black teens who needed me to stay present and bear witness to this scene. I was shaking. I was overwhelmed with shame. I protected myself. I chose my safety and comfort over the needs of the young people. As I walked away, I knew I had failed them. As I increased my distance, I could still hear the man yelling, "No!" and banging on the hood of their car.

I wish I had done a million things other than walk away. I wish I had pulled out my cell phone and recorded the situation. I wish I had put myself in between the two scared Black teenagers and the angry White man. I wish I had called the police and explained that the young Black teens were innocent and being harassed by an older White man.

But I didn't. I walked away, carrying shame, embarrassment, and fear. I had been too consumed with my own feelings of fragility and propelled by my fight-or-flight response that I hadn't been able to consider the safety of the young Black teenagers.

I never learned what became of this incident, whether these Black youth made it safely in reverse. I have no way of knowing if someone more courageous than me stopped the White man from continuing his actions. When I got home, I checked the police logs to see if they included any incidents that had occurred at the park. I saw none.

People often look to me for solutions to know how to act when conflict happens. As a way to be open and transparent about failure, I shared this story on my social media account. I wanted to confess that I had done the wrong thing. I wanted to highlight that I do not always do what is right, just, and active.

Almost immediately, White friends comforted me, told me I was right to walk away, and encouraged me to show myself some grace. Black friends openly shared they were upset, disappointed, and frustrated. Black friends told me I had failed; I had become yet another person in their lives who had good intentions but who didn't actually walk the walk. One friend wrote, "Liza, that could have been my son in that car. It could have been my son who needed help, who needed a witness, and who needed a mom to stay with him." Another friend wrote that I should have known better. I was trained to address these issues. If she couldn't count on someone like *me* to stand up for young Black people, whom could she trust?

This incident still lives in the pit of my stomach, in the quickening of my heartbeat, and in the shallowness of my breath. I share this story because sometimes, people think that given all the right tools, they will always do the right thing. They won't. I didn't. At this point in the book, you have probably realized the identity-related areas that are comfortable for you to talk about and those that make you feel uncomfortable. Nothing about this work is perfect. In fact, the work is often much messier than we think. Because of this messiness, it is highly probable that you will make mistakes. If you are engaging in difficult conversations about identity, you will experience discomfort, and sometimes you will fail.

In this chapter, I ask that you journey with me as we face some of our greatest mistakes, our failures. I'll talk about how to respond to failure during the identity-conscious practice. Making mistakes is part of the process, but by embracing failure, you can learn to see mistakes as opportunities for growth. Despite their desire to do no harm, educators will inevitably recognize harm in the course of their work with students and peers. You'll look at an example of how the identity-conscious practice provides tools for naming and repairing harm. In addition, you'll expand your skills by exploring how a desire for comfort can become a distraction. When the ally journey becomes too painful, we need tools we can rely on to help us recover from failure so that it doesn't keep us stuck or distracted. Activities at the end of the chapter will help you build awareness and create plans for moving into action.

ESSENTIAL QUESTIONS

- What does it mean to fall short in your work on identity?
- What role do failure, discomfort, and disappointment have in identity work?
- How can educators shift from making people feel better to encouraging them to do better?

Embracing Failure as Part of the Identity-Conscious Practice

In part I of this book (page 13), you learned that conflict is an inevitable part of the identity-conscious practice; if you don't want discomfort to become a barrier to your practice, you have to build skills for moving through it. This chapter applies that same mindset to failure. Failure is an inevitable part of the identity-conscious practice. It's not an indication that you're not ready for the practice or that you don't have what it takes to be an ally. It's actually confirmation that you're on the journey; *it's part of the process*. What happens next is up to you. How will you respond to your failures?

Stanford University psychologist Carol Dweck (2007) writes about a growth mindset versus a fixed mindset. A *growth mindset* is when a person believes they can develop talents through hard work, effective strategies, and feedback from others, whereas a *fixed mindset* occurs when a person believes they have innate gifts—they are either good at something or they are not (Dweck, 2007). But people don't operate in this binary; rather, each of us exhibits both a growth and fixed mindset at different times. We can practice moving from a fixed mindset to a growth mindset by observing the feelings that come from a fixed mindset—defensiveness, threat, insecurity—and thinking about why those feelings occur (much like the reflection exercises provided in this book). The experience can illuminate ways to move forward, learn, and achieve our goals. The example I provided about my experience in the park is a helpful map for moving from fixed to growth: I experienced an event. I had strong feelings and emotions that stopped me from moving forward. I questioned the feelings and recognized action items I could take to shape behaviors and outcomes more aligned with my commitment to equity and justice.

While failure can sometimes lead us to feel apathetic and discouraged, it can also be a great motivator. Joyce Russell (2019), dean of the Villanova School of Business, reminds us that failure is a necessary part of success: "You can't develop resilience with just success in your life. You have to experience setbacks in order to build resilience, but the good news is that your resilience gets stronger each time you overcome challenges or obstacles." Common sense and life experience tell us this is true. And yet, we're still afraid to fail! Fear of failure can be so overwhelming, almost paralyzing. How can teachers combat this fear of failure and avoid getting stuck? Research indicates that self-compassion might be the answer. Studies show that engaging in a self-compassionate state leads people to take more responsibility for their roles, view failure as something they can change, remedy shortcomings, and move to action (Breines & Chen, 2012).

Educators often feel self-imposed pressure to be right and to avoid failure. Yet failure sometimes stems from gaps in training that teachers and leaders have no control over. For example, assistant professor Karen Acton (2021) interviewed elementary principals in Ontario to explore decision making, leadership, and the change process. Acton (2021) found that principals lacked the kind of training needed to be change agents and, instead, relied more on informal networks with others. This gap in knowledge meant that principals were making decisions without the tools they needed for educational reforms, oftentimes leading to failed outcomes.

Given this insight, what might it look like to move from failure to success? Principal preparation programs could commit to integrating knowledge about change and providing tools for future school leaders to be successful. Current principals could undertake professional development related to transformational school leadership. In addition, teacher training and residency programs can also do a better job supporting preservice teachers in embracing failure. At this early stage of practicum, teacher candidates learn how to teach in a safe environment where, ideally, there is productive mentoring and advising.

If we let it, failure will be a pathway to growth. Educational researchers David Marshall, Michael Scott, and Guofang Wan (2021) explored the connection between failure and reflections in a teacher residency experience and found that failure is important in teacher training. One participant in their study defined an experienced teacher as someone who "is going to make mistakes, and I think the main difference between . . . a successful teacher and one who struggles is you are willing to adjust your own practice and to respond to and solve problems in the classroom that are beyond your control" (p. 168). Identity-conscious practice requires teachers to embrace failure and commit to reflecting about the difficult issues it brings up. Simply turning away from these challenges stalls our growth. But when we acknowledge our shortcomings and learn from them, our identity-conscious practice improves.

Although I was ashamed, embarrassed, and dismayed by the incident in the park, that experience of failure turned me toward action. I am no longer willing to look away or continue on the path of my own safety, particularly at the expense of Black people. If I am truly engaged in being an accomplice to Black people, I must put something on the line. I have to risk something. That experience taught me how to move toward others. I am willing to do difficult things. Knowing that reflecting on our failures can provide meaningful opportunities for growth, what failures do you experience as part of your identity-conscious practice? How do they provide chances for you to grow?

Recognizing Harm

It is commonly known that medical professionals take an oath to do no harm, which guides them to consider risk in the treatment of a patient. Yet, medical scholars state that the directive to do no harm is not actually possible (Shmerling, 2020). Think about the act of cutting someone open during surgery, which can cause illness, or of providing chemotherapy, which can cause side effects—both instances cause harm, but perhaps at less risk than the original condition requiring surgery or chemotherapy.

Educators also commit to doing no harm. They commit to learning, teaching, and advising in ways that invite the whole child into their classroom. Teachers and school leaders strive to cultivate community, collaboration, and growth for students and them-selves. Yet, how often do educators do harm? Below are just a few examples of ways in which students experience harm in schools:

- A student's outburst in class is rooted in an emotional situation at home. The teacher responds with punitive discipline. Unfortunately, the teacher shames the student and misses the opportunity to address the root cause of the behavior.

- A class curriculum employs a deficit model, teaching the history of Black people through a single narrative of enslavement and violence against Black bodies. Students don't have the chance to consider the many Black inventors, entrepreneurs, activists, and communities that shaped U.S. history and resisted structural racism and oppression.

- A teacher singles out a student and separates them from the rest of the class, further contributing to the student's feelings of shame and guilt.

- A guidance counselor redirects a student who is interested in applying to college. The counselor's biases lead them to hold false assumptions about this student's academic potential. As a result, the counselor suggests the student focus on less challenging courses below the student's academic achievement.

- A teacher refuses to recognize a transgender student's name, pronouns, and identity.

These scenarios are all too common in schools, and they cause real and lasting harm for students. As teachers and school leaders build an identity-conscious practice, they must commit to recognizing harm in their schools. They must use their authority to make amends, reshape school policies, and create identity-safe environments for all students.

In addition to responding to harm, teachers can take a proactive stance by providing ways for students to see themselves reflected in their schools. In 1990, Rudine Sims Bishop, professor emerita of education at The Ohio State University, introduced the concept that pieces of literature can function as *windows*, *mirrors*, and *sliding glass doors* for students.

> Books are sometimes windows, offering views of worlds that may be real or imag-ined, familiar or strange. These windows are also sliding glass doors, and readers have only to walk through in imagination to become part of whatever world has been created and recreated by the author. When lighting conditions are just right, however, a window can also be a mirror. Literature transforms human experience and reflects it back to us, and in that reflection we can see our own lives and expe-riences as part of the larger human experience. Reading, then, becomes a means of self-affirmation, and readers often seek their mirrors in books. (p. ix)

Bishop (1990) wrote about how important it is to use books as opportunities for self-affirmation, particularly for Black children. Her scholarship has provided a helpful framework for many teachers to incorporate windows, mirrors, and sliding glass doors into their classroom curriculum. Chenoweth (2019) describes the profound impact Bishop's initial work still has:

> Bishop has somewhat of a cult following among educators, researchers and graduate students. . . . The metaphor continues to be cited in academic journals, textbooks, conference presentations and university classrooms. It's the subject of TEDx talks and blogs. Teachers the world over stock classroom bookshelves based on its insights.

Yet, if teachers are so aware that books, programs, and opportunities can serve as helpful tools of self-affirmation, why are North American educators still teaching from a Eurocentric curriculum (page 43) that privileges the voices of White authors, explorers, scientists, mathematicians, leaders, and writers? When we fail to engage in identity-conscious reflection, we perpetuate norms that cause harm.

The identity-conscious practice allows teachers to recognize harm and act to remedy it. In the example of Eurocentric curricula, that means going beyond stocking the class library with diverse authors. Sandra L. Osorio (2018), associate professor of teaching and learning at Illinois State University, states, "While having multicultural literature in the classroom is extremely important, it is just as important what you do with the literature" (p. 47). Based on Osorio's (2018) work, I've identified four ways teachers can implement the framework of windows and mirrors in classrooms using multicultural literature: (1) promote or develop an appreciation for diversity, (2) honor students' voices, (3) connect to students' rich linguistic and cultural backgrounds, and (4) promote critical consciousness. Table 9.1 (page 154) exemplifies this four-step framework and describes activities that teachers can utilize to incorporate it into the classroom.

> Why are North American educators still teaching from a Eurocentric curriculum that privileges the voices of White authors, explorers, scientists, mathematicians, leaders, and writers? When we fail to engage in identity-conscious reflection, we perpetuate norms that cause harm.

Osorio (2018) further states that teachers can use multicultural literature as a tool to facilitate deep conversations by shifting from the traditional role of teacher—or keeper of information—to a facilitator who centers the experiences of students. Here, there is a practical difference between teaching and facilitating. Teaching places the teacher in the center of knowledge creation, sharing information about a particular text or event, passing on knowledge to students, and deciding what students should know. A facilitator provides opportunities for exploration, discovery, and collaboration among students by getting out of the way of their learning and creating space for student voices to emerge.

TABLE 9.1: Multicultural Literature as a Classroom Tool

Tool	Example	Activity
Promote or develop an appreciation for diversity.	Make connections between a student's cultural experience and experiences from other cultures. Osorio (2018) shares a story of a Spanish-speaking student reading a book about an Asian girl learning English and her ability to connect to the character's struggles.	Read *Same, Same but Different* by Jenny Sue Kostecki-Shaw (2011). Choose a book from the curated list on Teaching for Change's Social Justice Books (n.d.) website (http://socialjusticebooks.org/booklists).
Honor students' voices.	Use storytelling to allow students to connect their lived experiences to what they are reading.	After reading a book, provide students the opportunity to write or tell stories about how they connect, or do not connect, with the story.
Connect to students' rich linguistic and cultural backgrounds.	Don't underestimate the rich cultural experiences students bring to the classroom. Students often understand more than adults assume, so create structures for them to contribute this knowledge in the classroom. Connect stories to what students know about the world around them.	Highlight areas of the text where you might want to go a bit more in depth. For example, ask students to research or learn more about a passage or section of the book, describe what was happening during the time the book takes place, and connect it to any real-world experiences in their own life to deepen that mirror connection that Bishop (1990) describes.
Promote critical consciousness.	Provide students prompts to think deeply about and beyond the text—for example, "How does the text serve as a tool for us to think about the community and the world around us?"	Discuss with students: • What are some challenges the characters in this book face? • How are these challenges the characters face similar to or different from challenges you see around you? • How do the characters talk about or address these challenges? What actions do they take? How are these similar to or different from what you see around you?

Source for framework: Adapted from Osorio (2018).

In a facilitated dialogue, the teacher decenters their own needs, knowledge, and experience and instead follows students' discovery based on prompts or probing questions. When we listen deeply to the words of our students and make connections to their lived experiences, we can support active learning and activism for and with our students.

In the same way that Osorio (2018) shares tools for using multicultural literature to advance racial equity, researchers Amy L. Masko and Patricia L. Bloem (2017) encourage educators to use literature to further their understanding of equity: "Literature provides predominantly White, middle-class (pre-service teaching) students with a safe space to explore their own processes of understanding racism and come to terms with their own privilege while building empathy through reading about the fictional experiences of children" (p. 57). Teachers can look to literature to make meaningful connections among stories (like the ones shared at the beginning of each chapter in this book), social science research, and their own lived experiences. They can reflect—as you've done through the activities in this book—to examine their relationships to identity, create action plans for their learning, and choose to become agents of change when they recognize harm.

Noticing When Comfort Is a Distraction

Throughout this book, you have engaged in learning that has challenged how you see yourself, how you teach, how you learn, and how you approach your work with young people. As you have read each chapter, engaged in reflection, dialogued with others, and then implemented some of the activities from the book in your classroom, what has come up for you? How has it gone? What did it feel like to try something new? What did your students experience?

Perhaps at some point during your work, you have had strong feelings about your reading material, your reflections, or some of the activities. It would also be understandable if, during your peer group discussions, you encountered resistance, got upset, or were moved to tears. These are normal reactions to difficult conversations and challenging experiences. I never underestimate the power of emotions in this work. But what happens when emotions become a distraction? What happens when big feelings get in the way of doing the work that brings about change? From an identity-conscious lens, what impact do race, class, sexual orientation, gender, and disability (or other identities) have on emotions?

> What happens when big feelings get in the way of doing the work that brings about change? From an identity-conscious lens, what impact do race, class, sexual orientation, gender, and disability (or other identities) have on emotions?

An emerging topic in conversations about race is the impact of White women's tears. *White women's tears, Liza? What do you mean?* In 2007, Mamta Motwani Accapadi, vice provost for university life at the University of Pennsylvania, wrote about how the emotions of White women can be oppressive to people of color. In difficult conversations about race and racism, when the going gets tough and tears begin to fall, White women often receive comfort from others. If a woman of color is sharing a story about racism, and a White woman begins crying, the attention almost always goes to easing the discomfort of the White woman and ignoring the pain of the woman of color (Accapadi, 2007).

Progressing in your identity-conscious practice requires moving through discomfort. It is through discomfort that we identify our growth edges—opportunities to deepen and sustain our practice. It's natural to seek comfort, validation, and affirmation, but we must cultivate an awareness of ways we seek to center our own comfort. The identity-conscious practice calls us to notice how we respond to discomfort and pain and then empowers us to create tools for moving through the experience instead of becoming distracted by it. As an activist, educator, and identity-conscious leader, I've learned this is not easy. Engaging in diversity, equity, inclusion, and justice work often brings about my insecurities. I often wonder, *Am I doing this right? What if my efforts cause harm? Will someone question my motives, my actions, and my intentions?* I wrestle with the feeling of not succeeding. I worry about failure. *But* I know that failure is part of the process. I'm mindful that my failure might unintentionally cause harm, *and* I know that my job is to make sure I reduce that harm. When I have harmed someone—intentionally or unintentionally—my job is to name, own, and interrupt that discomfort. *Why am I uncomfortable? What about my thoughts, attitudes, behaviors, and beliefs contributes to this discomfort? And what do I need to do to disrupt or interrupt this feeling?* Here is an important truth: It is not up to those I have hurt to comfort me. It is not the job of those who are most marginalized to make me feel better when I am confronted with privilege. The job is mine alone to work through the discomfort, to recognize failure, and to do my best not to repeat it.

> Progressing in your identity-conscious practice requires moving through discomfort. It is through discomfort that we identify our growth edges—opportunities to deepen and sustain our practice.

If I wait to be perfect—to do this work without any risk—then I simply am not being courageous enough. To be in a constant state of discomfort, for me, means that I am placing myself in conditions where learning occurs. To simply wallow in my sadness and self-pity contributes very little to the cause and, in fact, can be a harmful distraction. This approach to failure simply stalls our growth. If we are actively trying to build more inclusive communities and a more intentional identity-conscious practice, then we must learn how to use our failures as an opportunity to do better. We must build the habits and skills for recovering from failure.

Recovering From Failure

You will make mistakes along the journey to building your skills as an identity-conscious educator. If you can get curious about those mistakes, they can become opportunities to discover the tools you need to recover from failure. It's easy to agree with this idea, but it's hard to do in practice.

Common mistakes people must confront as part of their practice are microaggressions and macroaggressions. What are micro- and macroaggressions? *Microaggressions* are verbal, behavioral, and environmental slights and insults directed toward a targeted group or person. Sometimes microaggressions are referred to as small cuts. But there is nothing micro about microaggressions. These small cuts—the brief and commonplace insults—add up, creating significant damage and trauma. Examples of microaggressions include calling a person of color the name of a different person of color, assuming a person of Asian heritage does not speak English, and assuming a heterosexual relationship or marriage when asking about a person's spouse. *Macroaggressions* refer to compliance with "systemic forms of oppression rather than interpersonal forms of bias or discrimination" (Gorski, 2014, p. 6). Examples of macroaggressions include passing over a person of color for a promotion and offering it to a less qualified White candidate, choosing books for class that use the N-word or not including texts that amplify Black excellence, and maintaining pervasive discipline policies that disproportionately target Black students. Whether a person perpetrates micro- and macroaggressions consciously or unconsciously, they are harmful and discriminatory. It can be painful to recognize those behaviors in ourselves, but by honestly exploring the roots of those actions and the beliefs that inspire them, we can name our mistakes and recover from them.

As a starting point, I'd like to offer a few helpful suggestions. Think of a mistake you've made or an experience you've identified as a personal failure, and consider it through four steps.

1. **Name it:** Identify exactly what the mistake was. Did you misgender someone by using the wrong pronouns? Did you use the term *African American* when the person identifies as Black? Did you make a comment that was classist or ableist? Naming the mistake brings clarity about what went wrong, the part you played in the event, and the responsibility you have in that situation.

2. **Own it:** By now, you know how to engage in reflection. Owning the mistake means identifying where your thoughts, attitudes, behaviors, and beliefs come from and how those may have informed and impacted your words, interactions, or assumptions.

3. **Interrupt it:** Create pathways to disrupt your problematic behaviors and beliefs so that you do not repeat the mistake in the same way. Focus on how your own identities and experiences shape your views by connecting to the

identities and experiences of others. Create action items by asking yourself: "What is one thing I can start doing to get closer to my identity-conscious practice?" "What is one thing I can stop doing?" "What is one small change I can make in my practice to align with equity?" "What is one thing I can continue doing because it is already aligned with an identity-conscious practice?"

4. **Take responsibility:** Finally, you need to take responsibility for your impact, even if you didn't intend to cause harm. Taking responsibility means addressing ownership in the micro- or macroaggression.

When you are addressing a mistake, failure, or micro- or macroaggression, this four-part framework can help you respond to the event in the moment and in your later reflections. Review the scenarios in table 9.2 to see the different steps in action.

Why is dealing with failure such an emotional experience? It's natural to take your mistakes personally, to get stuck in a story about what your failures mean about your worth, value, or goodness as a person. When we look at behavior through an ethical lens, we'd like to think that all we have to do to avoid mistakes is abide by our principles. But in their book, *Blind Spots: Why We Fail to Do What's Right and What to Do About It*, leading ethicists Max H. Bazerman and Ann E. Tenbrunsel (2012) note that a person's moral judgment is not enough to account for failure to do the right thing. They write that there can be a "gap between who you want to be and the person you actually are" (Bazerman & Tenbrunsel, 2012, p. 1) and that "our ethical behavior is often inconsistent, at times even hypocritical" (Bazerman & Tenbrunsel, 2012, p. 4). You may have encountered ethical dilemma scenarios such as the trolley problem: A trolley is speeding down some tracks. Five people are tied to the tracks ahead of the trolley. You can choose to save the five lives by pulling a lever to switch the trolley to a side track, where only one person is stranded. Do you refuse to act and spare only one life, or do you divert the trolley and sacrifice the one life in exchange for the five? (Merriam-Webster, n.d.). Such scenarios require us to make a decision based on our morals and provide a corresponding rationale for that decision. You only have to spend a few minutes thinking about such a dilemma to notice the complexities. Bazerman and Tenbrunsel (2012) argue that our unexamined psychological constructs are the problem, and that we must become aware of "the blind spots that prevent all of us from seeing the gap between our own actual behavior and our desired behavior" (p. 5). This commitment to awareness is at the heart of the identity-conscious practice.

Acting in line with one's principles isn't always simple, right? Life is complicated. Identity informs and impacts a person's experiences. Every person, at one time or another, makes decisions that do not align with one's stated goals and beliefs. This is where identity-conscious practice can be helpful by giving us tools for reflecting on our attitudes, beliefs, and choices. A helpful tool for reflection is thinking in terms of *proximity*, getting close to those experiencing injustice or those we wish to help. Founder and executive director of the Equal Justice Initiative, Bryan Stevenson, says, "We cannot create justice without getting close to places where injustices prevail. . . . We have to get

TABLE 9.2: Name It, Own It, Interrupt It, Take Responsibility

	Scenario 1	Scenario 2	Scenario 3	Scenario 4
Name it	You misgendered a colleague by using the wrong pronouns.	You used classist language when referring to different types of jobs by saying "just hourly workers."	You made a comment about race, college admission, and affirmative action that implied people should get into college on their merit and not on their race.	You failed to provide accessible technology in the form of closed captioning or access to an ASL interpreter for a conference with parents and caregivers.
Own it	That happened because you are not used to using those pronouns for this person.	You have had limited exposure to different types of employment, and you have only worked jobs that provided a salary.	You grew up in a culture where people believed in meritocracy—that if you work hard, you'll succeed.	Your proximity to different disabilities means you did not think about providing accommodations for greater accessibility.
Interrupt it	You will not misgender or use the wrong pronouns when referring to or speaking with this colleague.	You recognize that your experience has limited your worldview, and the impact of that is showing up in your language. You will challenge your assumptions about class and employment.	You broaden your understanding of the impact of class and access to schooling, as well as the impact of that access on opportunities. You create structure for yourself to better understand the intersections of identity and opportunity.	In advance of a program, you create a standard practice of identifying if participants need accommodations, or you provide accommodations to your meetings as a general practice.
Take responsibility	You say, "I apologize for not using your pronouns. I acknowledge I may have caused hurt and frustration. I take ownership of that mistake and will not repeat it."	You say, "The comments I made were classist and were informed by stereotypes I have about different jobs. It is my responsibility to expand my understanding, and I will challenge my stereotypes about class."	You say, "I stated generalizations about the connection between trying hard and succeeding, which erased the impact of racism and systemic inequality. I will work to shift my beliefs that put emphasis solely on the individual and learn more about how systems create conditions of inequity."	You say, "I did not set up the meeting for success, because I did not make arrangements for accessibility. I will create a structure that does not rely on individuals' disclosing or telling me they need accommodations, and instead, I will create conditions that provide greater access to all."

proximate" (as cited in Ford, 2020). For teachers, this means asking, "How often am I making decisions that might harm others who hold identities that are close to my own? How often am I making decisions—or avoiding decisions—that harm others who hold identities and experiences that are very different from my own?" That proximity, or lack thereof, can be a blind spot in our decision making.

In my example at the beginning of the chapter (page 147), I felt a distance from the identities of the young Black teenagers and a distance from the White man in the park. Perhaps I would have acted differently if I'd shared an identity with the teens—if they were Asian, if they were moms, or if they were women. As part of my practice, I think about how identity informed and impacted my actions and inaction that day, and I commit to seeing a closeness, rather than distance, in future situations. What might this reflection look like for classroom teachers and school leaders? How does closeness to or distance from the identities of students, colleagues, and parents and caregivers impact how you teach, lead, and engage with others?

According to educational leadership professors Whitney Sherman Newcomb and Katherine Cumings Mansfield (2014), teachers and school leaders must focus on transformation for social justice and change. There are a few ways that teachers and school leaders can take responsibility for their learning:

1. Challenge your commitment to dominant norms and values (which you may have learned in school and teacher preparation courses) and their influence on practices and policies in K–12 schools.

2. Identify teachers and school leaders who are committed to social justice and identity-conscious work. Collaborate to build capacity for change.

3. Examine how students connect to the values of your classroom or school and the ways in which they make sense of those values.

4. Engage in courageous conversations about school and create habits of dialogue within the school community, even if it causes some discomfort.

5. Develop habits and skills for reflecting, building awareness, and moving to action to create more inclusive communities.

Table 9.3 provides examples of what it might look like for teachers to take responsibility for their learning in the preceding five ways.

While the journey to building an identity-conscious practice is designed to empower, strengthen, and improve the work of teachers and school leaders, failure is part of the process. The work of building an identity-conscious practice is difficult, and it takes time. There are no quick fixes or immediate solutions to this work. Practice acknowledging failure, reflecting on why it happened, and creating meaningful action to learn and recover from it. As we fail, we also grow and commit to doing better.

TABLE 9.3: Action Items to Take Responsibility for Your Learning

Action Item for Teachers	Example
Challenge your commitment to dominant norms and values (which you may have learned in school and teacher preparation courses) and their influence on practices and policies in K–12 schools.	Brainstorm the existing policies, programs, practices, procedures, and traditions at your school that contribute to dominant group advantages. Explicitly name how White cultural norms inform and impact teaching, evaluating, leading, and learning. Identity-conscious practice: *What identities do I hold that are privileged in current norms at school?*
Identify teachers and school leaders who are committed to social justice and identity-conscious work. Collaborate to build capacity for change.	Commit to professional development, peer learning groups, and dedicated time for teachers and leaders to examine current practices that support activism and change in education. Identity-conscious practice: *What professional development opportunities do I seek out? Do I seek out those that are different from my experience?*
Examine how students connect to the values of your classroom or school and the ways in which they make sense of those values.	Invite students to provide feedback about their school experiences, listen to them, and make meaningful change in partnership with the students. Follow the "never about us without us" motto and have students or families sit on decision-making committees. Identity-conscious practice: *How are my values affirmed in school? What values of other identities may be in conflict with or not represented in the school community?*
Engage in courageous conversations about school and create habits of dialogue within the school community, even if it causes discomfort.	Explore existing protocols that can provide structure for difficult and critically productive conversations, such as Courageous Conversation (https://courageousconversation.com). Identity-conscious practice: *How does identity shape our conversations about conflict? How might certain groups feel more empowered to engage in conversations? How might some groups feel hesitant about engaging in conversations?*
Develop habits and skills for reflecting, building awareness, and moving to action to create more inclusive communities.	Create opportunities for people to explore their learned biases that inform and impact how they experience school, teaching, leading, learning, and advising. Develop action items from these learned experiences. Identity-conscious practice: *What voices do we uplift or amplify in our teaching and learning? What stories or voices are often missing? How can we represent greater diversity of voices in our curriculum or in our leadership?*

Source for action items: Newcomb & Mansfield, 2014.

Activities for Engaging With Failure

What do K–12 educators need to know, do, and demonstrate in order to respond to their mistakes in a productive way as part of the identity-conscious practice? The three activities in this chapter will guide you to reflect on a past experience with failure, understand the impact of your action and inaction, and consider your proximity to various identities.

Activity 1: Naming It, Owning It, Interrupting It, and Taking Responsibility

Addressing failure requires you to identify why you failed, how you failed, how you can disrupt the failure in the future, and how you can make your learning transparent. Think about a time when you failed, a situation that has stayed with you since the incident occurred—something that keeps you up at night or that replays in your mind. In the chart provided for this activity, use the following prompts to write about the experience. I've included an example for each step, showing how I wrote about the event I shared at the beginning of the chapter.

1. **Name it:** What was the failure—or multiple failures—that occurred?

   Example: *I failed to be in solidarity with the young Black people in the car who were being treated unfairly and aggressively by a White man. I failed to show them that they were not alone. I failed to communicate that what was happening to them was wrong.*

2. **Own it:** Why did that failure occur? What messages informed your (in)actions? What did those (in)actions protect you from? How true was the risk that you feared, if it existed?

   Example: *The failure occurred because I was afraid of what the White man would say to me or do to me. In retrospect, I'm not sure the White man would have done anything to me, other than scare me. I thought of my identities as a woman and a woman of color. I thought about what I was wearing on that day and how I felt vulnerable in my identities.*

3. **Interrupt it:** If you were to have intervened or acted differently in this situation, what would you have done? What would you have experienced in this new situation?

   Example: *I wish I had pulled out my phone and recorded what was happening. I wish I had not run away. I wish I had stayed or at least talked only to the Black teens to tell them they weren't alone. I wish I had told them I'd stay with them and be a witness in case the police came. I wish I had told the man it wasn't safe for these teens to drive in reverse. I wish I had told others who were walking on the path to help me help the young people in the car.*

4. **Take responsibility:** What lessons did you learn about yourself in this situation? What did you learn about others? If you could talk yourself through that past incident, what would you say to yourself step by step?

   Example: *I learned that sometimes my fear is a barrier. I learned that my identity as an Asian woman could have been helpful in this situation. I learned that my gut reaction is to look away, and I need to be more mindful so that I do not repeat looking away from future confrontations.*

Name it	
Own it	
Interrupt it	
Take responsibility	

Activity 2: Understanding Your Impact

A helpful way to address failure is to try to understand the impact of your (in)actions in a particular incident. Using your scenario from activity 1 (page 162), construct a narrative of the incident from the perspective of the person or persons you failed. Consider the following questions, and then write your story in the space provided.

- What did they see?

- What did they notice?

- What did they experience?

- What do you imagine they wished you had done? What outcome did your (in)actions have for them?

_____

_____

_____

_____

Read the following reflection questions, and record your thoughts and experiences in the space provided.

- What was challenging about this activity?

- What did you notice about yourself in this narrative?

- How true do you believe this narrative was for the other person or persons?

- What did you experience as you wrote this narrative?

_____

_____

_____

_____

Activity 3: Considering Proximity

Your experiences are often informed by your proximity (closeness or distance) to identities. Identifying your proximity to different identities and experiences can help reveal areas where you might have strengths. Mapping out your proximity also helps reveal identities and experiences that you might not be close to or know much about. By knowing the identities you are least proximate to, you can recognize your capacity to commit micro- and macroaggressions against students, colleagues, and other members of your community. Proximity helps us to identify areas where we may want to do more research, learning, and exploring. Through this activity, you will better understand the relationship of your own identities to those around you. This activity comprises three steps.

Step 1: Locate Yourself

The first step is to look at the list of identities in the first column. In the second column, write identities you hold for each category. If you do not have any relationship to a category, or if you are unsure of what that category or your relationship to it is, you can leave the middle column blank. In the third column, write identities in that category that you do not hold. You do not need to write every possible identity there, but just enough to give you a sense of other identities within that category.

Identity Category	How You Identify Within That Category	Identities in That Category You Do Not Hold
Race		

Identity Category	How You Identify Within That Category	Identities in That Category You Do Not Hold
Class		
Gender		
Sexual orientation		
Ability or disability		
Religion or faith traditions		
Sex		
Family structure		
Mental health		
Immigration status		
Citizenship or nationality		
Language		
Age		

Identity Category	How You Identify Within That Category	Identities in That Category You Do Not Hold
Body size and shape		
Political beliefs		
Family shaped by adoption		
Incarceration experiences		
Education experiences		
Employment experiences		
Military experience		
Socioeconomic status		

Step 2: Map Your Proximity

Your second step is to *map your proximity*—your closeness or distance—to these identities and experiences. The graphic for this step illustrates three areas of proximity. Read the following description of each area, along with the example I've provided, and then use the graphic to map your proximity to various identities.

- **Area 1** (the white center of the body in the graphic) represents the identities that are at the core of who you are, meaning you cannot distance yourself from these identities because they are drivers to everything you are and do.

  Example: *My identity as an Asian American and Filipina are central to who I am. I wake up as an Asian American. I eat breakfast as an Asian American. I go throughout my day as an Asian American. I cannot get any distance from this at all.*

- **Area 2** (the light gray area just outside the body) represents identities that you have closeness to but can also choose to distance yourself from in certain areas, spaces, or situations.

  Example: *My husband and children identify as Black/Latinx and multiracial. While these identities are very important to my experience and my life, I have some distance from their everyday experiences because I do not walk around this world as a Black/Latinx and multiracial person. They are close to me, but those are not identities that drive my own experience.*

- **Area 3** (the dark gray area farthest from the body) represents identities that you do not have closeness to. There is an aspect of distance between you and those identities.

  Example: *I am not close to the Indigenous and Native American lived experiences. While I care about issues that impact Indigenous and Native people, I do not experience their issues or world with any degree of closeness.*

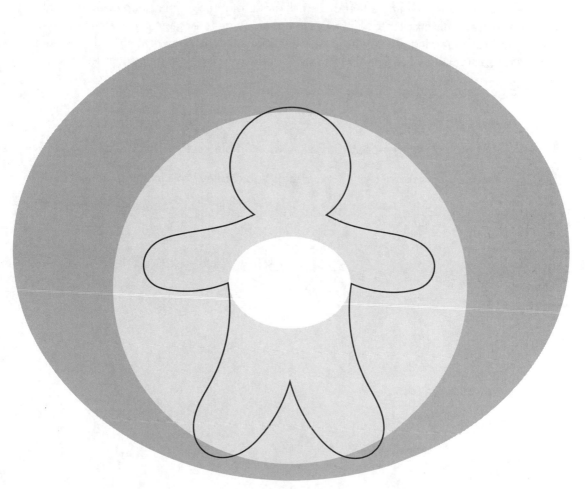

The Identity-Conscious Educator © 2022 Solution Tree Press • SolutionTree.com
Visit **go.SolutionTree.com/diversityandequity** to download this free reproducible.

Step 3: Reflect on Your Proximity

Now that you have mapped out your proximity—your closeness or distance—to identities, consider the following questions.

- What story is this map telling you?

- How might this proximity inform and impact your work as a teacher or school leader?

- What action items come from mapping out your proximity in this way?

Discussion

This guide provides structures for you to think deeply about identity and difficult conversations. To advance this beneficial work, engage in conversations with others using the following discussion prompts.

1. Have a conversation with a partner or a small group of three to four people. Go through each activity in this chapter together. Leave enough time to engage in conversation that does not rush learning. Be sure to create intentions for the conversation and expectations for participation. See Bringing People Together on page 8 to help set expectations.

2. In a larger group, engage with the following questions.

   ○ What did you experience as you did the activities in this chapter?

   ○ What did you notice about yourself as you completed these activities?

   ○ What do you believe is your next step as you continue this learning process?

CHAPTER 10

Tools for Extending Your Learning

Most workshops I facilitate are sixty-minute sessions for faculty and school leaders on topics related to diversity and inclusion. For these sessions, I carefully craft a scope and sequence, learning outcomes, and experiential activities (like the ones you've worked with in this book) for participants to learn, reflect, and engage. At the end of each session, I ask participants to open their notebooks and write down action items that will move them forward in this work. Teachers and school leaders busily fill in lines of to-do items.

I close out my visit by sharing my motto: "I provide, you decide. You have spent sixty minutes learning some new tools for engaging in identity-conscious practice. Now what? What will you do between now and the next time I see you?" Inevitably, during my next visit, I ask teachers and school leaders, "So, it's been a few months. How many of you completed the action items you wrote down in your notebook?" I smile as I recognize the same guilty look from teachers and school leaders that I get from the master's and doctoral students in my class. It's the look that says, "Oh no, I didn't do the homework."

I assure participants that they are in good company—something happens in between the excitement and energy of the live workshop and that moment when they realize they're on their own. Soon after our meeting, they are off to grade papers, plan for the next lesson, prepare dinner for themselves or their families, throw in a load of laundry, or head to a committee or community-based meeting. Almost immediately, the work of identity-conscious practice moves from *priority number 1* to *priority when I have time*. It makes sense. However, if we educators are going to make change, if we are going to see any difference in the condition of education and create more equitable structures, then we must make this work a top priority. What can educators do to incorporate this work into their lives in a sustainable and lasting way?

In this chapter, you'll explore tools for extending learning beyond this book. How do you keep learning about identity-conscious practice when you have so many competing priorities? As a first step, I'll note that staying organized by creating a system for storing and accessing your materials will allow you to sustain your practice for the long term. You'll then look at Glenn E. Singleton's (2015) Courageous Conversation protocol as a model for how to keep showing up for those difficult discussions along the way. It's important to understand that every person's practice is unique. We educators may not start the identity-conscious journey from the same place, but we are all on the path together, which means we can rely on one another as we move through discomfort in the context of community. Finally, you'll look at a framework for preparing for difficult encounters with students, peers, and stakeholders. Activities at the end of the chapter will help you build awareness and create plans for extending your learning and moving to action.

ESSENTIAL QUESTIONS

- What do I do with the tools in this chapter and throughout the book?

- How do I stay committed to building an identity-conscious practice?

- What does accountability look like in my classroom, in my school, and in my personal life?

Staying Organized

In this book, you've read about personal experiences with identity-based issues, reflected on your identities, and developed classroom-based strategies for having difficult conversations. In order to continue your work beyond the scope of this book, you'll need to create a system for staying organized. Think about initiatives you've taken on in the past. How did you organize those initiatives? How did you identify your priorities? What factors determined whether you continued the work or let it fall away? There are two main things I want to communicate here: (1) cultivate accountability to a group of peers, and (2) organize your materials.

The work of the identity-conscious practice is too big, challenging, and demanding to do alone. Having accountability from peers will make your practice sustainable for the long term. It's the best way to ensure you have people there to support you through tough seasons and to celebrate your progress. Todd Corley (2020), a senior executive in diversity and inclusive leadership, states, "Raising awareness does not automatically lead to improvement. Accountability should be positioned as a tool of empowerment and effectiveness. It should inspire ownership of personal and professional growth and development" (p. 32). Partnering with other members of your teaching team and your school administration will empower you to create more inclusive classrooms. Develop a cohort of peers who are also willing to engage in building an identity-conscious practice. Meet every week or twice a month to discuss your learning from this book. Find ways to expand beyond the small group and create school-wide dialogues about building skills for an identity-conscious practice. Invite your school leadership team to explore how their decisions are impacted by identity.

A key piece to supporting this initiative is time. School leaders should make time for teachers to engage in this work individually and with peers. Teachers are often asked to put in extra time after school or weekends to learn about topics like diversity and inclusion. Instead, schools should structure time within the existing schedule for teachers to learn, reflect, and create action. While many schools have professional development days on the calendar, these tend to be filled with important and timely topics. Diversity, inclusion, and identity must be included in the list of important and timely topics.

As your identity-conscious practice grows beyond the scope of this book, keep your work organized so you can flip through your reflections, ideas, and action items and access resources you've gathered for future use. And put that work in a place where you will always be reminded of it. As an example, I'll share how I organize my work. I use an orange spiral-bound notebook to house the learning, reflecting, and planning I do as part of my identity-conscious practice. I keep the orange notebook on my desk where I can access it frequently. Whenever I start a new lesson plan or change my syllabus (which I do at the start of every year in order to reflect and provide windows and mirrors for each of my students' identities), I bring out my proximity map from chapter 9 (activity 3, page 167). I use the map to locate the identities I might privilege in my curriculum and highlight the ones I leave out. For example, though none of my current students identify as Native American or Indigenous, I make sure we read articles written by Native and Indigenous scholars and practitioners so that as a group, we do not continue to perpetuate the invisibility and erasure of Native and Indigenous voices in education. In turn, my students take this scholarship and critical dialogue to their schools and classrooms, where they have conversations with their peers and their students.

In addition to the paper method, I recommend the following digital tools:

- Keep a digital folder to organize any reading materials you'd like to save on a device.

- Use the save or bookmark function on social media sites (such as Facebook and Instagram) to access resources at a later time.

- Create an electronic document, such as a notepad or Word document, to house links you wish to access later. Simply copy and paste links into the document and write a short summary describing the resource.

Whatever system you create, be sure to include a process for engaging with the materials. It can be tempting to fall into a pattern of gathering resources that sit untouched. Make time in your daily, weekly, and monthly schedule to read through the resources you've gathered, write down your reflections, and identify action steps to extend your work.

How will you organize your tools and resources so that the identity-conscious practice becomes sustainable in the long term and accessible when you need to draw on it? What tools would you use in a faculty meeting? What tools make sense when working with students independently? What tools work best when introducing a difficult lesson? Build your list of helpful tools, and organize them based on when you would use them in your daily practice.

Having Courageous Conversations

In 2018, I attended the National Summit for Courageous Conversation, a conference hosted by Pacific Educational Group. This was the first time I had learned about the Courageous Conversation protocol, a process for engaging, sustaining, and deepening dialogues about race. Prior to this conference, I simply approached the work of engaging in conversation with a get-it-done mentality. But when I encountered the Courageous Conversation protocol, I learned that engaging in dialogue is a process. It gave me competencies for moving through difficult conversations instead of just diving into them. I learned to connect more deeply with others and gain insight during difficult moments.

Founder and president of Pacific Educational Group, Glenn E. Singleton (2015), developed the Courageous Conversation protocol to support teachers and school leaders in the discussions needed to make progress regarding tough subjects like race, racism, ethnicity, and privilege. He outlines this protocol in his book *Courageous Conversations About Race: A Field Guide for Achieving Equity in Schools* (Singleton, 2015). The protocol comprises four agreements (see table 10.1): (1) stay engaged, (2) experience discomfort, (3) speak truth, and (4) expect and accept non-closure.

Per the last agreement—expect and accept non-closure—Singleton (2015) reminds us that courageous and difficult conversations are ongoing. There is no quick fix for issues such as racism, and there is no technical solution; but we can move toward greater collaboration through mutual understanding. Difficult conversations require us to bring our whole selves into the conversation—our attitudes, behaviors, beliefs, and ideas.

> There is no quick fix for issues such as racism, and there is no technical solution; but we can move toward greater collaboration through mutual understanding.

Difficult conversations require us to invite the other people to bring their whole selves into the dialogue. And as you know by now, those experiences and interactions are never identity neutral; they are always informed by identity and experience.

TABLE 10.1: Courageous Conversations

The Courageous Conversation Agreement	What It Means	Why It's Important	What It Might Sound Like
Stay engaged.	We are morally, relationally, and emotionally involved and present.	We commit to fostering understanding and relationships. We must be fully present in the dialogue.	"In order for me to stay engaged in this conversation, I need you to leave some space for me and to not monologue." "To stay engaged, for me, means to put your phone away and really listen."
Experience discomfort.	Courageous conversations are difficult and challenging. But having them is how we build our muscle for creating a culture of courageous conversations.	Discomfort looks different to different people. We need to be transparent about what discomfort looks and feels like so that we are not making assumptions about others.	"When I experience discomfort, I tend to get really quiet in the conversation, but it's usually because I'm so worried I'll say the wrong thing." "Experiencing discomfort is hard for me because I grew up being a people pleaser, and when discomfort is present, I try to do everything to minimize it."
Speak truth.	Oftentimes, what brings us to a difficult and courageous conversation is that something happened between us, in a meeting, or in our relationship. Speaking truth allows us to listen, make room for the other person, and be honest about our feelings and emotions.	Speaking truth can be difficult, especially when individuals are trying to work through divergent viewpoints. It is important to remember that a courageous conversation is not a debate or an opportunity to prove people right or wrong. It is a commitment to listen and learn.	"Speaking truth is difficult for me because I sometimes feel like people don't understand my experience or how I developed my views. I worry that my truth will be misinterpreted by others." "We have to create conditions where we can speak truth. I think we are in this situation because we were not honest with our thoughts or feelings previously."
Expect and accept non-closure.	We commit to ongoing dialogue and resist the urge to find a quick fix.	In a courageous conversation, we know that the work is not easily solved in a meeting or two. Rather, we benefit from identifying how we can have ongoing conversations and dialogue together.	"How will we know when it is time to revisit this topic and conversation?" "What steps can we take to make sure we continue this work?"

Source for agreements: Singleton, 2015.

A difficult conversation about identity relies heavily on our identity consciousness and fuels the work of our practice as we open to the identities and experiences of others. What are we aware of about ourselves? What are we unaware of about ourselves? What blank or blind spots do we have about particular identities? The activities in this book were designed for you to engage in both reflective practice and active dialogue about identity. Through your work, you've learned how identity informs and impacts how you act, how you interact, and how you see the world around you. And those views, in turn, inform and impact how you teach, learn, and lead. Committing to engage in courageous conversations is an effective way teachers can ensure their learning continues.

Understanding That Every Practice Is Unique

It is important to acknowledge that we live in a racialized society. Teachers and school leaders not only teach through a racialized lens but also were educated through a racialized lens. What does that mean? It means that every person's practice will be unique to their experience. For example, teachers who were educated in North America learned about the history, achievements, and struggles of their region through the lens of race—through the lens of Whiteness. A major feature of their identity-conscious practice will be noticing the ways that lens informs their beliefs, attitudes, and actions as well as decentering White advantage in their teaching. Table 10.2 identifies some ways this perspective shows up in the language of Eurocentric teaching and offers alternatives for decentering White advantage.

Every person's journey of identity consciousness is unique; educators each start from a different point and place in their learning process. While many people of color have long known and understood the impact of race, Whiteness, and power throughout their lives, they must examine other areas of privilege in their identities. The people of color you engage with in conversation may not start from the same place you do, but they are on the journey alongside you, learning about other identities and experiences, engaging in reflection about their proximity to marginalized identities, and identifying ways to act as allies. As an Asian American, middle class–raised, able-bodied, cisgender, heterosexual woman, I've had to dive deep into learning about identities that were unfamiliar to me or distant from my experience. I continue to use the activities in this book to move me through that journey.

Moving Through Discomfort in Community

Early in my teaching career, I was asked to teach sixth-grade health. This curriculum was pretty straightforward and included topics like friendships, hygiene, and communication. The teacher who had the seventh-grade health class taught a very different curriculum. Her topics included the human body and sexual health. I asked her, "How

TABLE 10.2: Language Centering and Decentering White Advantage

Language Centering White Advantage	Language Decentering White Advantage
Teachers often say "manifest destiny." "It had been decided by God that we should take this new land, and the West was open for manifest destiny."	Instead, say "White supremacy." "White supremacy, a belief that White colonizers were better than Native and Indigenous people, was a reason colonizers used to justify taking land, declaring it their own, and creating rules for how society would be governed on land that was not theirs."
Teachers often say "explorers." "The explorers came from England and landed in what would soon be called America."	Instead, say "invaders" or "colonizers." "People were here on their land, living their lives, and then invaders came in boats and declared this land found."
Teachers often say "westward expansion." "The colonists began to move westward to discover new land."	Instead, say "westward invasion." "Indigenous people were here on their land, living their lives, and then invaders showed up saying they wanted to expand west. This was a westward invasion."
Teachers often say "discovered." "The Europeans discovered the new land."	Instead, say "invaded." "The people came from afar and invaded land that already had people living on it."
Teachers often say "slaves." "Africans were brought over as slaves."	Instead, say "Africans who were enslaved." "Africans were stolen from their families and communities and enslaved by colonizers who kidnapped them, captured them, and subjected them to brutality, the effects of which are still very present today in our laws, policies, and practices."

do you get over the discomfort of middle schoolers spending an entire semester talking about genitalia?" She responded:

Well, in my first class, I let them know that our bodies are important. And learning words to accurately describe and define our bodies is important. So, we spend the first class just saying the words out loud and, soon enough, they become comfortable saying them. I let them know we sometimes feel shame or embarrassment in these words. In the beginning, every one of them is embarrassed. But, by the end of the semester, the words are just part of their everyday sentences, and I teach them why the right words are important. I want them to learn the actual names for the parts of their bodies and not just cute or silly nicknames.

Essentially, her strategy was to keep saying something and keep dialoguing about it until that discomfort turned into comfort. She never told the students to just get over it; instead, she taught them to move through the discomfort.

You know by now that engaging in difficult conversations about identity will likely bring up discomfort. In fact, the reflections, writing prompts, and conversations you've engaged with in this book may have brought up some discomfort for you. How do you react when you experience discomfort? If your earliest messages were to avoid discomfort at all costs, then this has likely been a challenging book for you. As you continue to put yourself in situations where you can move through discomfort, you will build the skills you need to be more confident in having tough conversations; you will become more comfortable with time and practice.

Moving through discomfort and practicing your skills within the context of community are especially powerful for reinforcing your learning. That's why the discussion questions are a repeated feature of this book. While it is a good step to think, learn, and process on your own, the real change happens when you dialogue and work with others in community. Practice engaging in dialogue about these issues related to identity. Practice adding some aspects of identity into your class discussions. Practice bringing up topics about identity with your friends and family. They, too, might experience some discomfort, but these are all opportunities to learn and grow.

Ultimately, there are no set measurements for ensuring cultural competence. We don't have grades or assessments for this. There is no standard of completion, no award for achievement: "Yes! Congratulations! You have reached cultural competence!" The identity-conscious practice is an ongoing process of thinking, feeling, and acting. While it is difficult to measure whether people are culturally competent, it is much easier to identify when they are not. Their microaggressions, insistence on upholding harmful traditions, or exclusionary attitudes indicate they are not engaging in the work of becoming conscious of identity and committing to an inclusive culture.

I have asked several people whom I consider to be identity conscious whether they consider themselves culturally competent. The answer they typically give me is, "Yes; however, I am always learning. I am still a work in progress. I don't have it all figured out." Because this work is ongoing, I talk about *building* an identity-conscious practice, not *achieving* an identity-conscious practice. I'm not sure it's possible to have expertise in every aspect of identity. However, we can increase identity consciousness and gain skills for difficult conversations by building our practice. Table 10.3 outlines hallmarks of the ongoing practice along with suggested action items.

TABLE 10.3: Hallmarks of Building Your Identity-Conscious Practice

Practice	Action Items
Be in an ongoing process of understanding yourself and your identity.	Use the format of reflection in this book. While the book covers a few identities teachers see most often in schools, there are many more to examine. Use the Engaging in Reflection questions in the Activities section of each chapter, and change the identity category (for example, family structure, immigration status, language, and so on) as appropriate.
Be willing to ask yourself reflective questions about how early messages you received informed and impacted your identity.	Biases are often informed and impacted by early messages you received. Engage in a practice of asking yourself, "Why do I think that?" and "Where did I learn that?" Then, imagine your current students are answering those questions. What do you want them to say about their experiences with you? What do you want them to say they learned from you about an aspect of identity?
Learn about your thoughts, attitudes, behaviors, and beliefs about conflict and conflict resolution.	Avoiding conflict often keeps you from the difficult conversations that must occur in this work. Write about your approach to conflict and what you might model for your students.
Be mindful of judgments and assumptions you make about other people, their identities, and their earliest messages.	Make a habit of engaging in identity-conscious practice by examining your reactions to situations. When judgment comes up around a topic, ask, "Where is that reaction coming from?" and "How is my reaction a reflection of my biases?"
Listen and be curious about the experiences of others.	Practice a "seek to understand" mentality in this work. Use questions like, "Would you like to say more about your experience?" or "Are there questions you'd like me to ask you?"
Practice engaging in dialogue with others about identity.	Create a structure and schedule to keep these conversations going. Engage in the peer learning dialogues that are provided in your group, and be open to participating in a number of different groups. Even if the questions are the same, the conversations and answers can differ from group to group.

Preparing for Difficult Encounters

The skills we've explored in the previous chapters involve reflecting on past experiences and influences. The identity-conscious practice allows us to examine early messages we received, attitudes we wish to change, and alternative actions we hope to take. But how might you lean on your practice to prepare for difficult encounters you anticipate in the future? Because identity informs our attitudes, actions, and interactions, we can invoke the lens of identity as we engage in difficult encounters. In those cases, it's helpful to have a framework for addressing unfolding situations that are heavily influenced by identity and require your input as a leader.

Teachers and leaders are problem solvers. They spring into action when an event occurs, address it in the moment, and move forward. However, there are times—particularly when identity is involved—when teachers and leaders must pause, engage in thoughtful reflection, and create actions that are informed by the identity-conscious lens.

Looking through the lens of identity when anticipating difficult conversations at school, teachers and school leaders can use a threefold process: (1) *prepare* to address conflicts of identity by understanding the situations, stories, and experiences of those involved; (2) *process* their relationship and proximity to the situations; and (3) *proceed* thoughtfully, intentionally, and flexibly. Table 10.4 illustrates the prepare, process, and proceed framework as it might play out at school; suggests questions to ask at each stage; and provides corresponding examples.

You have done some powerful work by engaging with the activities throughout this book! In order to extend your identity-conscious practice beyond the pages of this book, you'll need to create systems for sustainability. If you haven't already done so, begin gathering a group of peers around you who can hold you accountable. Consider what tools and systems you need to create to stay committed to your practice, able to gather and organize resources, and prepared to take action.

TABLE 10.4: The Prepare, Process, and Proceed Framework

	Questions to Ask	Example
Prepare	• What do you need to know about this conflict or situation? • How might different stakeholders tell this story? • What has contributed to this conflict or situation?	At recess today, there was an incident on the playground where a White child, Kate, told a Black child, Shanelle, "You can't play princess with us. Princesses are White." Kate and Shanelle usually get along in the classroom. I am unsure if this happened because recess is an unstructured time or if it has happened in the classroom and I have missed clues and didn't address them in class. Based on the racial language, I anticipate a consistent retelling of the story but anticipate this impacting the students differently.
Process	• How do your identities inform and impact this situation? • What parts of this scenario feel familiar to you? Unfamiliar to you? • How does your own identity consciousness show up in this situation? • What is your relationship to this issue? To the individuals involved in this conflict? • How are experiences with privilege and oppression showing up in this situation?	As an Asian American who grew up in a predominantly White environment, I was constantly made fun of on the playground. Hearing this story brings up some of those memories for me. I was always the made-fun-of child, and I'm not sure how to relate to the child who said this. I feel so close to this scenario of being othered or told I could not participate in something simply because of my race. When incidents like this happened, my teachers ignored them. I never felt like I could speak up or advocate for myself.
Proceed	• What protocols for dialogue might be used for this difficult conversation? • What actions can you or the group take to address privilege or oppression in this conversation? • What does it look like to stay engaged in this conversation together? • What would each child need in order to be able to speak truth? • What would expecting and accepting non-closure look like here? • What information needs to be addressed?	I'm going to ask the students to write down their perspective of what happened and what led up to this moment on the playground. I'm going to place the narratives side by side and notice where the deviation is, if there is one, in the stories. Though I am nervous, I am not afraid to talk about race in this scenario given the comment that was made. I am aware that replaying the story can bring up hurt, and I am cautious not to have Shanelle relive this comment that was made on the playground. If Shanelle does not want to be in this conversation, she does not have to be. She might not be ready for a courageous conversation in this moment, and I can revisit that if Shanelle wants to do it. Otherwise, I'll focus my attention on Kate to address this comment, where it came from, and how identity informed this incident.

Activities for Extending Your Learning

What do K–12 educators need to know, do, and demonstrate in order to extend their learning along the identity-conscious journey? The three activities in this chapter will guide you to practice the prepare, process, and proceed steps; reflect on the identity work you've undertaken so far; and practice articulating your needs to others during difficult conversations.

Activity 1: Reviewing Case Studies for Prepare, Process, and Proceed

Classroom teachers and school leaders have a responsibility to address bias in the school community. Use the prepare, process, and proceed steps (see table 10.4, page 179) to work through the following case studies. As you examine each case study, remember that none of this work—teaching, leading, advising, collaborating, coaching—is identity neutral. Identity informs our perceptions, actions, and interactions with others. The purpose of these case studies and the prepare, process, and proceed framework is to help you uncover how aspects of your identity might inform and impact how you see each scenario, how you act, and how you interact with those involved.

Scenario 1: Team Teachers

Jennifer and Cheryl have been team-teaching second grade for the past two years. Cheryl is a veteran teacher of eighteen years and has taught second grade at this school her whole career. Jennifer has been teaching for a total of five years and has spent the last two years team-teaching in a classroom with Cheryl. In her first three years of teaching, Jennifer taught second grade at another school.

In their first year of team-teaching, Cheryl took on a mentoring role with Jennifer. Jennifer felt supported and was glad to know her new school had a process for providing onboarding on the school, the classroom, the students' families, and the culture. The relationship seemed appropriate during the first year, as Jennifer was learning a new place and a new curriculum. However, entering the second year of team-teaching, Jennifer wanted to take a more independent role. Given Cheryl's constant supervision, Jennifer began to feel that Cheryl did not have confidence in her. Jennifer was an experienced teacher, but Cheryl's "motherly" approach at times came off as condescending.

As the second year of team-teaching continued, Jennifer became more agitated as Cheryl treated her like an assistant teacher rather than a co-teacher. Cheryl also noticed a behavior change in Jennifer. When Cheryl gave her feedback that she believed was helpful, Jennifer was quick to snap at Cheryl. This unaddressed tension became palpable. During free periods, Jennifer left the room quickly and only returned as students arrived back to the classroom. Jennifer was agitated by Cheryl's condescending approach; Cheryl was agitated by Jennifer's avoidance. While they were professional and friendly in front of the students, they grew impatient with each other between classes.

After a particularly tense day, Cheryl and Jennifer were cleaning up the classroom when Cheryl told Jennifer her attitude had been very poor that day and she was disappointed Jennifer was not being a team player. Cheryl said, "You don't seem like you enjoy teaching." Jennifer replied, "I like teaching. I just don't like teaching with you." Cheryl began to cry and left the room. Jennifer was upset that she now had to finish cleaning up the classroom on her own, and she worried about how Cheryl would treat her the next day.

page 1 of 5

You have heard about some of the tensions between Cheryl and Jennifer. These tensions surprised you at first because the two teachers seemed like such a good fit in their initial year of team-teaching. Together, they bring diversity of experience and identity to the classroom: Cheryl is a White woman, she is an eighteen-year teaching veteran, and she has spent her career at this school; Jennifer is a Black woman, she is a five-year teacher, and she has brought new energy and ideas to the classroom and school. You have heard, on different occasions, that both teachers are thinking of not returning for the next academic year.

Use the prepare, process, and proceed framework to get ready for a meeting you will have with Jennifer and Cheryl. Consider the following questions, and write a response in the space provided.

1. **Prepare:** What do you need to know about this conflict or situation? How might different stakeholders tell this story? What has contributed to this conflict or situation?

2. **Process:** How do your identities inform and impact this situation? What parts of this scenario feel familiar or unfamiliar to you? What is your relationship to this issue or to the people involved in this conflict? How are experiences with privilege and oppression showing up in this situation?

3. **Proceed:** What protocols for dialogue might be used for this difficult conversation? What actions can you or the group take to address privilege or oppression in this conversation? What does it look like to stay engaged in this conversation together? What would expecting and accepting non-closure look like here? What information needs to be addressed?

_____

_____

_____

_____

Scenario 2: The Gay Pride Parade

For the past few years, your school has deepened its commitment to diversity, equity, and inclusion. With the support of the faculty and staff and the board of trustees, you hired a new director of diversity, equity, and inclusion, who is charged with assessing the school's current climate and taking actionable steps to make your community more inclusive.

After surveying the community, the director found that many people feel the school has not taken action to be more inclusive of LGBTQ students and families. The director set up focus groups, held affinity group meetings with LGBTQ families, and conducted an assessment of what other schools in the area are doing to be more supportive of the LGBTQ community. The director, along with families from the LGBTQ affinity group, noted that a number of local schools march in the city's Gay Pride parade. Together, you and the director decide that this would be an important step toward signaling inclusion of LGBTQ families and agree to move forward. The director advertises the event as a community-building experience and begins the process of signing up the school for the parade.

The next morning, you have a meeting on your calendar regarding the Gay Pride parade. You are told this is a meeting with a very concerned spouse of a current board member. She is appalled that the school is participating in this parade because she claims it is highly inappropriate and not something students should see. She has openly disparaged the new director of diversity and has called for the director's resignation. She has also made it very clear that her family will be withholding a sizable donation to the school unless the school doesn't participate in the parade and fires the director. You realize that this person's threat to withdraw a donation is credible and understand that she will likely rally parents who contribute financially to the school.

Use the prepare, process, and proceed framework to get ready for this meeting. Consider the following questions, and write a response in the space provided.

1. **Prepare:** What do you need to know about this conflict or situation? How might different stakeholders tell this story? What has contributed to this conflict or situation?

2. **Process:** How do your identities inform and impact this situation? What parts of this scenario feel familiar or unfamiliar to you? What is your relationship to this issue or to the people involved in this conflict? How are experiences with privilege and oppression showing up in this situation?

3. **Proceed:** What protocols for dialogue might be used for this difficult conversation? What actions can you or the group take to address privilege or oppression in this conversation? What does it look like to stay engaged in this conversation together? What would expecting and accepting non-closure look like here? What information needs to be addressed?

_____

_____

_____

_____

Activity 2: Doing Identity Work

Now that you have done some deep and reflective work throughout this book, complete the following sentences. As you read them, make note of how you are feeling, how you are reacting, what feels familiar, and what feels unfamiliar to you. Complete some of the sentences with identities that are listed in activity 2 of chapter 1 (page 22).

- The identity of mine that I feel most comfortable with is _____.

- The identity of mine that I feel least comfortable with is _____.

- The identity that brings me the most joy is _____.

- The identity that brings me the most worry is _____.

- The identity that affords me the most privilege is _____.

- The identity that I feel the most oppression with is _____.

- The identity that I have most in common with other people in my life (students, peers, and friends) is _____.

- The identity that I have least in common with other people in my life (students, peers, and friends) is _____.

- The identity I would like to bring more reflection to is _____.

- The identity I would like to dialogue about more often is _____.

- I feel _____ about difficult conversations in my personal life.

- I feel _____ about difficult conversations in my professional life.

- One takeaway I have from the work I've done in this book is _____.

- One action item I want to focus on related to identity is _____.

- One action item I want to focus on related to difficult conversations is _____.

Activity 3: Having Difficult Conversations

Having courageous conversations can be difficult because you are unsure of what other people need, what they understand, or what they have learned about difficult conversations. Use the chart for this activity to help clarify your needs and articulate these needs to others when you find yourself in a difficult conversation.

In order to stay engaged in this difficult conversation, I need:	When I am feeling uncomfortable in a conversation, I tend to:

What I need from you when we are in a difficult conversation is:	What I believe I can offer in a difficult conversation is:

Read the following reflection questions, and record your thoughts and experiences in the space provided.

- What did you experience when you filled out this chart?

- What did you notice about yourself?

- What would you experience when you share this information with someone else?

- How might this level of transparency inform and impact your conversation?

_____

_____

_____

_____

Discussion

This guide provides structures for you to think deeply about identity and difficult conversations. To advance this beneficial work, engage in conversations with others using the following discussion prompts.

1. Have a conversation with a partner or a small group of three to four people. Go through each activity in this chapter together. Leave enough time to engage in conversation that does not rush learning. Be sure to create intentions for the conversation and expectations for participation. See Bringing People Together on page 8 to help set expectations.

2. In a larger group, engage with the following questions.

   ○ What did you experience as you did the activities in this chapter?

   ○ What did you notice about yourself as you completed these activities?

   ○ What do you believe is your next step as you continue this learning process?

CHAPTER 11

From Practitioner
to Facilitator

In 2013, I was invited to participate in the filming of a documentary about race called *I'm Not Racist . . . Am I?* (Greene & Lee, 2014). To learn more about the film, visit the film's website (http://notracistmovie.com). The filmmakers had gathered a group of teenagers and filmed their conversations during a series of workshops about race and racism. I met the teenagers toward the end of their time together, and my job was to facilitate a conversation about the impact of privilege. As I prepared for my workshop, I thought, *Great! I am so glad I'm working with a group of people who have done the heavy lifting of identity consciousness. We can skip all of that beginning work and go deeper into issues of oppression, inequities, and relationships. I'll just do a brief hook to warm us up.*

The *brief hook*, which I expected to be a two-minute exercise, turned into one of the most transformative moments of our time together and of the documentary. Instead of being a warm-up exercise, our conversation served as a pivotal point in the teens' experience as they realized the impact of their words and of their silence.

I began the session by passing out a dry-erase board to each of the students, saying, "As a way for me to get to know you, please write down some topics on your dry-erase board that your group has avoided talking about up to this point." As a facilitator, I was trying to gather information to help make the workshop more personal for the participants. I wanted to cover topics they felt they had not had a chance to explore. I fully expected this to be an introductory exercise.

Within seconds, though, the students laughed, whispered to one another, and looked around the room suspiciously as they wrote on their dry-erase boards. One by one, they read off the words they had written. I could feel tension building in the room. It turned out these were hurtful words and phrases that had been used repeatedly during their year together but had gone unchecked during the workshops. One young White girl felt that her peers were attacking her because she had used many of the words and phrases. Our conversation came to a standstill when she stormed out of the room crying. As a facilitator, I encountered an unexpected moment; honesty and discomfort had made their grand entrance, and now, we were faced with a difficult conversation.

The work you have been doing in this book follows a particular pattern: build knowledge, engage in reflection, move to action. As you build your practice and implement your action plans with students and peers, you might be asked to facilitate dialogues on your team, in your school, or in your community. I'd like to share with you the tools I've learned for identity-conscious facilitation to support your ongoing growth in this work.

In this chapter, you'll learn how to expand your skills to facilitating conversations about identity. The facilitator's job is to follow the conversation, read people's engagement, and keep the discussion moving forward by responding to challenges. You'll discover a framework for noticing participant cues. And you'll learn six strategies for responding to challenges that arise in tough conversations. Activities at the end of the chapter will help you build awareness and practice the tools you've encountered for facilitating challenging conversations about identity.

ESSENTIAL QUESTIONS

- What steps can I take to work through a difficult conversation?

- What skills do I need to practice as a facilitator of identity-conscious conversations?

- What potential challenges might I face when facilitating these types of dialogues?

Noticing Participant Cues

By this point in the book, you've likely started having challenging conversations in your classroom. You've learned how to open doors for students to address topics and issues that are difficult. By working through the activities in this book, participating in group discussions, and taking time for personal reflection, you've built identity consciousness. And you've become more adept at moving through discomfort. Noticing the ways you've grown and the courageous actions you're taking as an ally, your colleagues have invited you to facilitate discussions about identity.

As a facilitator, you need to notice the *ABCs*—*attitudes*, *behaviors*, and *curiosities*—of a group dynamic in a difficult conversation and respond, as appropriate, to participants' cues. Pay attention to the words people use and don't use that express their beliefs (attitudes), the way they use body language and positioning (behaviors), and the questions they ask (curiosities). Table 11.1 outlines the ABCs of facilitating a group, including examples of each element and possible ways a facilitator might respond.

TABLE 11.1: The ABCs of Facilitation

	Definition	Examples in a Discussion	Possible Responses
Attitudes	The thoughts and belief systems people have that shape their views or experiences	Saying things like, "I think that if you try hard enough, anything is possible. I'm tired of people making excuses that they can't achieve something or that things like racism are the reason why they can't succeed. Just try harder."	"Thank you for your comment. I'm curious about what experiences you have had that inform your comment. Where does your comment come from?" "I hear you saying that racism shouldn't be a reason why people don't succeed. I hear you saying that if they just try harder, they should be successful. What would it mean, however, if it were true that racism was a barrier? What would we have to address if that were, in fact, true?"
Behaviors	The visible expressions people show in conversations	Crying when the conversation is difficult Crossing one's arms and legs during a difficult conversation Turning off one's camera (if participating in an online workshop)	"I'm noticing you are having an emotional response to this conversation. What steps can you take right now to both acknowledge your response and keep it from getting in the way of our work together?" "I am noticing your arms and legs are crossed as you listen to this information. Tell me a bit about what you are experiencing in your body." "I am checking in with you, as I can't read your facial or body language at this time. What, if anything, would you like to share with me about the choice to turn off your camera during this topic?"
Curiosities	The questions people ask or the things they wonder about a topic or a comment	Asking questions like, "I just don't understand. If people chose to come to this country, why can't they just speak English? Why do we have to have so many services in different languages?"	"Thanks for your question. I'm hearing you ask about people's decision to come to the United States and their inability to speak English. What assumptions might be embedded in your curiosity?"

> The effective facilitator knows how to read the room, notice the experiences of participants, and respond in a way that meets people's needs and moves the conversation forward.

The effective facilitator knows how to read the room, notice the experiences of participants, and respond in a way that meets people's needs and moves the conversation forward. Looking for the ABCs will allow you to ground yourself in the unfolding conversation and meet whatever challenges arise moment to moment.

Responding to Challenges

As a resident assistant in college, I took part in a professional learning exercise called Behind Closed Doors where my fellow resident assistants and I role-played our responses to possible scenarios. We were supposed to imagine knocking on a room's door, unsure of what would appear on the other side, and practice a response. The scenarios varied from room to room. Sometimes, we encountered a party where there was underage drinking. Sometimes, we found a student who was experiencing a depressive episode. Sometimes, we were called in to investigate a noise complaint. As we ran through a dozen scenarios in our training exercise, our supervisors emphasized, "You just never know what you're going to find behind closed doors. We can prepare you to the best of our ability, but you will always find a scenario that you didn't train for."

The same advice applies to facilitating difficult conversations about identity. There are so many scenarios you could practice as you prepare to facilitate. You could imagine dozens of variables: the size of your group, the demographics of your group, the readiness of your participants (students, peers, parents, or families), and so on. Sometimes, the variations have to do with time. Maybe you're facilitating a lesson on the last day of the last period before vacation. Maybe you're facilitating a conversation right before lunch, everyone can smell pizza aromas wafting up from the cafeteria ovens, and you hear stomachs grumbling across the classroom. *Yes, both of these have happened to me.*

While you can't prepare for every eventuality, you can rely on universal strategies and draw from them in unforeseen circumstances. At this point in the book, it should be no surprise to you that many of these strategies involve reflecting on your thoughts, attitudes, behaviors, and beliefs. After all, you and your experience are the only things within your control. Just like in the Behind Closed Doors activity, you can't always anticipate or control the actions and behaviors of others; however, you can prepare for this work by building your practice. The following six strategies—(1) breathe, (2) acknowledge and validate, (3) be curious, (4) speak from experience, (5) move to reflection, and (6) follow through—will help you center your identity-conscious practice in your facilitation style.

Breathe

Think back to a moment when you were put on the spot in class or caught off guard in a peer discussion and you didn't know how to answer. Can you remember what happened in your body? Your heart rate quickened. Your face went red. You shifted in your seat. Your nervous system shifted into a fight (become aggressive) or flight (run away) response. According to the Cleveland Clinic (2019), the fight-or-flight response is meant to help you during stressful situations and life-threatening scenarios. In our classrooms, we might not be running from bears or swerving out of dangerous traffic, but we might perceive our stress to be very high in these dialogues.

Your body will respond in a similar way when you encounter uncertainty or discomfort as a facilitator. When you experience one or a combination of these physical responses, it's your cue to pause. Breathe. Fight the urge to answer quickly, as your answer might be rooted in your stress response. Though you might feel pressure to respond, take two seconds to inhale and exhale. You can nod while you breathe to acknowledge you are listening or thinking. But, before you speak, just breathe. Get oxygen back into your body. Relax your shoulders. Allow the stress response to recede.

Acknowledge and Validate

In conversations about identity, participants—students, peers, and leaders—usually share a personal story or experience. They often use their personal narratives to express their connection to or disconnection from a topic you have introduced. This is your cue to *acknowledge and validate*. Acknowledge that you heard their contribution and you recognize their feelings. For example, you might respond to a question with, "Thank you for your question. I noticed the passion in your voice as you shared your story and followed up with a question." By acknowledging a contribution, you allow the participant to feel heard and included. Sometimes, you may find that people ask difficult questions or make difficult statements because they want to be heard. Let them know you heard their question or statement.

Next, even if the person's perspective brings up challenging content, validate the contribution. When participants share an experience or a feeling, they take a risk. To validate their feelings, their experiences, and their emotions reinforces the shared sense of safety you're creating in the group. For example, if a participant shares a difficult experience or story, I often say, "Your feelings, as you are expressing and showing them, are very real," or "That anger that I hear in your voice is understandable."

Validating participants' feelings, however, does not necessarily mean that I agree with their sentences. For example, when I facilitated a difficult conversation about religion and sexual orientation, a participant expressed that they grew up hearing that being LGBTQ is a choice. While I do not agree with this, I could still validate that person's feelings. By responding, "Your feelings are real. Thank you for sharing your response," I was able to validate the person's feelings without agreeing with their position.

If appropriate, you can share your own experience. Continuing with the example from the previous paragraph, I said, "Thank you for sharing. Your feelings are real. My experience with that topic does not align with yours, because I was taught that being LGBTQ is not a choice, and therefore, my thoughts, attitudes, behaviors, and beliefs look very different from yours." Take your cue from the unfolding conversation, and remember to look for the participant ABCs as you determine the most appropriate response moment to moment.

Be Curious

A great tool a facilitator has is the ability to ask reflective questions. It's natural to feel judgment arise when a participant shares an experience, opinion, or belief that does not align with your experiences, opinions, or beliefs. In order to remain curious when you encounter moments like that, ask yourself, "What is my reaction saying about me?" Turn the judgment back to your identity-conscious practice. Because our reactions to situations are often reflections of ourselves, being curious about our reactions requires us to be identity conscious.

As news broke about the origins of COVID-19, many people, including high-ranking U.S. government officials, placed blame on China, Chinese practices, and Chinese people. This displacement of anger gave rise to a surge of hate crimes in North America. Between March 2020 and May 2020, Stop AAPI Hate (2020)—a nonprofit organization created to track and respond to incidents of hate, violence, harassment, discrimination, shunning, and bullying against Asian Americans and Pacific Islanders—received 1,843 reports of anti-Asian discrimination due to COVID-19.

In January 2021, after a year of ongoing quarantine and surges in COVID-19 that resulted in lockdowns and restrictions across the United States, a new surge of anti-Asian violence erupted. While the violence against the Asian American community had continued throughout the summer of 2020, national attention had been drawn to justice for Black people, Black lives, and Black communities after video emerged of George Floyd's killing by a Minneapolis police officer. And yet, many activists continued to work in solidarity across racial lines to address violence and hate in and among communities of color.

During the ongoing violence against the Black and Asian communities (in addition to the ongoing systemic separation of families that disproportionately impacted Latino and South American families as well as the ongoing systemic racism against Native and Indigenous communities related to COVID-19 responses), I was facilitating a workshop on the topic of Asian American and Black solidarity when a participant asked me, "Why should Black people even stick up for Asian Americans at all? It's not like they have ever helped us. So, I'm not interested in helping people that have never helped me." My face got red, and my heart rate quickened. I felt angry, defensive, and taken aback by this comment. I wanted to disconnect from the conversation, telling myself, "See, Liza! It's not worth it. Why do you keep doing this work?" I wanted to call it quits. But I reminded myself to *breathe*. I reminded myself to *acknowledge and validate*. I reminded myself to *be curious*.

I replied, "Thank you for your comment. Your comment is understandable given the history of our two communities. I'm not sure you are looking for a particular answer, but I am curious to know where your comment comes from. Would you like to say more about what was behind your statement?" The participant shared that, growing up, he was one of the few Black students in the honors classes in high school. There were lots of White students and several Asian students. This person was picked on by both White kids and Asian kids in class, and he shared that it stung more when the Asian students teased him because he felt like they were all supposed to be in it together as people of color. He felt betrayed. He experienced that Asian students never stood up for him. Since then, he'd noticed that he could only really count on his own people to have his back.

If I had simply dismissed the man's statement or responded in a defensive manner, I would have shut down his sharing, his pain, and his anger. While it was never his responsibility to teach anyone in that workshop or to share his experience, the process of getting curious opened the door for him to share, if he chose to. By leaning into my identity-conscious practice, I was able to defuse my defensive response and remind myself that I, too, have been in the position of feeling hurt by people of color. Creating a pathway for him to share, if he chose to, also created a pathway for me to connect to his story, which, in the end, was not so different from my own.

Speak From Experience

It's natural for teachers to feel they should have all the answers. Yet, conversations about identity often bring up unresolved questions and uncomfortable statements you may be unprepared to address. Expect this to happen when you facilitate discussions about identity. How should you respond to the unexpected? Lean into your practice. When a participant asks you a question you don't know how to answer, pause before you speak, and notice what's happening in your body. How do you feel when you realize you can't provide the answer? What fears, stories, or compulsions show up in response? Feel free to ask for clarification: "What makes that question important to you?" or "What's behind your question?" or "How will information support you right now?"

From that place of awareness, you can make a conscious choice. I'll share two potential responses I see to this scenario: You could say, "Thank you for your question. I am not close enough to that issue to have an answer. Where do you think we could turn as our first step to finding that answer?" This allows the participant to take responsibility for the process. Or you could simply respond, "Your question isn't one I can answer based on my own experiences. Is this question rooted in an experience you've had that might help us find an answer?"

Sometimes, a participant will make a statement that runs counter to the purpose of a workshop. For example, as I was facilitating a faculty meeting at a local high school, I asked the faculty to engage in a reflective practice about their experiences related to gender identity. A White male faculty member spoke up and said, "I think giving kids too many choices about gender just confuses them. They are too young to think about these choices. We should stick with the two we know: boy and girl, male and female. Too many choices make them confused."

The man's statement triggered an emotional response for me. I felt my heart race, my face turn red, and my anger start to build. But I was able to get myself together, remind myself I was a facilitator of this difficult conversation about identity, and answer him by saying, "Thanks for your comment. I hear you connecting these choices with confusion. Your statement about choices and confusion doesn't align with my experiences of working with many young people who have found comfort in choice and who have felt freedom from fitting within two expectations. In my experience, young people say that these choices actually help them feel better and understand their world better. It actually leads to less confusion about who they are. How possible is it for you to hold some of that as truth as we move through this workshop together?"

The faculty member shrugged his shoulders. I replied, "Thank you. I imagine my job is not to convince anyone of one way or another in the next sixty minutes, but perhaps to open up some possibilities of different beliefs and understandings."

Move to Reflection

In difficult conversations about identity, it's normal for participants to get heated, passionate, and emotional. It is therefore helpful to anticipate these big moments and to have a few tools for shifting these tensions.

Inviting participants into reflecting, writing, and thinking time is an effective way to defuse tensions and refocus energy. Those tasks help participants regulate their breathing and stay curious, and they provide time for you, the facilitator, to rethink, regroup, and reset the room.

In 2020, nearly all my classes moved to a virtual platform to uphold protocols during the COVID-19 pandemic. One day in my class on race and leadership, students were talking about how racial identities inform and impact their work. While this class's topics almost always focus on the scholarship of racial identities, the students began talking more openly about their experiences in the class. They were exhausted from being online, suffering quarantine fatigue, and managing work and school in addition to their duties as spouses, parents, partners, and family members.

As we were discussing an assigned reading about the experiences of Black graduate students, one student said, "It's difficult being a Black student right now, with the pandemic and with such racism against Black people." The student began listing the names of other Black students in class, saying, "The five of us, we are really hurting. We are really having a tough time." Another student spoke up. "Wait a minute. You left me off of that list. I identify as Black too, you know." The room quieted; the faces on the screen registered shock and confusion. The rest of the students had not realized that this student identified as Black; they had only heard the classmate identify as Latinx. The conversation quickly escalated. "Who gets to decide how a person racially identifies?" "How far back does one have to go in their heritage to claim a Black identity and experience?" "Who are you to tell me I'm not Black?" This was a moment of discomfort, anger, frustration, rage, and hurt.

In my classes, I *encourage* challenging and difficult conversations, particularly about race. However, I recognized this conversation had veered into unproductive territory. It was my time to intervene and to move participants into reflection about what was happening in the room. I stepped in and said, "First, thank you for this important conversation. I'm noticing expressions of anger, hurt, frustration, and agitation. Those all are understandable reactions, especially given our topic and the comments that were made in these last few minutes. It's time to examine the dialogue that is happening now, which we will continue in productive ways. Please turn to your notebooks as we process what is happening in this class. Please respond to the following prompts." And then I introduced them to these five questions and the parenthetical sentence stems, which they could use in their responses.

1. What did you notice happening in this room? ("I noticed that . . .")

2. What thoughts came to mind for you during this difficult conversation? ("I thought that . . .")

3. What are you curious about, or what do you wonder? ("I wonder . . .")

4. What do you think should happen for us to move forward in this dialogue? ("To move forward, we should . . .")

5. What do you need in order to either step in (if you haven't engaged) or step back (if you contributed a lot in the last conversation)? ("In order to step in/ step back in this conversation, I need . . .")

I posted the questions and then asked students to take a ten-minute break, to walk away from their screens, and to find nourishment—by going outside, getting a drink of water, or simply finding a space to sit quietly away from their computers. I let them know we would pick up the conversation in a way that would provide pathways for curiosity, reflection, and action.

Follow Through

Many conversations you facilitate will happen within time constraints. Perhaps you scheduled a forty-five-minute block in your teaching schedule or a sixty-minute evening workshop for your peers or community. This means that action items and follow-through are important to create accountability; without them, participants get caught in a cycle of "all talk, no walk."

Though you cannot always achieve closure when a difficult conversation has occurred, you can and should follow through by providing concrete action items after a session is complete and checking in with people who were impacted by the difficult conversation in the session. I use the motto, "Check in with the most vulnerable in the room." Who was most impacted by the conversation? Who might have feelings they need to express, explore, or process after this session? And how can you support that person after this conversation?

As the facilitator of the dialogue, you should always build in time for checking in and checking out, even if it means you don't cover all the content you had planned to cover. Remember that these difficult conversations about identity are a journey, and many people are sharing experiences that are personal. Be sure to make time for processing, learning, and debriefing.

When difficult conversations occur in the classroom, in a meeting, or in a professional learning space, it's tempting to pretend they didn't happen or they didn't impact relationships or team dynamics. Unfortunately, unresolved issues, conversations, or hurts can leave an impact and may affect a person's willingness to engage in future conversations about identity. As the facilitator, you should acknowledge when a difficult experience or interaction happened and help participants come to an understanding of what it means to move forward. For example, at the start of the next class, you might say, "In our last class, we experienced difficult conversations. And, at the end of class, we did not quite resolve our conflicts or differences. What do you need from me or from your classmates in order to move forward?"

While facilitating conversations about identity is rewarding, it presents a unique set of challenges and requires you to develop additional skills. The six strategies offered in this chapter aim to support you in hosting difficult discussions in your classroom, department, leadership team, and community. Table 11.2 lists the six strategies along with the purpose of each and an example to illustrate how you might employ that strategy. Before you facilitate or lead a discussion, take time prior to your event to think about how your identity-conscious practice might inform and impact how you act, interact with participants, and engage in the dialogue.

Practice, practice, practice. The best way to build your confidence and skills as a leader in identity-conscious conversations is to place yourself in situations where you are leading the discussion. Start by engaging in this work in your classroom. Then think about how you might lead difficult conversations with your grade-level team or department. How might you extend this learning to your school or your district?

TABLE 11.2: Strategies for Responding to Difficult Moments

Strategy	Purpose	Example
Breathe.	This allows you to slow down your fight-or-flight response in moments of stress; it provides the opportunity to think and respond clearly and with intent.	"Thank you for your question. I'm going to take a moment to give your question some consideration before I answer."
Acknowledge and validate.	This affirms for your participants that you have listened to them and heard their contributions; sometimes, people make comments or ask questions because they want to be heard and to have a voice in the dialogue.	"I hear you saying that you felt hurt during that interaction. That response is understandable."
Be curious.	This creates pathways for new possibilities, open-mindedness, and opportunities for learning; this also places you in a learning zone when dialogue becomes difficult.	"I appreciate your comment. I'm not as familiar with that perspective. What would you like to say about how your perspective was shaped?"
Speak from experience.	This creates connection between what is being shared and your identity-conscious practice; sometimes, you might have experiences with the topic, and other times, you might not have a close connection to the topic.	"I am hearing you say that if people would just work hard, then they should be successful. What you just said doesn't align with my experience, because I have known people in my life who worked very hard but who still faced significant barriers to moving forward."
Move to reflection.	This provides your students (and you) some time to think about the process of dialogue and how this conversation is going. It is important to reflect on the process of dialogue to build habits and skills for future conversations.	"What are you noticing about our dialogue so far? What do you wonder about yourself or others?"
Follow through.	This allows you to commit to ongoing dialogue and resolution. It is possible conversations will have to end prior to any resolution because of the constraints of class time or meeting time, so it is important to articulate action items or next steps.	"Priscilla, I know we had a difficult interaction in that meeting. Are you open to a courageous conversation with me sometime this week about what happened between us?"

Activities for Moving From Practitioner to Facilitator

What do K–12 educators need to know, do, and demonstrate in order to extend their learning along the identity-conscious journey? The three activities in this chapter will guide you to reflect on your experiences with facilitating conversations, review your strategies, and practice your strategies for addressing challenges in difficult conversations.

Activity 1: Engaging in Reflection

There is certainly a leap from building your knowledge and reflecting to taking action. Begin by reflecting on your experiences with facilitating conversations and how those experiences might inform and impact your willingness to host discussions about identity. Read the following reflection questions, and record your thoughts and experiences in the space provided.

1. Think back to a difficult conversation you participated in. What went well in that conversation? What did not go well?

   _____

   _____

   _____

   _____

2. Think about a time you participated in a professional development training or workshop that went well. What did you notice about the facilitator? How did that person build your knowledge? How did that person make you feel during that workshop? If you do not remember anything—or if the training or workshop did not leave an impression on you—why do you think it was easily forgettable?

   _____

   _____

   _____

   _____

3. When you facilitate a difficult conversation or a professional development workshop, what do you hope your students or participants feel at the end of your lesson or workshop? What do you hope they know or understand at the end of your lesson or workshop?

   _____

   _____

   _____

   _____

4. What personal challenges do you feel you need to face to be an effective facilitator of difficult conversations? What is one step you can take to address each challenge?

_____

_____

_____

_____

Activity 2: Reviewing the Strategies

Before using the six strategies you've read about in this chapter, reflect on your proximity to these strategies and how connected to or disconnected from the suggestions you feel.

• Which of the six strategies feel familiar to you? Which feel unfamiliar?

_____

_____

_____

_____

• What is missing from these strategies?

_____

_____

_____

_____

• How supported do you feel by your school, leadership, or team to have difficult conversations with your class, with your peers, or in the community?

_____

_____

_____

_____

- What worries or fears do you hold about having difficult conversations with your class?

  _____

  _____

  _____

  _____

- How might identity consciousness or the activities in this book get you closer to addressing those worries or fears?

  _____

  _____

  _____

  _____

Activity 3: Practicing Your Strategies

This chapter identifies six strategies for addressing challenges in difficult conversations. You can find more details about these strategies in table 11.2 (page 195).

1. Breathe.

2. Acknowledge and validate.

3. Be curious.

4. Speak from experience.

5. Move to reflection.

6. Follow through.

Read the following scenarios, and practice using the strategies by writing in the space provided.

Scenario 1: The Descendant of Pilgrims

You have structured your lesson plan to talk more directly about issues of injustice in history. This material is somewhat new for you, given that you learned about history from the viewpoint of White settlers and colonizers. You have done more research on the experiences of Native and Indigenous people, and you have built your knowledge in preparation for these next few lessons.

As you are beginning your lesson, a student raises his hand and says, "This is *not* accurate. The Pilgrims landed at Plymouth Rock, and they were friends to the Native Americans. They treated them very well, and that's why we celebrate Thanksgiving: to show how much we value our friendships. My mom's ancestors came over on the *Mayflower*, so I know this history well. Every Thanksgiving, we tell the story of how the brave Pilgrims came to this country and made peace with people who were so different from them. The Pilgrims brought over lots of new tools and ways of living that helped the Native Americans and changed their lives for the better. I'm tired of everyone saying that Pilgrims were bad. It wasn't their fault they had to leave their country and come here. It happened, so we should just get over it and not always focus on the negative things. The Pilgrims' coming here was positive. If they didn't come, I never would have been born here."

You notice some students in the class nodding in agreement. Other students are rolling their eyes while the student makes his comment. Others look confused by what is going on.

How might you address this scenario in your classroom? Examine each strategy and its purpose, and then record your response in the right-hand column of the chart for this scenario.

Strategy	Purpose	Your Response
Breathe.	This allows you to slow down your fight-or-flight response in moments of stress; it provides the opportunity to think and respond clearly and with intent.	
Acknowledge and validate.	This affirms for your participants that you have listened to them and heard their contributions; sometimes, people make comments or ask questions because they want to be heard and to have a voice in the dialogue.	
Be curious.	This creates pathways for new possibilities, open-mindedness, and opportunities for learning; this also places you in a learning zone when dialogue becomes difficult.	
Speak from experience.	This creates connection between what is being shared and your identity-conscious practice; sometimes, you might have experiences with the topic, and other times, you might not have a close connection to the topic.	

Strategy	Purpose	Your Response
Move to reflection.	This provides your students (and you) some time to think about the process of dialogue and how this conversation is going. It is important to reflect on the process of dialogue to build habits and skills for future conversations.	
Follow through.	This allows you to commit to ongoing dialogue and resolution. It is possible conversations will have to end prior to any resolution because of the constraints of class time or meeting time, so it is important to articulate action items or next steps.	

Scenario 2: The Diversity Dilemma

Your school faculty and leadership team have been leaning into conversations about identity over the past few months, and you know it is time to bring the parents and caregivers up to speed on the work you have been doing as a school at a family forum. Your team has collected data from the past few years, and you've noticed a pattern that many honors classes at your school lack racial diversity and are, in fact, filled by nearly all White students. You begin to ask questions about why this is and what, if anything, faculty and school leadership can do to address this issue. You are reminded of the tools you have learned for identity-conscious practice, and you encourage school leadership to think about how issues of identity might be creating this condition.

Your school leaders bring up that racial diversity in the honors program is something they will be closely examining over the next year. At the family forum, a parent raises a hand and says, "I am a parent of a current honors student. And I have two other children who have also gone through the honors program here at our school. I am all for racial diversity and believe it is important. However, I hope that you are not thinking of lowering the academic standards of the honors program just to make it more diverse. No offense, but part of what makes the honors program so special is that it is so hard to get into. And if you loosen those standards just for diversity, then I believe you are compromising the integrity of the entire honors program and the reputation of honors students. If word gets out, then this honors designation will mean nothing, and that will make it harder for our children who deserve to be in the honors program to get into competitive colleges. My child has worked very hard and deserves the right to have an honors program. Again, I believe in racial diversity. But I do not believe in lowering standards just to achieve it and making other people suffer for this cause."

How might you address this situation at the family forum? Examine each strategy and its purpose, and then record your response in the right-hand column of the chart for this scenario.

Strategy	Purpose	Your Response
Breathe.	This allows you to slow down your fight-or-flight response in moments of stress; it provides the opportunity to think and respond clearly and with intent.	
Acknowledge and validate.	This affirms for your participants that you have listened to them and heard their contributions; sometimes, people make comments or ask questions because they want to be heard and to have a voice in the dialogue.	
Be curious.	This creates pathways for new possibilities, open-mindedness, and opportunities for learning; this also places you in a learning zone when dialogue becomes difficult.	
Speak from experience.	This creates connection between what is being shared and your identity-conscious practice; sometimes, you might have experiences with the topic, and other times, you might not have a close connection to the topic.	
Move to reflection.	This provides your students (and you) some time to think about the process of dialogue and how this conversation is going. It is important to reflect on the process of dialogue to build habits and skills for future conversations.	
Follow through.	This allows you to commit to ongoing dialogue and resolution. It is possible conversations will have to end prior to any resolution because of the constraints of class time or meeting time, so it is important to articulate action items or next steps.	

Discussion

This guide provides structures for you to think deeply about identity and difficult conversations. To advance this beneficial work, engage in conversations with others using the following discussion prompts.

1. Have a conversation with a partner or a small group of three to four people. Go through each activity in this chapter together. Leave enough time to engage in conversation that does not rush learning. Be sure to create intentions for the conversation and expectations for participation. See Bringing People Together on page 8 to help set expectations.

2. In a larger group, engage with the following questions.

   ○ What did you experience as you did the activities in this chapter?

   ○ What did you notice about yourself as you completed these activities?

   ○ What do you believe is your next step as you continue this learning process?

CHAPTER 12

Beyond *The Identity-Conscious Educator*

My teenager came home from school one day incredibly frustrated. "What's wrong?" I asked. "I just hate math," they replied. "Why do I even need to know the quadratic formula anyway? Like, really? When am I ever going to use this? Nothing I do is going to involve the quadratic formula. Do you and Dad use the quadratic formula? Did the quadratic formula help you get through college, graduate school, get a job, buy a house, or anything that adults would need to do? What is this tool actually going to help me solve in the real world? I'm so over it."

I smiled. That only made them more upset. "Let's be clear," I started. "Some people actually *do* use the quadratic formula on a daily basis and have gone to college, graduate school, and other professions where the quadratic formula is really relevant. But, if you are asking if I use it on a daily basis, then, no, I do not."

"See! I knew it!" they replied excitedly.

"However," I quickly followed up. "Engaging in complex math problems helped me to think critically, to solve problems with abstract factors, and to try to think beyond what I can see or what I know. It's not a tool I use every day, but it did help me to build the habits and skills of solving for things that are unknown."

"Well, I can still not like it," my teenager replied. "But I guess I can see how learning the quadratic formula is at least building some other skills." And with that, they put down their backpack, grabbed a snack, and turned their attention to the two dogs waiting for them.

The tools in this book do not cover every single possible example of identity in schools. And it's possible there are scenarios covered in this book that you may never encounter. However, I'll share the same message with you that I shared with my teenager. These tools help you think critically about the five identities in this book by providing you with a formula: build knowledge, engage in reflection, move to action. In part II (page 37), you had the opportunity to examine five core identities that commonly show up in school: (1) race, (2) class, (3) sexual orientation, (4) gender, and (5) disability. Based on your location and the context of your community, other identities are likely represented at your school. Given my work in North America and across the globe, I appreciate that many readers might wish to explore other identities, including religion and faith traditions, family structures, geographic location, mental health, health experiences, language, immigration status, and country of origin, just to name a few. The purpose of this book is to support your personal and professional growth in building an identity-conscious practice. Wherever you go from here, I encourage you to focus on the process; you now have a working model for exploring identities beyond the scope of this book.

In this final chapter, you'll review the framework we've created throughout the book for building your identity-conscious practice and examine how you'll use it to incorporate additional identities. First, I'll discuss laying the groundwork, creating context for an identity you'd like to explore. From there, you know the drill: building knowledge, engaging in reflection, and moving to action. I'll end by talking about why it's important to refresh your perspective from time to time as you carry your practice into the future. You'll notice that, unlike the rest of the chapters in this book, this final chapter doesn't contain activities or discussion questions at the end. Consider this a graduation of sorts: by the time you finish this chapter, you'll have all the tools you need to shape your practice going forward. What kinds of activities will you bring in as you continue the work you've begun? And what kinds of discussion groups will you seek out as a next step?

ESSENTIAL QUESTIONS

– How do I explore other identities that are not covered in this book?

– What resources should I use to build knowledge, and what questions will help me engage in reflection?

– How do I structure action items for building an identity-conscious practice?

Laying the Groundwork

While the first step of the identity-conscious practice is to build knowledge, it's helpful to lay the groundwork before you begin—namely, asking, "Why do I want or need to explore this identity?" Every chapter of this book began with a short narrative where I shared my personal connection to the chapter's main theme. These narratives each serve as a way for you to connect to me, understand my interest in the topic, and trust my expertise on the subject, but they also offer examples of how to create context for working with a particular identity. Now it's your turn. Reflect on the following questions as you lay the groundwork for exploring an identity for the first time.

- What is the issue or identity you want to explore?

- What makes this issue or identity important? Why do you need to explore it?

- What are your goals in exploring this identity? What are you hoping to achieve?

- How will exploring this identity impact or inform your teaching?

- How proximate (see activity 3 from chapter 9, page 164) are you to this identity or experience?

Now that you have context for incorporating a new identity into your practice, you can begin the process at step 1, building knowledge.

Building Knowledge

Building knowledge is the first step in the identity-conscious practice. Each chapter in this book is informed by scholarship and academic research. While you may not need to do a deep dive into scholarly articles found in peer-reviewed journals or in research databases to build knowledge, it is important to survey different perspectives and approaches to identity-conscious work.

There are two key considerations for building knowledge: (1) where your information is coming from and (2) how that information is informed. The internet provides easy access to a depth and breadth of information, which means it also provides access to a wealth of misinformation. Every time you access new information, *consider the source* and *think critically* about the information you find.

Rely on organizations that are rooted in the field of education. For example, in building the research base for this book, I searched online for topics such as "race in education," "disabilities and education," and "class disparities in education." Those education-specific search results will give you a broad list of where to begin. As a next step, turn to academic research by using Google Scholar (https://scholar.google.com) as well as the library and any database privileges you may have. Prioritize journals that have a long-standing reputation in education or in that identity topic.

You'll inevitably come across websites and organizations that do not align with your purpose of building an identity-conscious practice. Rather than dismiss those sources, however, use them as a helpful critical lens, allowing you to better understand why some people prefer to avoid talking about identity. If you come across an article or source that reflects the belief that identity does not matter, read it. Engage with it critically. Notice any bias evident in the source. Consult the AllSides Media Bias chart (www.allsides.com /media-bias/media-bias-ratings) to identify bias in news media. The site intends to make media bias transparent so that readers can engage with different perspectives and draw their own conclusions.

In writing this book, I followed the "never about us without us" approach to research and engagement. I was careful to draw on voices of people who have direct experience with or hold identities I write about in the chapters on race, class, sexual orientation, gender, and disability. As you build your knowledge, prioritize sources that speak from experience and with expertise on the identities you're exploring. For example, if I am trying to learn more about the experiences of Indigenous people on North American land, I need to find resources and stories as told by Indigenous people of that land, such as Roxanne Dunbar-Ortiz's (2014) book *An Indigenous Peoples' History of the United States*. Seek direction from groups that focus on an identity's truth and experience. If you're looking for thoughtful examples of Indigenous and First Nations groups who provide culture-centric recommendations, consider the First Nations Development Institute (n.d.; www.firstnations.org /knowledge-center/books) and the work of Debbie Reese, a Nambé Pueblo American Indian scholar and educator, who has compiled a thorough list and analysis of American Indians in children's literature (https://americanindiansinchildrensliterature.blogspot.com).

Consider the following questions as you build knowledge.

- What do you currently know about this identity or experience? What have you heard or read, prior to conducting your research?

- What, if anything, did you learn during your own schooling and education in terms of formal knowledge about this identity or experience?

- As you read and build knowledge about this identity or experience, what do you learn that is new or different from what you knew prior to this research?

- How does the identity of the author (of the website, article, book, or post) impact the knowledge that is being shared?

As you build your knowledge, prioritize sources that speak from experience and with expertise on the identities you're exploring.

Engaging in Reflection

Throughout this book, you have learned new habits and skills for connecting your attitudes and beliefs to the knowledge you've built. This is where reflection fits into the identity-conscious practice. Consider the knowledge you've built around the identity you're exploring, and engage in reflection by connecting your attitudes, behaviors, and beliefs to what you now know. In figure 12.1, complete the reflection worksheet by inserting the identity you're exploring into the questions, then record your thoughts and experiences in the space provided.

Reflection Worksheet

1. Reflect on the earliest messages you received about _____. What did you learn or notice about _____? What did you hear, see, or experience related to _____?

    _____

    _____

    _____

2. Educators are responsible for creating an affirming, safe, and courageous environment for all students. What are some examples of how _____ is represented in your classroom community? How might it be misrepresented or not represented at all?

    _____

    _____

    _____

3. Complete the following sentences as you reflect on your learning about _____.

    • In thinking about this identity, I wonder _____

    _____.

    • In thinking about this identity, I hope _____

    _____.

    • In thinking about this identity, I am looking forward to _____

    _____.

    What do your answers in the sentences tell you about the first messages you received about this identity? What impact have these first messages had on your approach to this identity or experience?

    _____

    _____

    _____

FIGURE 12.1: Reflection worksheet.

*Visit **go.SolutionTree.com/diversityandequity** for a free reproducible version of this figure.*

Moving to Action

I like to think of building the identity-conscious practice as work that lives in your body. It becomes part of you—how you move, how you breathe, how you take up space in this world. When I think about where this work is located in the body, here's how I envision it: Building knowledge happens in the head space, engaging the mind.

Reflecting happens in the heart space, engaging thoughts and beliefs. Some people stop at this head-and-heart space. They read all the books, watch all the TED Talks, and listen to all the podcasts. They feel so emotional, so moved by the information and their reflections, that they hang out there. But the full practice calls us one step further: into action. Action shows up in our voices—when we speak up for a more inclusive and identity-conscious community. Action shows up in the space we take up—the meetings we attend and every space where we make ourselves visible in this work. Action shows up in our everyday interactions with students, families, and each other. Action shows up in our proximity—our closeness and our distance from one another.

> I like to think of building the identity-conscious practice as work that lives in your body. It becomes part of you—how you move, how you breathe, how you take up space in this world.

Action requires movement and evidence. Action is something we do and others can do with us. Action requires thoughtful motion. Use figure 12.2 to complete the action item worksheet. First, read the questions. Then, in the space provided, write action items you're compelled to undertake based on the knowledge building and reflecting you engaged in around this identity.

Refreshing Your Perspective

Someone once told me that exploring your identity and your relationship to the world around you is like ascending a very tall spiral staircase; while you are going higher and higher, it sometimes feels like you're staying in the same spot. Though you're going around and around, you feel like you aren't moving. Yet, if you stop every so often to look around as you travel upward, you'll see that your perspective is different, your distance from where you started is greater than the last time you stopped, and you can now see so much more of the landscape than you could before. Building an identity-conscious practice is like that. As time goes on, although you're examining different identities, you come back to the same questions over and over again. You may feel like you keep going around in circles. Pause and take time to look out into the landscape. You'll see things that you haven't paid attention to before, you'll notice gaps in inclusive practices, and you'll more easily recognize solutions. It may seem like you're standing still, but your new perspective is evidence that, in truth, you're moving upward.

Read. Reflect. Rinse. Repeat.

As you continually build an identity-conscious practice, you root yourself in the process of building knowledge, engaging in reflection, and moving to action. And, then you do it all over again. Maybe you go a bit deeper into that identity. Maybe you focus on a new identity. You have built the skills for engaging in difficult conversations, for embracing success and failure, and for moving through discomfort. You have built the

Action Item Worksheet

1. Based on this new knowledge and reflection, what is one action, behavior, or step you can *start* doing in your classroom, with your students, in your community, or in your own practice?

   _____

   _____

   _____

2. Based on this new knowledge and reflection, what is one action, behavior, or step you can *stop* doing in your classroom, with your students, in your community, or in your own practice?

   _____

   _____

   _____

3. Based on this new knowledge and reflection, what is one action, behavior, or step you can *change*, *edit*, or *adjust* in your classroom, with your students, in your community, or in your own practice?

   _____

   _____

   _____

4. Based on this new knowledge and reflection, what is one action, behavior, or step you can *continue* doing in your classroom, with your students, in your community, or in your own practice?

   _____

   _____

   _____

5. What does accountability look like in these action steps? How will you hold yourself accountable for moving forward?

   _____

   _____

   _____

6. What will you do if you are met with resistance or failure? What steps will you take to move through or recover?

   _____

   _____

   _____

7. What will success look or feel like to you?

   _____

   _____

   _____

FIGURE 12.2: Action item worksheet.

*Visit **go.SolutionTree.com/diversityandequity** for a free reproducible version of this figure.*

habits of doing this work in every aspect of your teaching, leading, learning, advising, and coaching. And, maybe without even realizing it, you've started to see identity in your life outside of school and built the habits and skills of engaging in this work in your home, family, neighborhood, and community. You model this work for others, and you encourage them to build knowledge, engage in reflection, and move to action.

Read. Reflect. Rinse. Repeat.

EPILOGUE

In the early months of 2021, after enduring a year of the global health pandemic and six months of ongoing racial injustice against the Black community, the United States found itself addressing the transition to a new president. On January 6, 2021, a mob of people marched to the U.S. Capitol Building in Washington, D.C., intent on following through on conspiracy theories that the presidential election had been stolen.

On January 7, 2021, school leaders and educators wondered how, if at all, they were going to talk about the insurrection and violence they'd witnessed. Some schools leaned into these dialogues, explicitly naming the differences in how Black Lives Matter protesters were treated and how the majority-White mob was treated, the latter meeting little police preparation and no military resistance. Some schools believed it was their civic duty to engage in dialogues with their students, drawing in historical context, laws, and difficult conversations about race. Others believed there was no place to talk about the incident in schools, seeing it as a political issue that could upset and anger families depending on which political party they aligned with.

If not in school, where should students be learning about civics, government, democracy, and presidential elections? Was this conflict really about the appropriateness of the topic, or was it about the thoughts, attitudes, behaviors, and beliefs of adults? What aspects of identity drew teachers and school leaders toward or pushed them away from these conversations? What parts of our identities embrace conflict, and what parts run from it? What do we risk when we speak up?

I began writing this book at the end of 2019, months before the first outbreak of COVID-19 in the United States; before the killings of George Floyd, Breonna Taylor, Ahmaud Arbery, Tony McDade, and dozens of transgender people of color; before I heard about the reports of missing Native and Indigenous women; before I learned of the hundreds of missing children unaccounted for at the southern U.S. border; before the violent attacks on Asians in the United States; before the national debates about lockdowns, school closings, and standardized testing; and before the surge of mental health crises experienced by children and families. Even before all these incidents, people in the United States struggled to have difficult conversations about identity. The events of

2020 and beyond have only increased the need to build knowledge, engage in reflection, and create plans for action.

As this book was headed to peer review and editing, the trial of Derek Chauvin—the officer found guilty of the murder of George Floyd—was broadcast on national television. In international news, violence erupted between Israel and Palestine. Protests continued against the government in Colombia. The COVID-19 pandemic in India caused overwhelming loss, death, and destruction of families and communities. Vaccination rates increased in the United States, and mask mandates were lifted—and then reinstated—in many major cities and states. While this book ends, the work continues. The habits and skills you have learned through this book continue.

With so much going on in our communities and in our world, it is natural to feel overwhelmed by the need to address diverse identities and experiences. Educators often ask me, "What am I supposed to do?" I can't answer this question for you. But I can tell you to create a to-do list, just as you've done throughout this book. I created a to-do list for myself. I created action plans that work for my identities and experiences. If your action items are to be effective, you must inform them with your identity-conscious practice.

During the summer of 2020, I recommitted to addressing how my identity as an Asian American informed and impacted my work with the Black community. I have used the tools in this book to explore and commit to action as I build my identity-conscious practice to be a co-conspirator with the LGBTQ community. To do that, I have to bring in my identity as a Catholic, a cisgender woman, and a person who never learned about influential LGBTQ people in my education and schooling. *I have to build my knowledge.* What I have to do for action items might be different from what someone else who is not religious, who is not cisgender, or who had a more inclusive education than I did has to do. *I have to engage in reflection.* We might choose to read different books, go to different workshops, or engage in dialogue with different groups based on our unique set of identities. *I have to move to action.*

While we cannot share one common action list among us all, you can build an inclusive classroom, school, and community in a reliable and enduring way by building *your* identity-conscious practice. It is through your unique practice and the shared commitment and action among your peers that you will begin to engage in real action and change that will result in increased belonging, voice, and a sense of welcome among all stakeholders. I wish you well on this journey. I wish you courage, strength, and the readiness to see humanity in yourself and in others.

REFERENCES AND RESOURCES

Abolitionist Teaching Network. (2020, August). *Guide for racial justice and abolitionist social and emotional learning*. Accessed at https://abolitionistteachingnetwork.org/guide on June 8, 2021.

Aboud, F. E. (2008). A social-cognitive developmental theory of prejudice. In S. M. Quintana & C. McKown (Eds.), *Handbook of race, racism, and the developing child* (pp. 55–71). Hoboken, NJ: Wiley.

Accapadi, M. M. (2007). When White women cry: How White women's tears oppress women of color. *College Student Affairs Journal, 26*(2), 208–215.

Acton, K. S. (2021). School leaders as change agents: Do principals have the tools they need? *Management in Education, 35*(1), 43–51.

Ajuwon, P. M., Lechtenberger, D., Griffin-Shirley, N., Sokolosky, S., Zhou, L., & Mullins, F. E. (2012). General education pre-service teachers' perceptions of including students with disabilities in their classrooms. *International Journal of Special Education, 27*(3), 100–107.

Albert Shanker Institute. (2015). *The state of teacher diversity in American education*. Washington, DC: Author. Accessed at www.shankerinstitute.org/resource/state-teacher-diversity-executive-summary on June 8, 2021.

American Psychological Association, & National Association of School Psychologists. (2015). *Resolution on gender and sexual orientation diversity in children and adolescents in schools*. Accessed at www.apa.org/about/policy/orientation-diversity.aspx on June 7, 2021.

Americans With Disabilities Act Knowledge Translation Center. (2018). *Guidelines for writing about people with disabilities*. Accessed at https://adata.org/factsheet/ADANN-writing on June 7, 2021.

Americans With Disabilities Act National Network. (n.d.). *What is the Americans with Disabilities Act (ADA)?* Accessed at https://adata.org/learn-about-ada on November 17, 2021.

Amodio, D. M. (2014). The neuroscience of prejudice and stereotyping. *Nature Reviews Neuroscience, 15*(10), 670–682.

Annamma, S. A., Connor, D., & Ferri, B. (2013). Dis/ability critical race studies (DisCrit): Theorizing at the intersections of race and dis/ability. *Race Ethnicity and Education, 16*(1), 1–31.

Anti-Defamation League. (n.d.). *A brief history of the disability rights movement*. Accessed at www.adl.org/education/resources/backgrounders/disability-rights-movement on November 16, 2021.

Artiles, A. J., Rueda, R., Salazar, J. J., & Higareda, I. (2005). Within-group diversity in minority disproportionate representation: English language learners in urban school districts. *Exceptional Children, 71*(3), 283–300.

Ashby, C. (2012). Disability Studies and inclusive teacher preparation: A socially just path for teacher education. *Research and Practice for Persons With Severe Disabilities, 37*(2), 89–99.

Banks, J. A. (1993). Multicultural education: Historical development, dimensions, and practice. *Review of Research in Education, 19*(1), 3–49. Accessed at www.jstor.org/stable/1167339 on January 18, 2021.

Barnes, C., & Mercer, G. (2010). *Exploring disability: A sociological introduction* (2nd ed.). Malden, MA: Polity Press.

Bazerman, M. H., & Tenbrunsel, A. E. (2012). *Blind spots: Why we fail to do what's right and what to do about it.* Princeton, NJ: Princeton University Press.

Beach, H. (2021, February 12). *Why representation matters to BIPOC teachers and their students.* Accessed at https://xqsuperschool.org/rethinktogether/bipoc-teacher-representation/ on November 16, 2021.

Bell, D. A., Jr. (1980). *Brown v. Board of Education* and the interest-convergence dilemma. *Harvard Law Review, 93*(3), 518–533.

Bell, W. K., & Kondabolu, H. (Hosts). (2017, October 5). What did we learn? with Alicia Garza and Wyatt Cenac [Audio podcast episode]. In *Politically Re-active with W. Kamau Bell and Hari Kondabolu.* Earwolf. Accessed at https://podcasts.apple.com/us/podcast/what-did-we-learn-with-alicia-garza-and-wyatt-cenac/id1125018164?i=1000393102269 on January 24, 2022.

Bezucha, D. (2021, September 26). 'We're forgotten': New report draws long overdue attention to missing and murdered indigenous women, girls. Accessed at www.wpr.org/were-forgotten-new-report-draws-long-overdue-attention-missing-and-murdered-indigenous-women-girls on October 23, 2021.

Bird, R., & Newport, F. (2017, February 17). *What determines how Americans perceive their social class?* Accessed at https://news.gallup.com/opinion/polling-matters/204497/determines-americans-perceive-social-class.aspx on June 7, 2021.

Bishop, R. S. (1990). Mirrors, windows, and sliding glass doors. *Perspectives, 6*(3), ix–xi.

Blanchard, S. B., King, E., Van Schagen, A., Scott, M. R., Crosby, D., & Beasley, J. (2018). Diversity, inclusion, equity, and social justice: How antibias content and self-reflection support early childhood preservice teacher consciousness. *Journal of Early Childhood Teacher Education, 39*(4), 346–363.

Blum, G., Wilson, M., & Patish, Y. (2015). Moving toward a more socially just classroom through teacher preparation for inclusion. *Catalyst: A Social Justice Forum, 5*(1), 4–14.

Borja, M., Jeung, R., Horse, A. Y., Gibson, J., Gowing, S., Lin, N., et al. (2021, April). *Anti-Chinese rhetoric tied to racism against Asian Americans.* San Francisco: Stop AAPI Hate. Accessed at https://stopaapihate.org/wp-content/uploads/2021/04/Stop-AAPI-Hate-Report-Anti-China-Rhetoric-200617.pdf on July 16, 2021.

Brayboy, B. M. J. (2005). Toward a tribal critical race theory in education. *Urban Review, 37*(5), 425–446.

Breines, J., & Chen, S. (2012). Self-compassion increases self-improvement motivation. *Personality and Social Psychology Bulletin, 38*(9), 1133–1143.

Bronson, P., & Merryman, A. (2009, September 4). Even babies discriminate: A *NurtureShock* excerpt. *Newsweek.* Accessed at www.newsweek.com/even-babies-discriminate-nurtureshock-excerpt-79233 on August 12, 2021.

Brown v. Board of Education of Topeka, 347 U.S. 483 (1954).

Buterman, J. (2015). Meantime: A brief personal narrative of a trans* teacher. *Canadian Journal of Educational Administration and Policy, 173*, 28–49.

Calarco, J. M. (2011). "I need help!" Social class and children's help-seeking in elementary school. *American Sociological Review, 76*(6), 862–882.

Case, K. A., & Meier, S. C. (2014). Developing allies to transgender and gender-nonconforming youth: Training for counselors and educators. *Journal of LGBT Youth, 11*(1), 62–82.

CASEL. (n.d.). *What is the CASEL framework?* Accessed at https://casel.org/fundamentals-of-sel/what-is-the-casel-framework/ on November 17, 2021.

Castro-Atwater, S. A. (2016). Color-blind racial ideology in K–12 schools. In H. A. Neville, M. E. Gallardo, & D. W. Sue (Eds.), *The myth of racial color blindness: Manifestations, dynamics, and impact* (pp. 207–225). Washington, DC: American Psychological Association.

Centers for Disease Control and Prevention. (2021, April 19). *Health equity considerations and racial and ethnic minority groups*. Accessed at www.cdc.gov/coronavirus/2019-ncov/community /health-equity/race-ethnicity.html on June 7, 2021.

Chaet, A. (2020, June 6). *Watch the entire CNN/Sesame Street racism town hall*. Accessed at www.cnn .com/2020/06/06/app-news-section/cnn-sesame-street-race-town-hall-app-june-6-2020-app/index .html on June 8, 2021.

Chang, G. H. (2019). *Ghosts of Gold Mountain: The epic story of the Chinese who built the Transcontinental Railroad*. Boston: Houghton Mifflin Harcourt.

Chenoweth, R. (2019, September 5). *Rudine Sims Bishop: 'Mother' of multicultural children's literature*. Accessed at https://ehe.osu.edu/news/listing/rudine-sims-bishop-diverse-childrens-books on July 9, 2021.

Cherry, K. (2020, July 24). *How the attentional bias influences the decisions we make*. Accessed at www .verywellmind.com/what-is-an-attentional-bias-2795027 on October 29, 2021.

Children's Community School. (2018). *They're not too young to talk about race!* [Graphic]. Accessed at www.childrenscommunityschool.org/social-justice-resources on June 8, 2021.

The Chronicle of Higher Education. (2010). The almanac of higher education, 2010–2011. *The Chronicle of Higher Education, 57*(11).

Chughtai, A. (2021, July 7). *Know their names: Black people killed by the police in the US*. Accessed at https://interactive.aljazeera.com/aje/2020/know-their-names/index.html on October 23, 2021.

Clemens, C. (2017, June 5). *Ally or accomplice? The language of activism*. Accessed at www.tolerance.org /magazine/ally-or-accomplice-the-language-of-activism on June 7, 2021.

Cleveland Clinic. (2019, December 9). *What happens to your body during the fight or flight response? Your survival response explained*. Accessed at https://health.clevelandclinic.org/what-happens-to-your -body-during-the-fight-or-flight-response on June 7, 2021.

Corley, T. (2020). Creating accountability for inclusive, responsive leadership. *People & Strategy, 43*(1), 29–32.

Craig, L. (2017, April 11). *Racial bias may begin in babies at six months, U of T research reveals*. Accessed at www.utoronto.ca/news/racial-bias-may-begin-babies-six-months-u-t-research-reveals on November 15, 2021.

Crosby, S. D., Howell, P., & Thomas, S. (2018). Social justice education through trauma-informed teaching. *Middle School Journal, 49*(4), 15–23.

Cross, W. E., Jr., Seaton, E., Yip, T., Lee, R. M., Rivas, D., Gee, G. C., et al. (2017). Identity work: Enactment of racial-ethnic identity in everyday life. *Identity, 17*(1), 1–12.

Croteau, S. M., & Lewis, K. (2016). "Just like the other boys": Meeting the needs of gender diverse students. *Journal of Cases in Educational Leadership, 19*(4), 102–113.

C-SPAN. (2019, March 19). *We want to do more than survive* [Video file]. Accessed at www.c-span.org /video/?458837-1/we-survive on June 8, 2021.

Dankoski, M. E., Bickel, J., & Gusic, M. E. (2014). Discussing the undiscussable with the powerful: Why and how faculty must learn to counteract organizational silence. *Academic Medicine, 89*(12), 1610–1613.

Dessel, A. B. (2010). Effects of intergroup dialogue: Public school teachers and sexual orientation prejudice. *Small Group Research, 41*(5), 556–592.

Dhaliwal, T. K., Chin, M. J., Lovison, V. S., & Quinn, D. M. (2020, July 20). *Educator bias is associated with racial disparities in student achievement and discipline* [Blog post]. Accessed at www .brookings.edu/blog/brown-center-chalkboard/2020/07/20/educator-bias-is-associated-with-racial -disparities-in-student-achievement-and-discipline/ on September 16, 2021.

Disability Visibility Project. (n.d.). *Disabled people of color*. Accessed at https://disabilityvisibilityproject
.com/tag/disabled-people-of-color on June 8, 2021.

Downey, D., & Escobar, A. (2021, October 22). Riverside teacher placed on leave after mimicking Native
Americans during math class. *The Press-Enterprise*. Accessed at www.pe.com/2021/10/21/video-shows
-riverside-teacher-mimicking-native-americans-criticized-as-insensitive/ on November 17, 2021.

Dunbar-Ortiz, R. (2014). *An Indigenous peoples' history of the United States*. Boston: Beacon Press.

Dunham, Y., Baron, A. S., & Banaji, M. R. (2008). The development of implicit intergroup cognition.
Trends in Cognitive Sciences, 12(7), 248–253.

Dweck, C. S. (2007). *Mindset: The new psychology of success*. New York: Ballantine Books.

Education Encyclopedia. (n.d.). *Multicultural education*. Accessed at https://education.stateuniversity
.com/pages/2252/Multicultural-Education.html on July 6, 2021.

Education for All Handicapped Children Act of 1975, Pub. L. No. 94–142, § 89, Stat. 773 (1975).

Erevelles, N., Kanga, A., & Middleton, R. (2006). How does it feel to be a problem? Race, disability,
and exclusion in educational policy. In E. A. Brantlinger (Ed.), *Who benefits from special education?
Remediating (fixing) other people's children* (pp. 77–100). Mahwah, NJ: Erlbaum.

Every Student Succeeds Act of 2015, Pub. L. No. 114–95, 20 U.S.C. § 1177 (2015).

Fierros, E. G., & Conroy, J. W. (2002). Double jeopardy: An exploration of restrictiveness and race
in special education. In D. J. Losen & G. Orfield (Eds.), *Racial inequity in special education*
(pp. 39–70). Cambridge, MA: Harvard Education Press.

First Nations Development Institute (n.d.). *Books*. Accessed at www.firstnations.org/knowledge-center
/books on August 12, 2021.

Flaherty, C. (2021, June 9). Legislating against critical race theory, with curricular implications in
some states. *Inside Higher Ed*. Accessed at www.insidehighered.com/news/2021/06/09/legislating
-against-critical-race-theory-curricular-implications-some-states on October 11, 2021.

Ford, A. (2020, June 6). *Bryan Stevenson: Get proximate on issues of race and injustice*. Accessed at www
.tlu.edu/news/bryan-stevenson-get-proximate-on-issues-of-race-and-injustice on July 12, 2020.

Gere, A. R., Buehler, J., Dallavis, C., & Haviland, V. S. (2009). A visibility project: Learning to see
how preservice teachers take up culturally responsive pedagogy. *American Educational Research
Journal, 46*(3), 816–852.

GLSEN. (n.d.). *Developing LGBTQ-inclusive classroom resources*. Accessed at www.glsen.org/activity
/inclusive-curriculum-guide on November 16, 2021.

GLSEN. (2013a). *No Name-Calling Week, high school (9–12) lessons*. Accessed at www.glsen.org/no
-name-calling-week#snt--5 on June 7, 2021.

GLSEN. (2013b). *School climate in New York (State snapshot)*. New York: Author.

Goldstein, J. (2018, November 3). Elementary school teachers dressed up as Trump's proposed border
wall and Mexicans for Halloween. *People*. Accessed at https://people.com/human-interest/teachers
-dress-up-border-wall-mexicans-halloween/ on November 17, 2021.

Gonzalez, M., & McNulty, J. (2010). Achieving competency with transgender youth: School
counselors as collaborative advocates. *Journal of LGBT Issues in Counseling, 4*(3–4), 176–186.

Goodrich, K., & Barnard, J. (2019). Transgender and gender non-conforming students in schools: One
school district's approach for creating safety and respect. *Sex Education, 19*(2), 212–225.

Gorski, P. C. (2014). Consumerism as racial and economic injustice: The macroaggressions that make
me, and maybe you, a hypocrite. *Understanding and Dismantling Privilege, 4*(1), 1–21.

Graham, R. (2019, June 20). Don't be an ally. Be an accomplice. *The Boston Globe*. Accessed at www
.bostonglobe.com/opinion/2019/06/20/don-ally-accomplice/sdU0ulbN9q8SYLMgsxJfWI/story
.html on June 7, 2021.

Gray, L. (2019). *Educational trauma: Examples from testing to the school-to-prison pipeline*. London:
Palgrave Macmillan.

Greene, C. W. (Director), & Lee, A. R. (Producer). (2014). *I'm not racist . . . am I?* [Motion picture].
United States: Point Made Films.

Hammond, Z. (2015, April 1). *3 tips to make any lesson more culturally responsive*. Accessed at www
.cultofpedagogy.com/culturally-responsive-teaching-strategies/ on November 18, 2021.

Harbin, B. (2016). *Teaching beyond the gender binary in the university classroom*. Accessed at https://cft
.vanderbilt.edu/guides-sub-pages/teaching-beyond-the-gender-binary-in-the-university-classroom/
on November 16, 2021.

Haviland, V. S. (2008). "Things get glossed over": Rearticulating the silencing power of Whiteness in
education. *Journal of Teacher Education, 59*(1), 40–54.

Hayes, A. M., Dombrowski, E., Shefcyk, A., & Bulat, J. (2018, April). *Learning disabilities screening
and evaluation guide for low- and middle-income countries*. Accessed at www.ncbi.nlm.nih.gov
/books/NBK545498/ on October 27, 2021.

Helms, J. E. (1994). The conceptualization of racial identity and other "racial" constructs. In E. J.
Trickett, R. J. Watts, & D. Birman (Eds.), *Human diversity: Perspectives on people in context*
(pp. 285–311). San Francisco: Jossey-Bass.

Hernandez, D. A., Hueck, S., & Charley, C. (2016). General education and special education teachers'
attitudes towards inclusion. *Journal of the American Academy of Special Education Professionals*, 79–93.

Higgins, M. (2016). Decolonizing school science: Pedagogically enacting agential literacy and ecologies
of relationships. In C. A. Taylor & C. Hughes (Eds.), *Posthuman research practices in education*
(pp. 186–205). London: Palgrave Macmillan.

Hirschfeld, L. A. (2008). Children's developing conceptions of race. In S. M. Quintana & C. McKown
(Eds.), *Handbook of race, racism, and the developing child* (pp. 37–54). Hoboken, NJ: Wiley.

Holcombe, M. (2020, June 29). Students using Instagram to reveal what it is like to be "Black at"
private high schools. *CNN*. Accessed at www.cnn.com/2020/06/29/us/instagram-black-students
-at-pages-race-issues-trnd/index.html on September 13, 2021.

Holmes, K. A., Garcia, J., & Adair, J. K. (2018). Who said we're too young to talk about race? First
graders and their teacher investigate racial justice through counter-stories. In N. Yelland & D.
F. Bentley (Eds.), *Found in translation: Connecting reconceptualist thinking with early childhood
education practices* (pp. 129–147). New York: Routledge.

Hunt, C. S., & Seiver, M. (2018). Social class matters: Class identities and discourses in educational
contexts. *Educational Review, 70*(3), 342–357.

Husband, T., Jr. (2012). "I don't see color": Challenging assumptions about discussing race with young
children. *Early Childhood Education Journal, 39*(6), 365–371.

Hyde, J. S., Bigler, R. S., Joel, D., Tate, C. C., & van Anders, S. M. (2019). The future of sex and
gender in psychology: Five challenges to the gender binary. *American Psychologist, 74*(2), 171–193.

Indian Health Service. (n.d.). *Two-Spirit*. Accessed at www.ihs.gov/lgbt/health/twospirit on June 8, 2021.

Individuals With Disabilities Education Act of 1990, Pub. L. No. 101–476, § 104, Stat. 1103 (1990).

Institute for Policy Studies. (n.d.). *Income inequality*. Accessed at https://inequality.org/facts/income
-inequality/ on November 15, 2021.

Invisible Disabilities Association. (n.d.). *How do you define invisible disability?* Accessed at https://invisibledisabilities.org/what-is-an-invisible-disability on August 4, 2021.

Jett, C. C., & Cross, S. B. (2016). Teaching about diversity in Black and White: Reflections and recommendations from two teacher educators. *New Educator, 12*(2), 131–146.

Joffe-Walt, C. (Host). (2020). *Nice White parents* [Audio podcast]. *The New York Times.* Accessed at www.nytimes.com/2020/07/23/podcasts/nice-white-parents-serial.html on June 8, 2021.

Johnstone, D. (2001). *An introduction to Disability Studies* (2nd ed.). New York: Fulton.

Jones, S. P. (2020). Ending curriculum violence. *Learning for Justice.* Accessed at www.learningforjustice.org/magazine/spring-2020/ending-curriculum-violence on November 17, 2021.

Kaler-Jones, C. (2020, May 7). When SEL is used as another form of policing. *Medium.* Accessed at https://medium.com/@justschools/when-sel-is-used-as-another-form-of-policing-fa53cf85dce4 on November 17, 2021.

Katz, P. A., & Kofkin, J. A. (1997). Race, gender, and young children. In S. S. Luthar, J. A. Burack, D. Cicchetti, & J. R. Weisz (Eds.), *Developmental psychopathology: Perspectives on adjustment, risk, and disorder* (pp. 51–74). New York: Cambridge University Press.

Keengwe, J. (2010). Fostering cross cultural competence in preservice teachers through multicultural education experiences. *Early Childhood Education Journal, 38*(3), 197–204.

Kelly, D. J., Quinn, P. C., Slater, A. M., Lee, K., Gibson, A., Smith, M., et al. (2005). Three-month-olds, but not newborns, prefer own-race faces. *Developmental Science, 8*(6), F31–F36.

Kemple, K. M., Lee, I. R., & Harris, M. (2016). Young children's curiosity about physical differences associated with race: Shared reading to encourage conversation. *Early Childhood Education Journal, 44*(2), 97–105.

Kennedy Center. (n.d.). *Kennedy Center education.* Accessed at www.kennedy-center.org/education on June 8, 2021.

Killermann, S. (2017). *Genderbread person v4.0* [Poster]. Accessed at www.genderbread.org/resource/genderbread-person-v4-0-poster on June 8, 2021.

Kim, J. (2012). Asian American racial identity development theory. In C. L. Wijeyesinghe & B. W. Jackson, III (Eds.), *New perspectives on racial identity development: Integrating emerging frameworks* (2nd ed., pp. 138–160). New York: NYU Press.

Kingsbury, M. (2019, November 22). *Representation matters: 10 children's books with disabled characters* [Blog post]. Accessed at www.thinkinclusive.us/10-childrens-books-with-disabled-characters on June 8, 2021.

Kinzler, K. D. (2016, October 21). How kids learn prejudice. *The New York Times.* Accessed at www.nytimes.com/2016/10/23/opinion/sunday/how-kids-learn-prejudice.html on August 12, 2021.

Kokka, K. (2020). Social justice pedagogy for whom? Developing privileged students' critical mathematics consciousness. *The Urban Review, 52*, 778–803.

Kosciw, J. G., Greytak, E. A., Diaz, E. M., & Bartkiewicz, M. J. (2010). *The 2009 National School Climate Survey: The experiences of lesbian, gay, bisexual and transgender youth in our nation's schools.* New York: GLSEN.

Kosciw, J. G., Palmer, N. A., & Kull, R. M. (2015). Reflecting resiliency: Openness about sexual orientation and/or gender identity and its relationship to well-being and educational outcomes for LGBT students. *American Journal of Community Psychology, 55*(1–2), 167–178.

Kostecki-Shaw, J. S. (2011). *Same, same but different.* New York: Holt.

Kotler, J. A., Haider, T. Z., & Levine, M. H. (2019). *Identity matters: Parents' and educators' perceptions of children's social identity development.* New York: Sesame Workshop. Accessed at www .sesameworkshop.org/sites/default/files/2019-10/sw_identitymatters_screen.pdf on June 8, 2021.

Ladson-Billings, G. (1998). Just what is critical race theory and what's it doing in a nice field like education? *International Journal of Qualitative Studies in Education, 11*(1), 7–24.

Lapointe, G. (2019, November 13). *6 powerful books by disabled authors.* Accessed at https://bookriot .com/books-by-disabled-authors on June 8, 2021.

Lareau, A. (2011). *Unequal childhoods: Class, race, and family life* (2nd ed.). Berkeley, CA: University of California Press.

Lazzell, D. R., Jackson, R. G., & Skelton, S. M. (2018). Intersectionality is crucial for culturally responsive & sustaining environments. *Equity Digest, 2*(1). Accessed at https://greatlakesequity .org/sites/default/files/201816111632_equity_digest.pdf on January 17, 2022.

Lee, S. J. (2009). *Unraveling the "model minority" stereotype: Listening to Asian American youth* (2nd ed.). New York: Teachers College Press.

LeFevre, A. L., & Shaw, T. V. (2012). Latino parent involvement and school success: Longitudinal effects of formal and informal support. *Education and Urban Society, 44*(6), 707–723.

Leslie, L. M., Bono, J. E., Kim, Y. S., & Beaver, G. R. (2020). On melting pots and salad bowls: A meta-analysis of the effects of identity-blind and identity-conscious diversity ideologies. *Journal of Applied Psychology, 105*(5), 453–471.

Lingras, K. A. (2021). Talking with children about race and racism. *Journal of Health Service Psychology, 47*(1), 9–16.

Long, S., Souto-Manning, M., & Vasquez, V. M. (Eds.). (2016). *Courageous leadership in early childhood education: Taking a stand for social justice.* New York: Teachers College Press.

Love, B. L. (2019). *We want to do more than survive: Abolitionist teaching and the pursuit of educational freedom.* Boston: Beacon Press.

Love, B. L. (2020, June 12). An essay for teachers who understand racism is real. *Education Week.* Accessed at www.edweek.org/leadership/opinion-an-essay-for-teachers-who-understand-racism-is -real/2020/06 on June 7, 2021.

Luelmo, P., & Bindreiff, D. (2021, January). The disproportionality of Latinx students in special education. *Leadership Magazine.* Accessed at https://leadership.acsa.org/disproportionality-of -latinx-students-special-ed on October 27, 2021.

MacNell, L., Driscoll, A., & Hunt, A. N. (2015). What's in a name: Exposing gender bias in student ratings of teaching. *Innovative Higher Education, 40*(4), 291–303.

Mangin, M. M. (2020). Transgender students in elementary schools: How supportive principals lead. *Educational Administration Quarterly, 56*(2), 255–288.

Maranto, R., Carroll, K., Cheng, A., & Teodoro, M. P. (2018). Boys will be superintendents: School leadership as a gendered profession. *Phi Delta Kappan, 100*(2), 12–15.

Marshall, D. T., Scott, M. R., & Wan, G. (2021). Through failure and reflection: Conceptualizations of a successful teacher residency experience. *Action in Teacher Education, 43*(2), 160–175.

Masko, A. L., & Bloem, P. L. (2017). Teaching for equity in the milieu of White fragility: Can children's literature build empathy and break down resistance? *Curriculum and Teaching Dialogue, 19*(1–2), 55–67.

McCrimmon, A. W. (2015). Inclusive education in Canada: Issues in teacher preparation. *Intervention in School and Clinic, 50*(4), 234–237.

McGregor, H. (2012). *Decolonizing pedagogies teacher reference booklet.* Vancouver, British Columbia, Canada: Vancouver School Board. Accessed at https://blogs.ubc.ca/edst591/files/2012/03/Decolonizing_Pedagogies_Booklet.pdf on November 15, 2021.

McGuire, J. K., Anderson, C. R., Toomey, R. B., & Russell, S. T. (2010). School climate for transgender youth: A mixed method investigation of student experiences and school responses. *Journal of Youth and Adolescence, 39*(10), 1175–1188.

McMahon, J. (2020, August 10). *NY state completes investigation into mock slave auction in Watertown 4th grade class.* Accessed at www.syracuse.com/news/2020/08/ny-state-completes-investigation-into-mock-slave-auction-in-watertown-4th-grade-class.html on November 17, 2021.

Merriam-Webster. (n.d.). Next stop: "Trolley problem." In *Merriam-Webster.com dictionary.* Accessed at www.merriam-webster.com/words-at-play/trolley-problem-moral-philosophy-ethics on September 23, 2021.

Meyer, E. J., Tilland-Stafford, A., & Airton, L. (2016). Transgender and gender-creative students in PK–12 schools: What we can learn from their teachers. *Teachers College Record, 118*(8), 1–50.

Migliarini, V., & Annamma, S. A. (2020). Classroom and behavior management: (Re)conceptualization through disability critical race theory. *Handbook on Promoting Social Justice in Education, 1–22.* Accessed at https://doi.org/10.1007/978-3-319-74078-2_95-2 on January 17, 2022.

Miller, J., Donner, S., & Fraser, E. (2004). Talking when talking is tough: Taking on conversations about race, sexual orientation, gender, class and other aspects of social identity. *Smith College Studies in Social Work, 74*(2), 377–392.

Milner, H. R., IV, Pearman, F. A., III, & McGee, E. O. (2013). Critical race theory, interest convergence, and teacher education. In M. Lynn & A. D. Dixson (Eds.), *Handbook of critical race theory in education* (pp. 339–354). New York: Routledge.

Modica, M. (2015). Unpacking the "colorblind approach": Accusations of racism at a friendly, mixed-race school. *Race Ethnicity and Education, 18*(3), 396–418.

Morris, E. W., & Perry, B. L. (2017). Girls behaving badly? Race, gender, and subjective evaluation in the discipline of African American girls. *Sociology of Education, 90*(2), 127–148.

Movement Advancement Project. (n.d.). *Safe schools laws.* Accessed at www.lgbtmap.org/equality-maps/safe_school_laws on September 16, 2021.

Mude, W., Oguoma, V. M., Nyanhanda, T., Mwanri, L., & Njue, C. (2021). Racial disparities in COVID-19 pandemic cases, hospitalisations, and deaths: A systematic review and meta-analysis. *Journal of Global Health, 11,* 05015.

Mullaney, C. (2019, April 13). Disability Studies: Foundations and key concepts. *JSTOR Daily.* Accessed at https://daily.jstor.org/reading-list-disability-studies on June 7, 2021.

Nadal, K. L., Erazo, T., & King, R. (2019). Challenging definitions of psychological trauma: Connecting racial microaggressions and traumatic stress. *Journal for Social Action in Counseling and Psychology, 11*(2), 2–16.

Nagata, D. K., Kim, J. H. J., & Wu, K. (2019). The Japanese American wartime incarceration: Examining the scope of racial trauma. *American Psychologist, 74*(1), 36–48.

National Center for Education Statistics. (2021). *Characteristics of public school teachers.* Accessed at https://nces.ed.gov/programs/coe/indicator/clr on November 16, 2021.

National Council of Teachers of English. (2021). *Guidelines for affirming gender diversity through ELA curriculum and pedagogy.* Accessed at https://ncte.org/statement/guidelines-for-affirming-gender-diversity-through-ela-curriculum-and-pedagogy/ on October 26, 2021.

National Women's Law Center, & the Education Trust. (n.d.). *". . . and they cared": How to create better, safer learning environments for girls of color.* Accessed at https://nwlc.org/wp-content/uploads/2020/08/FINAL_NWLC_EDTrust_Guide.pdf on November 16, 2021.

Newcomb, W. S., & Mansfield, K. C. (2014). Purposeful presence: Situating social justice in leadership preparation. *Scholar Practitioner Quarterly, 7*(3), 279–290.

No Child Left Behind (NCLB) Act of 2001, Pub. L. No. 107–110, § 115, Stat. 1425 (2002).

O'Brien, L. T., & Gilbert, P. N. (2013). Ideology: An invisible yet potent dimension of diversity. In Q. M. Roberson (Ed.), *The Oxford handbook of diversity and work* (pp. 132–153). New York: Oxford University Press.

Office of Disease Prevention and Health Promotion. (2021). *Disparities.* Accessed at www.healthypeople.gov/2020/about/foundation-health-measures/Disparities on July 19, 2021.

Osorio, S. L. (2018). Multicultural literature as a classroom tool. *Multicultural Perspectives, 20*(1), 47–52.

Ozkaleli, U. (2011). Butterflies for girls, cars for boys: Gender in K–12. *Social Change, 41*(4), 567–584.

Parekh, G., Brown, R. S., & Zheng, S. (2021). Learning skills, system equity, and implicit bias within Ontario, Canada. *Educational Policy, 35*(3), 395–421.

Patton, B. (2017). You can't win by avoiding difficult conversations. *Journal of Business and Industrial Marketing, 32*(4), 553–557.

Payne, K. A., & Journell, W. (2019). "We have those kinds of conversations here . . .": Addressing contentious politics with elementary students. *Teaching and Teacher Education, 79*(3), 73–82.

Pearson, H. (2016). The impact of Disability Studies curriculum on education professionals' perspectives and practice: Implications for education, social justice, and social change. *Disability Studies Quarterly, 36*(2). Accessed at https://dsq-sds.org/article/view/4406/4304 on June 8, 2021.

Peters, T., Margolin, M., Fragnoli, K., & Bloom, D. (2016). What's race got to do with it? Preservice teachers and White racial identity. *Current Issues in Education, 19*(1), 1–22.

Plaut, V. C., Thomas, K. M., Hurd, K., & Romano, C. A. (2018). Do color blindness and multiculturalism remedy or foster discrimination and racism? *Current Directions in Psychological Science, 27*(3), 200–206.

Porosoff, L., & Weinstein, J. (2021). *Whose SEL is it? Toward social-emotional learning that empowers students* [White paper]. Accessed at https://mkt.solutiontree.com/l/77002/2021-04-28/62xy3j on January 17, 2022.

Poston, W. S. C. (1990). The biracial identity development model: A needed addition. *Journal of Counseling and Development, 69*(2), 152–155.

Reeves, R. V., & Nzau, S. (2021, June 14). *Poverty hurts the boys the most: Inequality at the intersection of class and gender.* Accessed at www.brookings.edu/research/poverty-hurts-the-boys-the-most-inequality-at-the-intersection-of-class-and-gender/ on October 17, 2021.

Reznick, A. (2021, July 31). *Deaths at the Arizona-Mexico border are on pace to be highest ever recorded.* Accessed at www.npr.org/2021/07/31/1023146100/deaths-at-the-arizona-mexico-border-are-on-pace-to-be-highest-ever-recorded on October 23, 2021.

Rice, P. C. (2017, November 15). Pronouncing students' names correctly should be a big deal (opinion). *Education Week.* Accessed at www.edweek.org/leadership/opinion-pronouncing-students-names-correctly-should-be-a-big-deal/2017/11 on October 22, 2021.

Riddle, T., & Sinclair, S. (2019). Racial disparities in school-based disciplinary actions are associated with county-level rates of racial bias. *Proceedings of the National Academy of Sciences, 116*(17), 8255–8260.

Russell, J. E. A. (2019, June 4). Failure is an option—if we learn from it. *Forbes*. Accessed at www.forbes.com/sites/joyceearussell/2019/06/04/failure-is-an-option/?sh=4502d10b3f82 on October 27, 2021.

Russell, S. T., Ryan, C., Toomey, R. B., Diaz, R. M., & Sanchez, J. (2011). Lesbian, gay, bisexual, and transgender adolescent school victimization: Implications for young adult health and adjustment. *Journal of School Health*, *81*(5), 223–230.

Serido, J., Shim, S., Mishra, A., & Tang, C. (2010). Financial parenting, financial coping behaviors, and well-being of emerging adults. *Family Relations*, *59*(4), 453–464.

Shafer, L. (2018, June 12). *The experiences of teachers of color*. Accessed at www.gse.harvard.edu/news/uk/18/06/experiences-teachers-color on June 7, 2021.

Shani, M., & Hebel, O. (2016). Educating towards inclusive education: Assessing a teacher-training program for working with pupils with special educational needs and disabilities (SEND) enrolled in general education schools. *International Journal of Special Education*, *31*(3), n3.

Shean, M., & Mander, D. (2020). Building emotional safety for students in school environments: Challenges and opportunities. In R. Midford, G. Nutton, B. Hyndman, & S. Silburn (Eds.), *Health and education interdependence* (pp. 225–248). Singapore: Springer.

Shmerling, R. (2020, June 22). *First, do no harm* [Blog post]. Accessed at www.health.harvard.edu/blog/first-do-no-harm-201510138421 on October 27, 2021.

Silverman, D. J. (2019). *This land is their land: The Wampanoag Indians, Plymouth colony, and the troubled history of Thanksgiving*. New York: Bloomsbury.

Simmons, D. (2021). Why SEL alone isn't enough. *Educational Leadership*, *78*(6), 30–34.

Simons, J. D., Beck, M. J., Asplund, N. R., Chan, C. D., & Byrd, R. (2018). Advocacy for gender minority students: Recommendations for school counsellors. *Sex Education*, *18*(4), 464–478.

Singleton, G. E. (2014). *Courageous conversations about race: A field guide for achieving equity in schools*. Thousand Oaks, CA: Corwin Press.

Singleton, G. E. (2015). *Courageous conversations about race: A field guide for achieving equity in schools* (2nd ed.). Thousand Oaks, CA: Corwin Press.

Smith, L., Mao, S., & Deshpande, A. (2016). "Talking across worlds": Classist microaggressions and higher education. *Journal of Poverty*, *20*(2), 127–151.

Snapp, S. D., McGuire, J. K., Sinclair, K. O., Gabrion, K., & Russell, S. T. (2015). LGBTQ-inclusive curricula: Why supportive curricula matter. *Sex Education*, *15*(6), 580–596.

Snellman, K., Silva, J. M., & Putnam, R. D. (2015). Inequity outside the classroom: Growing class differences in participation in extracurricular activities. *Voices in Urban Education*, *40*, 7–14.

Social Justice Books. (n.d.). *Booklists*. Accessed at http://socialjusticebooks.org/booklists on August 12, 2021.

Sonoma, S. (2021, January 7). *44 trans people killed in 2020, marking worst year on record for transphobic violence*. Accessed at www.them.us/story/44-trans-people-killed-2020-worst-year-for-transphobic-violence on October 23, 2021.

Soto, R. (2008). *Race and class: Taking action at the intersections*. Washington, DC: Association of American Colleges and Universities. Accessed at www.aacu.org/diversitydemocracy/2008/fall/soto on October 17, 2021.

Steffens, M. C., Jelenec, P., & Noack, P. (2010). On the leaky math pipeline: Comparing implicit math-gender stereotypes and math withdrawal in female and male children and adolescents. *Journal of Educational Psychology*, *102*(4), 947–963.

Steinmetz, K. (2020, February 20). Kimberlé Crenshaw on what intersectionality means today. *TIME*. Accessed at https://time.com/5786710/kimberle-crenshaw-intersectionality/ on October 16, 2021.

Stirrup, J., Evans, J., & Davies, B. (2017). Early years learning, play pedagogy and social class. *British Journal of Sociology of Education*, *38*(6), 872–886.

STOMP Out Bullying. (n.d.). *School responsibility*. Accessed at www.stompoutbullying.org/school -responsibility on June 8, 2021.

Stop AAPI Hate. (2020, May 13). *3-month report*. Accessed at https://stopaapihate.org/3-month-report/ on October 23, 2021.

Stryker, S. (2017). *Transgender history: The roots of today's revolution* (2nd ed.). New York: Seal Press.

Sue, D. W. (2010). *Microaggressions in everyday life: Race, gender, and sexual orientation*. Hoboken, NJ: Wiley.

Sue, D. W. (2015). *Race talk and the conspiracy of silence: Understanding and facilitating difficult dialogues on race*. Hoboken, NJ: Wiley.

Sue, D. W., Alsaidi, S., Awad, M. N., Glaeser, E., Calle, C. Z., & Mendez, N. (2019). Disarming racial microaggressions: Microintervention strategies for targets, White allies, and bystanders. *American Psychologist, 74*(1), 128–142.

Sue, D. W., Capodilupo, C. M., Torino, G. C., Bucceri, J. M., Holder, A. M. B., Nadal, K. L., et al. (2007). Racial microaggressions in everyday life: Implications for clinical practice. *American Psychologist, 62*(4), 271–286.

Sue, D. W., Lin, A. I., Torino, G. C., Capodilupo, C. M., & Rivera, D. P. (2009). Racial microaggressions and difficult dialogues on race in the classroom. *Cultural Diversity and Ethnic Minority Psychology, 15*(2), 183–190.

Sullivan, J., Wilton, L., & Apfelbaum, E. P. (2020). Adults delay conversations about race because they underestimate children's processing of race. *Journal of Experimental Psychology: General, 150*(2), 395–400.

Sydnor, C., & Jamison, C. (n.d.). *Roll with Cole and Charisma* [Video files]. Accessed at www.youtube .com/c/rollwithcole/videos on June 8, 2021.

Talusan, L. A. (2018, January 18). *Where's the water?* [Blog post]. Accessed at www.lizatalusan.com/to -loosen-the-mind/2018/1/18/wheres-the-water on August 12, 2021.

Taylor, R. W., & Ringlaben, R. P. (2012). Impacting pre-service teachers' attitudes toward inclusion. *Higher Education Studies, 2*(3), 16–23.

Theoharis, J. (2015). *The rebellious life of Mrs. Rosa Parks*. Boston: Beacon Press.

Toomey, R. B., Ryan, C., Diaz, R. M., & Russell, S. T. (2011). High school Gay–Straight Alliances (GSAs) and young adult well-being: An examination of GSA presence, participation, and perceived effectiveness. *Applied Developmental Science, 15*(4), 175–185.

Torino, G. C., Rivera, D. P., Capodilupo, C. M., Nadal, K. L., & Sue, D. W. (Eds.). (2019). *Microaggression theory: Influence and implications*. New York: Wiley.

The Trevor Project. (2021). *National survey on LGBTQ youth mental health*. New York: Author. Accessed at www.thetrevorproject.org/survey-2021/ on September 16, 2021.

Trickey, E. (2017, January 30). Fred Korematsu fought against Japanese internment in the Supreme Court . . . and lost. *Smithsonian*. Accessed at www.smithsonianmag.com/history/fred-korematsu -fought-against-japanese-internment-supreme-court-and-lost-180961967/ on November 15, 2021.

Tristani, L., & Bassett-Gunter, R. (2020). Making the grade: Teacher training for inclusive education— A systematic review. *Journal of Research in Special Educational Needs, 20*(3), 246–264.

Turner, C. S. V., González, J. C., & Wong, K. (2011). Faculty women of color: The critical nexus of race and gender. *Journal of Diversity in Higher Education, 4*(4), 199–211.

U.S. Department of Health and Human Services. (2020). *Healthy people 2020: Social determinants of health*. Accessed at www.healthypeople.gov/2020/topics-objectives/topic/social-determinants-of -health on June 7, 2021.

U.S. Department of Justice. (2016, May 13). *U.S. Departments of Justice and Education release joint guidance to help schools ensure the civil rights of transgender students* [Press release]. Accessed at www.justice.gov/opa/pr/us-departments-justice-and-education-release-joint-guidance-help-schools-ensure-civil-rights on June 8, 2021.

U.S. Department of Justice, & U.S. Department of Education. (2016, May 13). *Dear colleague letter on transgender students.* Accessed at www.justice.gov/opa/pr/us-departments-justice-and-education-release-joint-guidance-help-schools-ensure-civil-rights on June 8, 2021.

U.S. Office of Special Education Programs. (2007, July). *History: Twenty-five years of progress in educating children with disabilities through IDEA.* Washington, DC: Author. Accessed at https://files.eric.ed.gov/fulltext/ED556111.pdf on November 18, 2021.

Utt, J. (2018). A case for decentering whiteness in education: How Eurocentric social studies curriculum acts as a form of white/western studies. *Ethnic Studies Review, 41*(1–2), 19–34.

Valle, J. W., & Connor, D. J. (2019). *Rethinking disability: A Disability Studies approach to inclusive practices* (2nd ed.). New York: Routledge.

Washington, J., & Evans, N. J. (1991). Becoming an ally. In N. J. Evans & V. A. Wall (Eds.), *Beyond tolerance: Gays, lesbians and bisexuals on campus* (pp. 195–204). Alexandria, VA: American Association for Counseling and Development.

Welcoming Schools. (n.d.a). *Books.* Accessed at https://welcomingschools.org/resources/books on June 8, 2021.

Welcoming Schools. (n.d.b). *Lesson plans to create gender expansive classrooms and support transgender and non-binary students.* Accessed at https://welcomingschools.org/resources/lesson-plans/transgender-youth/transgender-with-books on June 8, 2021.

Welcoming Schools. (n.d.c). *Responding to questions.* Accessed at https://welcomingschools.org/resources/responding-to-questions on June 8, 2021.

The White House. (2021, March 21). *Fact sheet: U.S. efforts to combat systemic racism.* Accessed at www.whitehouse.gov/briefing-room/statements-releases/2021/03/21/fact-sheet-u-s-efforts-to-combat-systemic-racism/ on October 23, 2021.

Wingfield, A. (2015, September 13). Color blindness is counterproductive. *The Atlantic.* Accessed at www.theatlantic.com/politics/archive/2015/09/color-blindness-is-counterproductive/405037/ on September 15, 2021.

Women's Voices. (2019, July 8). *Ally, accomplice, co-conspirator* [Video file]. Accessed at www.youtube.com/watch?v=QZVILjJPreM&feature=emb_imp_woyt on June 8, 2021.

Woolley, S. W. (2015). "Boys over here, girls over there": A critical literacy of binary gender in schools. *TSQ: Transgender Studies Quarterly, 2*(3), 376–394.

Woolley, S. W. (2019). "When you don't believe something is real, you can't actually advocate for or support it": Trans* inclusion in K–12 schools. *Intersections: Critical Issues in Education, 3*(1), 25–43.

World Health Organization. (n.d.). *Gender and health.* Accessed at www.who.int/health-topics/gender#tab=tab_1 on October 26, 2021.

Zwicky, C., & Walls, T. (2020). Transforming curriculum, exploring identity, and cultivating culturally responsive educators. In T. Puckett & N. S. Lind (Eds.), *Cultural competence in higher education: Innovations in higher education teaching and learning (pp. 67–82).* Bingley, England: Emerald Group Publishing.

INDEX

A

ABCs (attitude, behaviors, curiosities), 186, 187

abolitionist teaching. *See also* from ally to abolitionist

    social-emotional learning and, 138

    striving for, 135–139

accomplices, 132, 133–134

accountability, 104–105, 170

acknowledging and validating contributions and feelings, 189–190

action, moving to, 207–208

action items for allyship, 132, 133

action items worksheet, 209

aggression, 40. *See also* macroaggressions; microaggressions

Airton, L., 88

Albert Shanker Institute, 91–92

allies. *See also* from ally to abolitionist

    accomplices and, 134

    action items for allyship, 132, 133

    becoming an ally, 130–132

"Ally or Accomplice? The Language of Activism" (Clemens), 133

American Psychological Association, 68

Americans with Disabilities Act National Network, 107, 108

Annamma, S., 47, 107, 110

Anti-Defamation League, 101

Apfelbaum, E., 44

Ashby, C., 103

attentional bias, 2

avoidance patterns, 28–30

B

Banks, J., 105, 106

Bazerman, M., 158

Behind Closed Doors, 188

Bell, D., 131, 134

Beyond Tolerance: Gays, Lesbians, and Bisexuals on Campus (Washington and Evans), 130, 131

bias

    attentional bias, 2

    equitable practices and, 55, 56

    gender and, 93

    macroaggressions and, 157

    race and, 44

    social-emotional learning and, 29

Bickel, J., 31

Bishop, R., 152–153, 154

"Black at" Instagram posts, 5

Blind Spots: Why We Fail to Do What's Right and What to Do About It (Bazerman and Tenbrunsel), 158

Bloem, P., 155

Bloom, D., 6

Bonilla-Silva, E., 41

breathing/deep breathing, 189

Bristol, T., 92–93

Brown v. Board of Education, 131

bullying and sexual orientation, 70–71, 72

Beyond Conversations About Race
Washington Collado, Sharroky Hollie, Rosa Isiah, Yvette Jackson, Anthony Muhammad, Douglas Reeves, and Kenneth C. Williams

Written by a collective of brilliant authors, this essential work provokes respectful dialogue about race that catalyzes school-changing action. The book masterfully weaves together an array of scenarios, discussions, and challenging topics to help prepare all of us to do better in our schools and communities.

BKG035

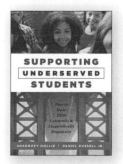

Supporting Underserved Students
Sharroky Hollie and Daniel Russell, Jr.

Discover a clear two-step road map for aligning PBIS with culturally and linguistically responsive teaching. First, you'll dive deep into *why* there is an urgent need for this alignment and then learn *how* to move forward to better serve all learners, especially those from historically underserved populations.

BKG010

Mindful School Communities
Christine Mason, Michele M. Rivers Murphy, and Yvette Jackson

Build a thriving school community that creates healthy, resilient, and successful students. A companion to *Mindfulness Practices*, this research-backed guide outlines how to teach self-regulation by fostering the five Cs of social and emotional learning and mindfulness: consciousness, compassion, confidence, courage, and community.

BKF912

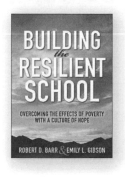

Building the Resilient School
Robert D. Barr and Emily L. Gibson

Overcome the effects of poverty in the 21st century by embracing an innovative new vision of public schooling. With the guidance of this practical, research-driven resource, you will discover a model for building resilient schools that support the whole child.

BKF836

Wait! Your professional development journey doesn't have to end with the last pages of this book.

We realize improving student learning doesn't happen overnight. And your school or district shouldn't be left to puzzle out all the details of this process alone.

No matter where you are on the journey, we're committed to helping you get to the next stage.

Take advantage of everything from **custom workshops** to **keynote presentations** and **interactive web and video conferencing**. We can even help you develop an action plan tailored to fit your specific needs.

Let's get the conversation started.

Call 888.763.9045 today.